CARO'S
Most Profitable
Hold 'em Advice

✦✦ The Complete Missing Arsenal ✦✦

ACKNOWLEDGEMENTS

Doyle Brunson
Avery Cardoza
Sara Cardoza
Diane McHaffie
Melissa Silberstang

CARO'S
Most Profitable
Hold 'em Advice

The Complete Missing Arsenal

Mike Caro

CARDOZA PUBLISHING

See FREE book offer on page 408

Cardoza Publishing is the foremost gaming publisher in the world with a library of over 200 up-to-date and easy-to-read books and strategies. These authoritative works are written by the top experts in their fields and with more than 10,000,000 books in print, represent the best-selling and most popular gaming books anywhere.

FIRST EDITION
Second Printing
Copyright © 2007 by Mike Caro
- All Rights Reserved -

MIKE ♠ CARO
The Advanced School of Winning!
POKER • GAMING • LIFE STRATEGY

This book is published in association with Mike Caro University of Poker. The official MCU online campus is at www.poker1.com.

Library of Congress Catalog Card No: 2007935913
ISBN: 1-58042-209-8

Visit our web site—www.cardozabooks.com—or write for a full list of books and computer strategies.

CARDOZA PUBLISHING
P.O. Box 98115, Las Vegas, NV 89193
Phone (800) 577-WINS
email: cardozabooks@aol.com
www.cardozabooks.com

ABOUT MIKE CARO

Mike Caro, the legendary "Mad Genius of Poker," is the world's foremost authority on poker strategy, psychology and statistics, and the author of more than a dozen best-selling poker and gambling books, videos and DVDs. Caro's work with Doyle Brunson on the bibles of poker, *Super/System* and *Super/System 2*, and his own revered classic, *Caro's Book of Poker Tells*, one of the most influential poker books ever written, have cemented his place as one of the all-time legends of poker.

Caro has lived the game of poker as a world-class professional player, researcher, theoretician, writer, and teacher. He's used mathematical analysis and his own revolutionary computer programs to pioneer the powerful modern poker strategies that thousands of world-class and serious professionals, plus millions of casual players, have relied on to win.

TABLE OF CONTENTS

1 INTRODUCTION

You're holding in your hands powerful ideas that represent my lifelong research into beating the game of hold 'em. On these pages, we're going to journey far beyond the traditional tactical tools offered in most poker books. You won't have to wade through this book separating what works from what doesn't, what's logical from what isn't. Everything in this book works and it's all logical and true. That's my pledge to you.

This book contains the entire missing arsenal of hold 'em strategies, tips and advice left out of everything you've ever seen or experienced in hold 'em—practical money-making strategies and the finishing touches you can use to destroy opponents. Many of these ideas, concepts, and powerful strategies will be new to you—they have never appeared in print from any other source before—and some you may have seen glossed over elsewhere. That is why the subtitle of this book is "The Complete Missing Arsenal."

I'm going to give you all the ammunition you need to win money at hold 'em. I've included hundreds of powerful concepts and 17 jam-packed chapters on beating no-limit and limit hold 'em. I'm also unveiling, for the very first time to the general public, my research on all 169 categories of starting hold 'em hands. This exclusive material—the most powerful starting-hand rankings in the world—was previously made available only to 800 world-class players and poker analysts (and sold for hundreds of dollars to serious players). It has never been published elsewhere.

My method of teaching is to reinforce concepts integral to your success as a poker player, so you'll see some repetition as we look at powerful ideas from different approaches. That's fine. I want to make sure that you fully absorb and understand these potent concepts so they're fully integrated into your game. What I'm not going to do is explain how to play every hand in every position by rote or what you should do on every possible flop. There are enough books out there to do that for you. Instead, I'm going to show you *how to think* and *how to approach* every situation you'll face in hold 'em as if you own the answers. And with the secrets you'll learn within these pages, you *will* own those answers.

The focus of this book is on making you money by extracting more profit in situations where you have the best hand, using powerful bluffs to get opponents with better hands to fold, recognizing when opponents are bluffing you, saving bets when you're beat, and much more. You'll also learn advanced betting concepts, how to use image, psychology, and manipulation to control situations, how to read players by using tells, and how to increase profits with professional and little-known techniques. I'll also show you how to play hold 'em like it's your business— and it will be when you're done with this book. You won't just learn strategies targeted at making more money, you'll get advice on keeping that money.

In the tradition of Doyle Brunson's *Super/System*, which I helped Doyle create back in 1976, this book reveals powerful revolutionary strategies that have never before appeared in print. I had refrained from combining these tactics into a single arsenal until my publisher, Avery Cardoza, finally convinced me to put them in writing, much as Doyle had prodded me into publishing some of my earlier secrets three decades earlier.

Now, in this book, you get to reap the results of my lifelong research and poker experience. These concepts and powerful strategies will open your eyes to a new and deeper way of making money at hold 'em. Now it's up to you to take this knowledge to the bank. Get ready for the big adventure.

—Mike Caro

2 BEGINNING THE JOURNEY

I want you to win. Those five words convey the essence of what I'm about, and I hope they lead us to friendship. You see, thirty-five years ago, I did *not* want you to win. I was a professional poker player who had spent much time analyzing and researching the game, at a time when there was scarcely any credible literature on the subject. I didn't want to share my secrets.

I'd lock myself in a room for days, doing statistical analysis and formulating theories on poker tells, strategy, and psychology that have blossomed into the foundation of my teaching today. But, in the 1970s, none of my work was intended for anyone else. What I'd discovered worked spectacularly at the poker tables. And I was one of those people who believed that it would be insane to enlighten other players.

DOYLE BRUNSON AND SUPER/SYSTEM

Then Doyle Brunson came into my life—the same Doyle Brunson who has won ten championship gold bracelets at the World Series of Poker. After claiming back-to-back world titles in 1976 and 1977, Doyle had been coaxed into writing a book, which was to become known as *Super/System – A Course in Power Poker.*

It had been decided that Doyle would write the whole book, but would consult with five other players that he considered to be the best in the world for each of the sections covering specific types of poker. He would create one section entirely by himself on no-limit hold 'em, the game where he won his two championships. Although I was honored to be chosen as an expert collaborator for two sections, statistics and draw poker, I was leery about contributing. Making public those long-guarded secrets that I used every day to make money at the tables wasn't something that inherently made sense to me. But Doyle was persuasive and charming.

I was further flattered when Doyle sought my statistical advice and analysis while putting together chapters in conjunction with his other expert collaborators, which included fellow hall-of-famer Chip Reese, former world champion Bobby Baldwin, and the legendary poker theorist David Sklansky. And perhaps the most gratifying decision of all was when Doyle said that he wanted me to write my sections in my own voice, under my own name—the only chapters not penned by Doyle himself.

So, it was Doyle's great vision that brought me into the public arena, kicking and screaming. And I've never regretted the decision. As soon as *Super/System* was published, I realized how desperately serious players sought legitimate, scientific poker advice.

I had once believed that publishing poker secrets would ruin the game. But I was wrong. It quickly became clear after *Super/System* was sold and changed poker forever, that the game was being enhanced, not hindered. For one thing, that book and the literature that followed was bringing more players into the poker arena. It was the beginning of poker's great revival. And not everyone who purchased a book benefited. Many seemed to misuse the information, or worse, just put the book on the shelf, partially read, and hurry to the tables with unjustified new confidence.

You can't treat a credible poker book that way. And I'm warning you not to use this book as magic medicine either. You bought this book, but now you must read and understand it. Just owning it will do nothing for your bankroll. You need to think about the tactics and techniques I'm about to share. If you do that, this will be the best hold 'em education you've ever encountered.

My Early Hold 'em Research

Shortly after Doyle unveiled his *Super/System*, I was showered with gratitude from players around the world. In the years that followed, I exponentially increased my devotion to analyzing the game, writing columns and books, and conducting seminars.

In 1983, I programmed an artificially intelligent hold 'em player able to compete at a world-class level. Following it's unveiling at the World Series of Poker, where it played against then world champion Tom McEvoy and Doyle Brunson, winning only one of three matches, it played a $500,000 match on national TV where it moved all-in and was called by casino owner Bob Stupak (who was publicly claiming to be the best in the world). My computer (called "Orac," which is Caro backwards) held three of a kind versus his top two pair. Unfortunately, there was an electrical glitch freezing the computer and the hand needed to be replayed, leading to Stupak's eventual victory. Who says bad-beat stories are reserved for humans!

That match marked the beginning of my emphasis on hold 'em. I even created *Mike Caro's Poker Engine* in the 1980s, using computers to do simulations of elaborate hand interaction in all forms of poker—again with a heavy emphasis on hold 'em.

I WANT YOU TO WIN

Something deep inside me had changed how I'd felt in my pre-*Super/System* years. I had reversed directions and my whole objective was now to share my discoveries. I know this will sound strange, but I began to feel a kinship for my fellow players. I truly wanted them to succeed. From a selfish standpoint, I wanted to be the one who made this happen.

My obsession with research secrecy had transformed into wanting others to win more than I wanted to win myself. What I like most is when players tell me that I'm responsible for their success. Whenever I hear that, it's magic, as if, strangely, I was the person who won. And so, when I say, "I want you to win," it's not just words, and it's not exaggeration. As I get older, I realize that getting you to win has grown beyond an obsession; it's my calling.

This book is a result of decades of my writing, research, teaching and playing poker. I've applied those concepts to hold 'em so you can learn them too. Much of this advice and many of the concepts apply to other forms of poker as well. And some can be extended to apply to games beyond poker and to life's broad arena itself. Often, such is the power and the nature of truth.

Trust me as a friend and believe me when I say, once again: *I want you to win.* I'd be honored if you'd follow me on this adventure as we walk through these pages, discovering profitable truths.

Let's get started.

3 PREFLOP CONCEPTS

HOW MANY HOLD 'EM HANDS SHOULD YOU PLAY?

How many times have you heard someone criticize another player by saying, "He plays too many hands" or criticize a different player by saying, "He just sits there and hardly ever plays any hands."

I'm about to tell you something shocking.

There are a whole lot of hands in hold 'em (as in all forms of poker) that are so inferior that almost everyone correctly throws them away without wagering. In contrast to that large category of unplayable hands, there are a relatively small number that are highly profitable. In the middle lies a huge ocean of marginal hands I call "borderline." As a group, these break about even.

Since the majority of hands you might consider playing are about break-even, you could decide to present an image as an active player and enter pots with most of them. Another skillful player could decide, instead, to almost never enter pots with any of these borderline hands. Guess what? It's entirely possible that you'll end up earning the same profit!

This is among the most amazing concepts in poker. People often ask questions about how many hands they should play. Since so many hands that you play have small-profit expectations, some players just fold most of these. It really happens that some winning players enter pots with twice as many hands as other winning players, yet their long-range profit is about equal.

Of course, this doesn't mean that either of these types of winners is maximizing his profit. There's much more to world-class poker than just how many hands you play. Later in this chapter, we'll go over my complete rankings for starting hands, but first, let's take a look at the Table of Misery.

TABLE OF MISERY

You and I know that a pair of aces is awesome and a pair of deuces is disastrous. Well, that isn't always true, is it? In rare situations a pair of deuces isn't quite so bad. For example, if you're playing against just one opponent, then a pair of deuces can hold its own against A-K. However, in the real world against a table full of players, the A-K is a better hand. And it isn't close.

Still, it's interesting to know what your chances are of liking a flop when you invest money on various pairs. It's hard to define a general set of rules for whether or not you like the flop since the game is so situational. Suppose you have A-A and the flop is A-K-K. Looks like a great flop, but are you perfectly safe? Obviously, a pair of kings held by any opponent will make you miserable. How likely is it that an opponent holds both remaining kings? Depends. If you bet and he passes, there's no chance whatsoever. If he didn't raise before the flop, he's less likely to hold kings, although with some tricky opponents exactly the opposite is true. We can make powerful and profitable estimates about what opponents hold, but we can seldom know as a certainty.

This is what we know for sure: If we don't take previous events into consideration and include only our pair of aces and the flop in our appraisal, then the odds are 11 to 1 against any opponent holding one king and something else—our most profitable scenario. And the odds are 1,080 to 1 against him holding both kings.

That's interesting, but not especially useful. However, the following Table of Misery Index will help you know how often to expect an unfavorable flop. It tells you how frequently the flop *won't* provide you with at least one more of your rank (thus making three-of-a-kind or rarely four-of-a-kind) and the flop *will* contain at least one card higher than your pair. If both these conditions are true—you don't make three-of-a-kind on the flop *and* there's at least one card ranking above your pair— you're miserable by this definition. Based on that simplistic assumption, this is the Table of Misery Index.

While this chart is deliberately elementary and ignores many concepts critical to professional hold 'em, it nonetheless illustrates a profound truth.

TABLE OF MISERY INDEX	
2-2	88.24%
3-3	88.22%
4-4	87.92%
5-5	86.97%
6-6	85.01 %
7-7	81.65%
8-8	76.54%
9-9	69.30%
10-10	59.57%
J-J	46.96%
Q-Q	31.12%
K-K	11.67%
A-A	0.00%

There isn't nearly as much difference between low ranks as there is between high ranks. Look at it this way. A pair of kings is much better than a pair of queens (and they're only one rank away from each other), but there's a much less dramatic difference between a pair of sevens and a pair of deuces (five ranks apart). Also, notice that, based on this simple premise, you're probably going to hate the flop unless you hold at least a pair of jacks.

THE TRUTH ABOUT ACES IN HOLD 'EM

Despite common advice, you do not want to raise with aces in order to chase players out of the pot before the flop in hold 'em. That pair of aces usually makes as much money or more with extra opponents chasing you. That doesn't mean you shouldn't raise. But it means when you do raise, you're usually doing so hoping opponents will call, not fold.

Thinning the field has its moments, but, contrary to what you've heard, raising with aces before the flop for that purpose isn't one of them.

POWERFUL BLIND CONCEPTS

If there are one or more blind bets in your hold 'em game (as is standard), powerful concepts come into play. Often, blinds are worth attacking. Often, blinds are worth defending. But because so much of the profit you will earn or fail to earn centers around decisions involving the blinds, you should take some time to examine what's what.

Blind bets are simply another way of making sure there is something of value to fight over before the cards are dealt. You are required to make these bets in order to stimulate action. An ante serves the same function in games where blind bets are not used. Sometimes both antes and blind bets are used together, but in any case, the extra money added to the pot has a significant effect on your expectation of winning and losing, and thus, your strategy.

FUNDAMENTAL SECRETS OF THE BLINDS

Most profit comes from correct play *in* the blinds and *against* the blinds. The blinds are a required sacrifice, and except in short-handed games where skilled players can profit, you will lose money while playing your blinds. One great secret to hold 'em profit is to minimize your average loss when you must bet blind. In a full-handed game, this specifically means that if you are required to put up, say, $50 as a blind bet, then even if you play perfectly from that point on, you won't earn enough in profit expectation to overcome that initial hit when you average all your hands together. You will lose money. If the blinds are the *only* hands you will ever play, you should not play at all. You should, instead, simply refuse to take the blinds if you could.

Of course, there is no overall disadvantage to taking the blinds in a regular game among equal players. That's because the players sacrifice in turn and everyone eventually has to suffer the same number of blind bets. Despite this disadvantage of making a required blind bet, you can profit greatly by losing less money in your blinds. Since so much of your dollar action comes when you're in the blinds or in a late position attacking the blinds, learning how to play these situations is monumentally important.

Here are seven concepts to consider:

1. You'll Play More Hands from the Blind

You'll play more hands in the blinds than in any other positions. You'll play more hands attacking the blinds than from early positions, assuming the game isn't so loose that you seldom get a chance to attack. This may seem obvious, but the implications are harder to grasp. In short, most of the profit you will ever make comes from powerful and frequent decisions regarding the blinds.

2. Consider Your Image

For maximum profit, you need to show that you're willing to gamble. Then, opponents will call you with weak hands, supplying you with extra money you wouldn't earn otherwise. The main flaw in your opponents is that they call too much. For this reason, an image that allows extra bluffs isn't usually as profitable as one that lures extra calls.

One of the best and most economical times to enhance your image is in the blinds. The image advantages are:

a. Everyone is watching you because you are the "target" who acts last on the first betting round.

b. You can play weaker hands aggressively, although you will usually opt not to do so except against the small blind or in a late position war.

c. Opponents simply tend not to remember that you were in the blind, so you get "credit" for playing weak hands when you got in for half price or even for free.

> *"An image that allows extra bluffs isn't usually as profitable as one that lures extra calls."*

3. When to Attack

You should attack the blinds more aggressively if they are either too loose or too tight. If they're too tight, you can sometimes bluff with total garbage. If they're too loose, you can bet semi-strong but weaker-than-normal hands and still make a profit if opponents call.

This runs contrary to the almost-universally-accepted, but flawed, notion that you should play loose against tight opponents and tight against loose opponents.

4. A Great Tactic

Try reraising with any semi-strong hand against a mid-position or late position player when you're on or just before the button. You'll benefit from chasing out the blinds, which lets you:

a. Split this dead money with the original raiser;

b. Enhance your loose image;

c. Put yourself in a position to act last on all future betting rounds.

5. Small Blind and Big Blind Calling

When the big blind isn't particularly aggressive and somebody has just called, you should usually call as the small blind. Even many weak hands will earn money, because it only costs you half a bet to call, and the average loss on those hands, if you had to put in the full bet, is less than half. For the same reason, you should usually call a single raise in the big blind if no one can still act behind you.

By the way, whether someone can still act behind you is an important consideration when calling in the big blind. If an opponent just called your blind and then another opponent raises, you can't "close the betting" by just calling. That original caller might subsequently reraise. But if the first player to voluntarily wager does so by raising and is then called by another player, you can close the betting with your call in the big blind. You're in no further danger and can immediately see the flop.

With borderline calling hands in the big blind—ones you can either fold or play without dramatically affecting your expected profit—here's how to resolve the dilemma:

a. Call if the first opponent was the raiser.
b. Fold if any other opponent was the raiser.

Remember: If anyone except the first player voluntarily entering the pot raised, this means that others will have a chance to reraise following your call. But when the first player raised and everyone else called, your borderline call is safer and more profitable.

6. Raising Concepts

Don't exercise your right to raise with the live blind very often. It's usually correct to just call with medium-strong hands and see what develops. However, tend to raise often if the small blind is the only caller. You'll have position throughout the hand.

Also, for the same reasons, you can reraise very liberally as the big blind when the small blind raises. I use this play almost routinely against many opponents. It enhances my image and I will be acting last through all future betting rounds. If I'm against an opponent who almost always raises the big blind given the opportunity, I will sometimes reraise with hands such as Q-7 offsuit or 7-6 suited. The sacrifice here is not what it appears to be. Against many opponents, reraising is almost as good as just calling with these fairly-weak hands, and in some cases, reraising is much more profitable.

7. Attacking the Blinds

You should tend to attack the blinds less when the players defending them are aggressive and unpredictable. "Tight and passive" are the best blinds to attack.

But, you should sometimes send a warning to aggressive and unpredictable opponents on your left by raiding their blinds from late positions. Remember, these players to your left have a positional advantage over you on most hands. And you may diminish their will to maximize their positional advantage on other hands when they're not the blinds.

So, although the advice to be less aggressive in attacking blinds of opponents who defend them is valid, there's also a time when you might want to attack those blinds, simply to make those opponents less aggressive in the future. It really depends on their dispositions. If you're going to push them toward revenge by attacking their blinds, don't do it. Remember that on most hands they won't have the blinds and since they're sitting to your left and act after you do, they're in better shape to punish you than you are to punish them. Strange game, poker.

SMALL BLIND VS. BIG BLIND: HOW TO GET THE MOST MONEY

Here's one of the areas of poker where I believe even strong players falter. Let's say you're playing limit hold 'em, just you and one opponent. Picture that. Now, erase that picture. We'll get back to it in a minute. Picture that same opponent, but this time you're in a regular ring game. Well, when you're in a full-handed game, you realize that if everyone folds and you're in the small blind, you don't really need a lot of strength to call or raise the big blind.

Should you usually stay in with 10-8 offsuit? Yes—either raise or just call. You shouldn't fold often, because played correctly against average opponents, that hand will earn a small profit. What about 9-5 offsuit? Well, that's a little trickier. Against many aggressive and sensible opponents, you'll probably lose money playing that. But it's close.

Why is it close? Let's say it's a $10/$20 game, and the blinds are $5 small and $10 large. This means you can just call for $5 and get 3 to 1 money odds at this point, provided your opponent doesn't raise. In a sense, you're getting a 50 percent discount over what it would cost if you had to call that $10 cold. Without being too picky about how we analyze it, just consider that if a play wouldn't lose $5 if you called the whole $10 cold, you probably should call for $5. And guess what? That 9-5 doesn't lose $5 if you call cold against many opponents with random hands.

So, what's the problem with calling? A couple of big ones:

1. You might get raised because the big blind is live.
2. Your opponent in the big blind has position over you and will be acting last on every future betting round. This turns out to be a pretty big issue. Players who think position doesn't much matter heads-up in hold 'em are quite wrong.

But, despite this positional disadvantage on all future rounds of betting, it's often worth calling. And you might even raise, hoping your opponent will surrender his big blind. In fact, you should raise frequently against too-conservative opponents. Opponents who don't defend their big blinds are good targets to put on your left, when you have a choice of seats. Generally, players on your left have a positional advantage and you'll lose money to them forever. So, players who don't maximize that advantage work to your benefit when positioned to your left.

Unless there is a great difference, favoring you, between your skill and theirs, you will probably lose money against players on your left for your lifetime. There's nothing much you can do about it except to minimize the advantage with prudent decisions. But don't despair. If you're a skillful player, you'll make considerably more than enough money from players to your right to cover this misfortune.

"You will probably lose money against players on your left for your lifetime."

Neutralizing the Disadvantage

When you have a player to your left who inadequately defends the big blind, you can go a long way toward neutralizing this overall positional disadvantage. So, in addition to other seating factors, consider changing to a seat where a player who doesn't defend the blind often enough sits to your left. This will allow you to make money with weak hands you would otherwise have thrown away. And many of the hands you would normally play will be more profitable, because you sometimes will win the blind without a contest—and the amount of the blind usually surpasses the average profit you could expect against an active opponent.

What hold 'em hands can you play in the small blind against the big blind after everyone else has folded? Your conclusion should be that—depending on the opponent, your image, and other factors—10-8 offsuit is very likely playable in the small blind, and 9-5 offsuit might be. Hands like 7-3 offsuit, 9-4 offsuit, and 7-2 offsuit or even suited usually shouldn't be played.

Now here's the deal. All that was about what you should do in a full-handed hold 'em game when you're the small blind versus a big blind. But, suppose instead that the game is two-handed from the get go. Now what?

Heads-Up Play

By convention, the blinds are reversed, as you've probably seen in a tournament when only two players remain. Except on the first round of betting, the small blind is in the dealing position and will act last. The big blind, except for the first betting round, will act first. This changes things. You will be able to consistently devastate opponents who don't adjust correctly. You don't need anywhere near as powerful of hands now to raise or call the big blind as you did in the full-handed game after everyone else folded.

Huh? But, Mad Genius of Poker, you just said that you didn't even need very much to call or raise previously. That's right. And now, in these circumstances, you often don't need anything at all. In some games against overly cautious opponents, you don't need anything specific to play. Absolutely everything will do!

There are two reasons for this:

1. There's something I call the **bunching factor**. This means that when players voluntarily fold, it tends to imply that better-than-average cards remain among the players yet to act. This is logical when you think about it, because opponents are more likely to fold bad cards than good cards. And this means that when everyone folds before you raise that big blind, then that big blind is more likely to hold a strong hand than if he were starting with a random deal. So, raising the big blind from the small-blind position in a full-handed game after everyone folds is not quite as good a deal as you might think. But usually, it is good enough. Raising the big blind from the small-blind position in a heads-up game is better than you might think.

2. Heads-up, you're going to be able to act last on the 2nd, 3rd, and 4th betting rounds. This positional advantage can make up a lot of ground. This reversal of position heads-up also means that you should usually be defensive with medium-strong hands from the big blind position and aggressive with them from the small-blind position. In other words, in a heads-up game from the big-blind position, you shouldn't three-bet against a raise as often as you would in a full-handed game if everyone folded

and then the small blind raised. You should also fold more hands in the big blind than you would in a ring game when the small blind raises.

LIMIT POKER: SIX TIPS ON PLAYING THE SMALL BLIND

How should you play the small blind in limit poker? Depends. When do you pass? When do you call? When do you raise?

There are no absolute answers for those questions. You'd have to specify exactly the type of game, exactly the hands held, and exactly the opponents you're facing. But here are six general concepts you should always keep in mind.

1. You Get a Discount

It's generally wrong to surrender and let the big blind win for free in limit hold 'em. If everyone passes and it's up to you in the small blind, you should usually at least call.

Remember what we've just learnd: The reason a call is correct has a lot to do with the value of that small blind, which already weighs in your favor. You're playing $10/$20 hold 'em with a $10 big blind and you're in the small blind position, having already been forced to wager $5. Everyone passes. It's just you and the big blind. If you had to call for the full $10, there would be a lot of hands you would fold.

But, it turns out that almost all of the hands you would fold lose much less than $5, on average, if played over and over. So, to state it simply, you can now call for just $5, because although calling for $10 may often be a bad investment, calling for just $5 is usually a good one. Fine. But what if your opponent raises? Well, then you're still getting a 25 percent discount, assuming you call. You will have to put in a total of $15 to first call the big blind and then call the raise. But it would have cost you $20 had you not automatically wagered the small blind. The

$5 that you've already entered makes a big difference. In fact, most hands you would normally fold if you had to put in $20 are worth playing at a 25 percent discount.

2. Depends Upon Your Opponent

Whether you should raise depends a lot on how often your opponent will fold. Unless you hold an overwhelming favorite, such as a pair of kings, the best thing that can happen is that you raise and your opponent throws his hand away. If it's a $5/$10 blind game, you'd win the big blind's $10 plus your $5 outright.

That $15 instant return is almost always more than your average earnings for playing many similar hands to their conclusion. But the real question is how often will the big blind surrender if you raise? If it's 20 percent of the time or more, you're almost always better raising with anything from a fairly weak to a moderately strong hand. However, if your opponent is very aggressive and likely to reraise with medium hands, you should be less willing to raise—and, in fact, be more willing to pass—with your weak hands.

3. Your Opponent Often Defends the Blind

If your opponent almost never surrenders the big blind, your main incentive for raising, which is taking the pot right now, is gone and you should consider just calling with weak to moderate hands. And you should fold with a greater number of weak hands than you normally would.

4. Calling is Better Than Raising if the Blind Will Call

Your dollar-for-dollar reward is more if you just call than if you raise a big blind who subsequently calls your bet. Let's say there are two blinds, your $5 blind and the big $10 blind. If you call, the pot affords you $15 to $5 or 3 to 1. If you raise to $20 (investing $15 more) and your opponent calls, you've invested

$15 in pursuit of $25 (your opponent's $20 plus your original $5). That's 1.67 to 1. Clearly, if all goes as planned, you'll get better pot odds by calling than by raising.

5. You're Out of Position

Don't forget that you're going to be in the worst position on all future rounds of betting when you're in the small blind to the dealer's left.

6. Come in Cheaply if Other Players Are in the Pot

If other players have already entered the pot, you should usually come in as cheaply as possible in the small blind. This means you should seldom raise or reraise. When you're the small blind against one or more opponents, besides the blinds, it's usually incorrect to raise or reraise with anything other than a top quality pair. An exception frequently arises if the raiser (or caller) is in a very late position. This often indicates the raise came with something less than an astonishing hand. Here you have the opportunity to assert yourself by reraising and freezing the big blind out of the pot. Anytime you can add forfeited money to the pot and end up head-to-head with prospects that are about as good as your opponent, you should consider doing it.

The problem with reraising as the small blind is that you'll always have to act first. This positional disadvantage usually overwhelms any incentive to take the initiative by aggressively reraising. In hold 'em, save those reraises for your very biggest pairs. Even hands such as A-K and A-Q tend to make more money overall if you just call a raise when you're in the small blind. In order to be less predictable, though, you should occasionally reraise—but only occasionally.

EARLY POSITION PREFLOP PLAY

If the game is full-handed, meaning there are eight to ten players dealt in, be excessively cautious in the first two to four positions. By "two to four," I mean specifically four positions, counting from the first seat after the big blind if there are ten players, three positions if there are nine players, and two positions if there are eight players.

For the purposes of this definition, you are always in an early, extra-cautious position if no one has yet voluntarily entered the pot and there are six or more opponents waiting to act after you.

Now that you know what I mean by early position in this discussion, do this: Unless there are compelling reasons to veto this advice and enter the pot, the only pairs you should always play without hesitation are aces, kings, and queens. The only non-paired starting hands you should always play are A-K suited, A-K of mixed suits, and A-Q suited. That's it.

And, yes, I'm talking about *both* limit and no-limit hold 'em. Going by the mathematicial explanations in the next chapter, Hold 'em Starting Hands, we know that there are six combinations for each of those large pairs, four combinations of A-K suited, twelve combinations of A-K of mixed suits, and four combinations of A-Q suited.

That gives us 36 absolutely playable combinations—hands you can play under all circumstances, unless there are unexpected tells or rock-solid information denying us the opportunity to play. That's a pitiful 36 out of 1,326 possible starting hands that we should almost always play—2.7 percent or 1 in 37. Wow! You're worried that you're going to seem too conservative and be considered a rock, right? But, remember, position makes a huge difference in poker. Without the luxury of acting after players on later rounds, your prospects for profit are severely handicapped. You can use other hands, from more commanding positions, to dispel your opponents' notions that you're a rock.

Of course, you *might* end up in the best position, even if you enter a pot early. Everyone except one of the blinds (or rarely even *both* of the blinds) might fold. Then you'll be against one or two players who will be forced to act before you on the last three rounds of betting. But if you play a hand early hoping this will happen, you're being far too optimistic. It's much more likely that at least one player between you and the blinds will enter the pot, leaving you in the uncomfortable situation of having to act first. Remember, the more players that remain to act between you and the blinds, the more likely you are to end up with inferior position on the future betting rounds. That's why you must be extra selective about the hands you play in early seats.

Now, I'm not saying you shouldn't liberalize this advice from time to time. I'm just saying that you must have valid reasons to do so, and in the absence of those reasons—which will be most of the time—you should religiously stick to this advice. If you play your hold 'em starting hands the way I recommend, you'll have plenty of opportunities to play a lively and aggressive game. But early positions won't account for much of that.

So, let's play a few hands…

NO-LIMIT STARTING HAND SCENARIO

Game description: No-limit hold 'em, $50/$100 blinds.

Players: 9

Your position: 2nd to act after the big blind.

Action so far: The player to your right (under the gun) has folded.

Other information: The game is comprised of both weak and aggressive opponents.

Your hand: 7♣ 7♦

Correct decision: Fold!

Reason: Often, you're going to be raised and will either fold or have to make a marginally profitable call. Your pair of sevens isn't large enough to call a big raise, because you could be dominated by a larger pair—and even if you aren't, you could meet disaster if a larger ranking card subsequently pairs your opponent. And you might be forced to surrender, even while holding the better hand on the flop, simply because you'll feel threatened.

Note that in some limit hold 'em games and a few no-limit ones where players allow you to see many flops cheaply, it might be okay to call the big blind. Normally, though, and whenever you're in doubt, you should fold. Much money is lost by players barging optimistically into a hold 'em pot in this situation, only to be punished.

LIMIT STARTING HAND SCENARIO

Game description: Limit hold 'em, $10/$20 blinds

Players: 10

Your position: 1ˢᵗ to act—under the gun.

Action so far: None. You go first.

Other information: The game is made up of very weak, non-aggressive opponents who call too often.

Your hand: A♦ J♠

Correct decision: Fold!

Reason: Anyone who thinks this hand is profitable doesn't understand the power of position in hold 'em. Here's a dirty little secret: Most players enter the pot with this hand. Another secret: Everyone who enters the pot with this hand can expect to experience a loss by doing so for their poker-playing careers. You might be tempted to play, but if you just trust me and throw this hand away automatically from the early positions in a full-handed game, you'll save a great deal of money.

The truth is that even A-K of mixed suits, although profitable in the long run, isn't as profitable as it might seem. Expect to average 10 percent or less in extra return on the money you place in the pot during this hand—assuming you play correctly.

(Putting it in the language of financial analysts, this means an immediate 110 percent ROI—*return on investment*.) A-Q of mixed suits from a very early position, can have a positive ROI, as well, although a very small one. You need to consider who's waiting to act behind you in gauging whether A-Q is profitable or not. Often, it isn't. A-J, even in the hands of a superstar, will average a loss from the first seat in a full-handed game. And it's even worse in no-limit games.

LATE POSITION PREFLOP PLAY

In later positions, you can be much more aggressive. In fact, the exact definitions of the cards you play hinges more on the traits and temperaments of your opponents at the moment. Also, the image you're trying to establish matters a great deal in middle and late positions.

If I'm on the dealer button and no one else has entered the pot, I'll consider the nature of the two players in the blinds. If they're both timid—meaning they throw away too many hands in blind positions and they aren't particularly aggressive when they have an advantage, I'll raise with almost anything. What does "almost anything" mean? Is 7-4 of mixed suits okay? Well, as ridiculous as it might seem, 7-4 might be okay.

Let's say you're playing in a limit hold 'em game with blinds of $50 and $100. There's $150 already in the pot, and it cost you $200 to raise. Assume that on average, the timid player in the small blind will fold 75 percent of the time and the timid player in the big blind will fold 60 percent of the time. Mathematically, this means that 45 percent of your raises will result in an immediate profit of $150. So, you're wagering $200 to win $150 right away.

If you're called, you might lose $200 or more. And if you're reraised, you'll have to consider whether to abandon your hand and forfeit the $200 or continue to pursue the pot. But the key is that 45 percent of the time you pocket $150 without a fight, and the remaining times—most of which you'll only be called by one or more of these timid foes—you're still in the hunt. You can get lucky and win, even with hands like 7-4, 8-7, and 5-4. Careful analysis of possible outcomes after the first-round betting shows that you make up the shortfall overwhelmingly by getting lucky on the flop and beyond.

I teach that it's best to be seated to the right of non-threatening, timid opponents, because they don't maximize their usual positional advantage of acting after you. But remember that when the opponents are in the blinds, they don't have positional advantage on the three future rounds of betting. You do. So, in hold 'em, that constitutes another powerful reason why you want unaggressive, tight players on your left. You can steal their blinds.

PLAYING MARGINAL AND GARBAGE HANDS

If the players in the blinds aren't timid, you need to be much more leery of playing garbage hands, because the chances of taking the pot immediately are severely reduced. Against typical opponents, from the dealer position, consider routinely folding all small hands ranking 10-9 of mixed suits and lower. With marginal hands, such as Q-10, K-9, and A-6, play some of the time, but not always. Frequent folding keeps astute opponents off guard, because you won't have an overabundance of this type of hand when you raise. So they won't be able to make assumptions about the probable strength of your dealer-position hands. You'll be playing a particularly deceptive and profitable game if you sometimes fold, sometimes call, and sometimes raise with such medium-strong, late-position hands. And actually, doing each about a third of the time often turns out to be about right.

PLAYING STRONG AND PREMIUM HANDS

With more substantial hands, like K-Q, Q-J, and A-10, you should usually raise. With the strongest hands, like A-A, K-K, Q-Q, J-J, 10-10, A-K (suited or mixed), A-Q (suited or mixed), and A-J suited, you should occasionally just call, hoping that your deception will trap the opponents in the blinds, causing them to make mistakes on later rounds of betting. But don't set this trap routinely. Usually raise, saving the deceptive call for rare occasions when it matters.

MORE LATE POSITION STRATEGY

When you're two or three seats before the blinds and no previous player has entered the pot, consider—in addition to the traits of the players in the blinds—whether the players immediately to your left might fold. You can gauge this either by considering their history of decision-making or by employing the tells we'll discuss later. If you can drive away the players between you and the blinds, you'll secure a positional advantage on all future betting rounds. Being aggressive two or three seats away from the blinds can be profitable if you do it at the right times and for the right reasons. But don't overuse this tactic.

While late position play accounts for a disproportionately large share of the hands you'll play, most of your play-or-fold decisions are made in early or middle positions. If you play correctly, you'll probably be surprised how often you fold when you're not in a late position. Remember that in choosing your starting hands, you'll need to paint your own canvas and be willing to shift playing styles in accordance with whatever resistance you encounter.

Let's play another hand…

NO-LIMIT STARTING HAND SCENARIO

Game description: No-limit hold 'em, $50/$100 blinds.

Players: 9

Your position: One seat before the dealer button.

Action so far: Everyone has folded so far.

Other information: The game is comprised of both weak and aggressive opponents, with only the player in the small blind position being unusually deceptive among those who remain.

Your hand: 6♥ 6♦

Correct decision: Raise $150, making it $250 total to play.

Reason: You're in a dramatically different situation than you were in the previous hand. Here, your pair of sixes is just under the raw strength of the pair of sevens that you folded, but now you only face three remaining players who could potentially beat you. In the previous example, there were seven remaining players who could hold better hands.

Sometimes you should just call, but usually you should raise. Ideally, you'd like to win the $150 in blinds right now without a fight. That amount of instant profit is more than you can expect to win, on average, if you play the pot through the river. Just calling invites too many players into the pot with probable higher-ranking cards that can easily pair above your sixes. You don't want that, so a raise is usually in order, although just calling is an occasionally correct tactic that will make your strategy less predictable.

A minimum allowable raise, doubling the big blind, is also a bit too timid and may invite more competition than you desire. The extra $50 has psychological impact and is much more likely to chase away players holding bigger ranks. One of your biggest goals here is to get the player on the button to fold. If you accomplish that, you'll be assured that you act last on all future rounds of betting.

Of course, there's nothing magic about $250. You might try $225, $275, or even $300. Or you might occasionally bet more.

The problem with making too large a raise is that you might trap yourself into either having to call a more significant reraise or, worse, find yourself folding the best hand and leaving a large wager undefended. All-in-all, $250 plays right.

If you don't succeed in winning the pot outright, you're hoping to contend with just one opponent. Your pair of sixes is less profitable if two or more opponents continue to pursue the pot.

Position and Hand Selectivity

The best advice I can give you is to try to control the game. Be selective about the starting hands you play, and always keep in mind what your likelihood is of ending up in last-to-act position on future betting rounds. The more likely that is, the more you can consider playing a hand. If it's unlikely that you will have a commanding position on future betting rounds, be extra selective about the starting hands you decide to play.

Q & A: LOOKING AT PROFIT
QUESTION

If you're a winning player, where does most of your profit come from in poker?

a. Most of your poker profit comes from staying out of pots with many opponents when you have speculative hands, such as when you're hoping to make a straight or a flush.

b. Most of your poker profit comes from the players to your right.

c. Most of your poker profit comes from the tightest opponents who are easiest to bluff.

d. Most of your poker profit comes from being able to quickly and correctly calculate the odds at the table.

ANSWER

The answer isn't A, because you usually don't want to avoid a lot of players when you're trying for a straight or a flush. A lot of active opponents is precisely what you want to see when you hold a speculative hand. This is especially true if the flush you are trying for is large, because you might beat a smaller flush in a showdown. Now, it's true that small flushes and straight attempts can lose value in some situations against many opponents, because of the risk of making the hand and still having it beat.

The general rule is that—when "on the come" hands collide—the best speculative hand has a profit expectation and other speculative hands often don't have any profit expectation at all. The problem with this concept in practice is that you often don't know whether you have the best, or the only, speculative hand. So, in general you want many players contesting for the pot when you're trying for a straight or a flush. That spells greater profit on the times you connect. And, of course, you still need to be selective about which speculative hands you decide to play.

And the answer isn't C. Most of your profit doesn't come from the tightest players. Yes, they are easier to bluff, but that doesn't mean you can bluff them very often, otherwise they'll adapt. And since they're in pots less frequently than loose players, the opportunities for profitable bluffs are relatively rare. More profit comes from loose players who are not selective and wager frivolously than from tight players who can be occasionally bluffed.

And most of your poker profit doesn't come from being able to quickly and correctly calculate the odds at the table (choice D) either. While it's good to be able to count the pot, estimate its eventual size, and weigh that against the projected size of all your future wagers in conjunction with the odds of making various final hands, this isn't something that's easy to do. It isn't easy even for experienced players. As long as you have a generally excellent awareness of pot odds and the likelihood of winning hands, you'll be able to profit by playing well, even if you can't quickly and correctly calculate exact odds.

Yep, the answer I was looking for was B. Most of your poker profit comes from your right. That's because each player has a positional advantage over those to the right, because they get to see what that player does before acting. That's why I teach that if you could put a weather satellite up in space and spy on a poker table, you'd see the money moving 'round and 'round the table mostly in a clockwise direction, with a few abnormal cross currents, as players take advantage of opponents to their right.

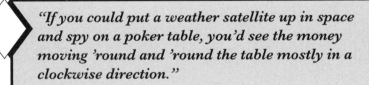

"If you could put a weather satellite up in space and spy on a poker table, you'd see the money moving 'round and 'round the table mostly in a clockwise direction."

And now on to the meat of preflop play: The starting hand selection.

4 HOLD 'EM STARTING HANDS

THE MATH BEHIND HOLD 'EM STARTING HANDS

In order to understand how to play your first two cards, you need to know how many different hold 'em starting hands you can possibly be dealt. The answer is 169.

There are 52 cards in a standard deck. Any of those 52 cards could come first and any of the remaining 51 cards could come second. So, if you multiply 52 times 51, what do you get? Well, you get the wrong answer if you're trying to figure out how many two-card combinations of starting hands are possible in hold 'em.

In order for you to see that, I'll simplify. Suppose that there were only three cards in the deck; the ace, king, and queen of spades. If you were dealt two of those three cards, how many possible hands could you get? You could have the A-K, A-Q, or K-Q. Nothing else is possible. These are the only three possible hold 'em hands.

But if you apply the incorrect method, you'd take three possible first cards multiplied by two remaining possible second cards and end up with six combinations—twice as many as the correct answer. That's because in hold 'em, you don't care about the *order* that your first two cards arrive. If you end up with A-K, it doesn't matter whether the ace came first or the king. So, you divide by two. You would get six (3 x 2) divided by two for a total of three combinations.

Now, since that's the correct kind of formula, let's apply it to hold 'em starting hands. Now it's 52 x 51 = 2,652 divided by two for 1,326 combinations. There! It's possible to get any of 1,326 starting hands.

So, why did I say there were only 169?

169 CATEGORIES OF STARTING HANDS

Well, that's the answer for how many different *types* of hold 'em starting hands there are. If you hold Q♣ J♦, your prospects are theoretically the same as if you looked down and saw Q♠ J♥. I'm not saying those hands are identical; I'm saying they are conceptually the same starting hands, because they have equal prospects. Of course, if the board ends up being A♣ K♣ 6♦ 3♣ 2♣, then with the first hand you have a nut flush that can't possibly be beat and with the second hand you don't even hold a pair.

But before the flop, there's no way of knowing which Q-J is better. Their strengths are identical, even though the cards are different. We call those two example hands, Q-J offsuit or Q-J of mixed suits. And they form a single category among the 169 categories. Similarly, there's no initial difference between K♥ 2♥ and K♦ 2♦. They also fit one of the 169 categories called K-2 suited (meaning of the same suit).

STARTING HAND CATEGORIES

The 169 starting hands form three classes: pairs, suited cards and mixed cards. Here's how the starting hands fit into these three classes:

1. **Pairs**: There are 13 categories, ranking from A-A down to 2-2.
2. **Suited Cards**: There are 78 categories, ranking from A-K down to 3-2. Notice that I don't specify that these must be unpaired, because with just one deck in use, there's no such thing as a pair of the same suit.
3. **Mixed Cards**: There are 78 categories of different ranks of different suits—for example 7♦ 6♣—also ranking from A-K down to 3-2.

Each category has different likelihoods of being dealt to you. For instance, even though a pair of aces is one category out of 169 and A-K *suited* is also one category, you're more likely to be dealt a pair of aces than A-K *suited*. As you know, a starting pair of aces is much more powerful than A-K suited. So shouldn't it be harder to get aces?

If you have a pair of aces, then the second ace must be one of the three other suits. And since it is unimportant which order the two aces arrived, we divide by two, as before, to arrive at the number of possibilities. We get 12 (4 x 3) divided by two for a total of six combinations. And, of course, that isn't just true of aces; it's true of any pair. There are 13 categories for pairs, one for each rank, and there are six equally powerful—or equally weak, depending on how you see it—exact instances of each pair. So, of the 1,326 total hands possible to start with when you play hold 'em, 78 of them are pairs, of which exactly six of them are a pair of aces.

That means that you'll start with a pair once in 17 hands (16 to 1 against)—5.9 percent of the time. This number is essential for you to remember. So, in a typical game, with a thirty-five hands-per-hour pace, expect to get dealt about two pairs an hour. And you'll start with a pair of aces (or any specific pair) less than ½ percent of the time (0.45 percent), with the odds 220 to 1 against (1 in 221 times). Figure on getting that pair of aces once every six hours or so.

There are only four possible hands that make up the category A-K suited, because there are only four suits in the deck. Obviously, there can only be four instances of A-K suited: clubs, diamonds, hearts, and spades. And that turns out to be true for each and every suited category, whether it be K-J suited, 7-6 suited, or the lowliest 3-2 suited.

That means of the 78 categories of suited starting cards, each has four members, for a total of 312. So, you'll be dealt cards of the same suit 23.5 percent of the time, and the odds are 3.25 to 1 against (or 13 to 4).

Understanding What to Expect

Now we're starting to understand expectation in hold 'em. The game will be really frustrating if you don't know what's normal and what's not. That's why I'm explaining these concepts. And in a minute, I'm going to show you how you can take these simple numbers straight to the bank.

With only six possible pairs of aces and only four possible combinations of A-K suited, you can see why it's easier to start with aces than the less profitable A-K suited hands. The ratio is six combinations to four combinations, or 3 to 2 in favor of the more common aces.

What about all those unpaired hands of mixed suits? Well, each of those has 12 possibilities. So, for those 78 categories, there are 936 qualifying hands, which is 70.6 percent of all 1,326 possible hands. This means that midway between two-thirds and three-quarters of the time, you should expect to start with unpaired, unsuited cards.

Of the remaining 29.4 percent, constituting just 390 hands, you'll have suited cards much more often than pairs. To be precise, there are 78 possible hands that comprise pairs (which, obviously, are never suited) and 312 that are suited.

The Anatomy of Preflop Cards

Now we're beginning to understand the anatomy you're working with before the flop.

- 5.9 percent of the time, you'll begin with a pair
- 23.5 percent of the time, you'll begin with suited cards (which can never be paired)
- 70.4 percent of the time, you'll begin without either a pair or suited cards

And that totals 100 percent, the whole universe of hold 'em starting hands. Each pair has six possibilities, each suited category (consisting of two different ranks) has four, and each non-paired, non-suited category has 12.

THE MAGIC CHART OF HOLD 'EM STARTING HANDS

Here's the tiny chart that will magically serve you for the rest of your hold 'em career:

CHART OF STARTING HANDS

Class of starting-hand categories[1]	Number of the 169 total hands possible[2]	Total hands out of 1,326	Percentage of hands	Number of exact qualifying hands[3]	Odds-to-1 against being dealt these hands[4]
Pair (A-A down to 2-2)	13	78	5.88	6	220-1
Suited (A-K down to 3-2)	78	312	23.53	4	330.5-1
Mixed-suit, not paired (A-K down to 3-2)	78	936	70.59	12	109.5-1

HOW TO READ THE CHART

1. There are three general classes of hold 'em starting hands: pairs, suited cards, and mixed cards that aren't paired.

2. Each category is defined by two specific ranks, so 10-10 and 6-6 are examples within the pair class, while A-K, Q-7 and 4-3 are examples within the other two classes.

3. These are the number of possible hands if you identify the exact suits. For example, there are six qualifying hands that comprise a pair of aces, four that comprise J-10 suited, and twelve that comprise 7-2 of mixed suits.

4. These are the odds of being dealt a type of hand, so the odds against being dealt 9-4 of mixed suits on your next hand are 109.5 to 1 against.

HOW TO USE THE CHART

Here's how this chart will be important to your hold 'em future. I'm about to provide you with important guidelines for how to play opening hands in hold 'em. Other books do that, too, although a few seem to be based more on guesswork than anything else and as such, stray into unprofitable territory. But, let's talk about that some other time. What's important is that most hold 'em authorities and expert players will give you sensible guidelines that harmonize with *their* particular styles of play.

So, one expert might say that in a tight nine-handed game, when you're first to act, you should only wager with A-A, K-K, Q-Q, or A-K (either suited or not). Fine. It's important to know how many hold 'em starting hands in the whole universe of possibilities is being defined. Well, now you can, thanks to the chart.

Examining that advice—which, by the way isn't bad for inexperienced players in a tight game—let's think about how often the expert is asking us to play. Look at the chart. Out of

1,326 possible starting hands, there are six pairs of aces, six pairs of kings, six pairs of queens, four instances of A-K suited, and twelve instances of A-K of mixed suits. Add that together and you get 34.

So, the self-appointed expert is saying that you should play just 34 hands out of 1,326. That gives us 2.56 percent. The expert is telling us to fold 97.44 percent of the time. Wow!

THE TOP 20 HOLD 'EM STARTING HANDS

Follow that advice and you'll only play a hand, on average once in 39 deals when you're first to act. The rest of the time, you'll fold. And, remember, I said that extra-conservative advice really isn't bad for inexperienced players. That's because early positions in hold 'em are treacherous to play, because you're leaving yourself open for many opponents to look down, find something special, and then beat up on you. Remember, unless they're in the blinds, when you act first, your opponents will have the positional advantage of acting after you on all future betting rounds, too. In hold 'em, just as in all forms of poker, getting to see what opponents do before your turn is a huge edge. And, when acting first, you don't have it.

In 1994, years before MCU existed, I used my *Pro Poker* newsletter to unveil my previously unpublished research on hold 'em starting hands. This section covers information that was made public only to 800 world-class players, poker analysts, and others serious about poker science who subscribed to that limited-circulation publication. It has never been published elsewhere. It's an approximation of the true strength for each of the 169 categories of starting hands, based on my computer research and analysis about how opponents typically play in pursuit of the pots.

In a minute, I'll let you examine the entire chart, but first I'll list the top 20 hold 'em starting hands. The list changes a little, depending on whether you're apt to face many opponents or just a few (which, itself, is largely dictated by how many players were dealt in).

CARO'S TOP 20 HOLD 'EM STARTING HANDS

Rank	Category	Class	Hands	Percent-age of hands	Odds-to-1 Against Being Dealt this Hand	Hands This or Better	Percent-age of Hands This Good or Better	Odds-to-1 Against Being Dealt This Hand or Better
1	A-A	Pair	6	0.45	220-1	6	0.45	220-1
2	K-K	Pair	6	0.45	220-1	12	0.90	109.5-1
3	Q-Q	Pair	6	0.45	220-1	18	1.36	72.7-1
4	J-J	Pair	6	0.45	220-1	24	1.81	54.25-1
5	A-K	Suited	4	0.30	330.5-1	28	2.11	46.4-1
6	10-10	Pair	6	0.45	220-1	34	2.56	38-1
7	A-K	Mixed	12	0.90	109.5-1	46	3.47	27.8-1
8	A-Q	Suited	4	0.30	330.5-1	50	3.77	25.5-1
9	K-Q	Suited	4	0.30	330.5-1	54	4.07	23.6-1
10	A-J	Suited	4	0.30	330.5-1	58	4.37	21.9-1
11	A-10	Suited	4	0.30	330.5-1	62	4.68	20.4-1
12	A-Q	Mixed	12	0.90	109.5-1	74	5.58	16.9-1
13	9-9	Pair	6	0.45	220-1	80	6.03	15.6-1
14	K-J	Suited	4	0.30	330.5-1	84	6.33	14.8-1
15	K-Q	Mixed	12	0.90	109.5-1	96	7.24	12.8-1
16	K-10	Suited	4	0.30	330.5-1	100	7.54	12.3-1
17	A-9	Suited	4	0.30	330.5-1	104	7.84	11.75-1
18	A-J	Mixed	12	0.90	109.5-1	116	8.75	10.4-1
19	8-8	Pair	6	0.45	220-1	122	9.20	9.87-1
20	Q-J	Suited	4	0.30	330.5-1	126	9.50	9.52-1

Note: All percentages were rounded off to two decimal places. The numbers in the odds-to-one against columns were rounded to whole numbers above 100, to one decimal place between 10 and 99, and to two decimal places below 10. If the last digit was exactly zero, further decimal places were not used. If the last digit was exactly five, an extra decimal place was provided to indicate the "halfway" status.

OBSERVATIONS

Isn't it strange that if you decide to be selective and play only the top 20 hands—which includes such often-troublesome holdings as A-J of different suits and a meager pair of eights—you're going to be involved less than one in ten hands. This points to a powerful truth in hold 'em: Most hands are quite vulnerable. Also, most hands ranking in the top 20 are unprofitable when played from early positions.

You would think that the top 20 hands would make up more than 10 percent of all hold 'em starting cards, simply because 20 is more than 10 percent of 169. But that's the peculiarity I'm teaching you. It isn't how many categories of hands you play; it's which class they fall into that determines how often you'll play.

In the top 20 chart, notice that there are nine categories of suited hands, with only four members each, while there are only four categories of mixed hands with 12 members each. As a consequence, in the whole spectrum of 169 categories of starting hands, you are more likely to be dealt hands toward the bottom than toward the top of the rankings.

One thing you didn't notice on the Top 20 chart was J-10 suited. I point this out because three decades ago, before hold 'em was analyzed scientifically, many experienced players believed that J-10 suited was the best hand in hold 'em, especially in no-limit. It seemed like common sense to them. That hand had moderately high cards and good possibilities of forming a straight or a flush (and a shot at a straight flush or royal). However, J-10 suited actually ranks 26th as a starting hand.

You're invited to visit the charts examining all 169 categories of hold 'em starting hands and the related discussion. We'll look at that now.

COMPLETE HOLD 'EM STARTING HANDS RANKINGS

I believe that in most games, just understanding hold 'em starting hands and playing selectively in accordance with this knowledge is enough to move you beyond break-even into the world of consistent profit. But, as you'll learn in this book, there's so much more to playing profitable poker. Now I want you to tackle something a little more technical.

OFFICIAL HOLD 'EM RANKINGS CHART

The following chart, my Official Hold 'em Rankings, shows the profitability rankings of all 169 hold 'em starting hands for most limit games. There are three columns of rankings, shown side by side.

The middle column, called "Many," is used when there are (or you can anticipate) three or more opponents in a hand. This column shows how the hands rank in multiway pots. When you have many opponents, hands that are speculative, such as 8♠ 7♠ or J♠ 9♠, tend to fare better than the same hands would against fewer opponents.

The last column, called "Few," is used when there are one or two opponents. This column shows, principally, how the hand plays heads-up, but also includes situations where three total players are involved and your opponents are all in late positions.

The first column, called "Main," is a compromise between the other two columns. This is the column you'd use to find the top hold 'em hands, assuming no other information is available. Obviously, other columns could have been created to handle more specific situations, but that would make this unnecessarily complicated. In fact, just learning the "Main" column is enough to give you good guidance for all limit hold 'em games.

The lists are divided into sections which show the top 5%, 10%, 15%, 20%, 25% 33.3%, 50%, and 75%, so that if you only want to play the top 10% most profitable starting hands, you can instantly see which ones they are. These sections do not fall perfectly within the percentages given. For instance, A-10 suited is the lowest-ranking hand in the "Main" column that qualifies within the top 5%. However, the group of hands in that column—from A-A down to A-10 suited—only accounts for 4.68% of the total possible starting hands (62 out of 1,326). But if I include A-Q unsuited in the top 5% category, it would encompass 5.58% of the total possible starting hands (74 out of 1,326).

That's why these groups are not exact. They are chosen by rounding off the statistical distribution to include only the most appropriate hands.

Reading the Chart

Note that the cards shown in the charts are only examples of the hands for the category they represent. For example, if you see a pair of eights, that means we're dealing with *any* pair of eights, regardless of the suits. The example is only one of six that could have been used. If you see two cards of the same suit, those stand for every combination of those exact ranks that are the same suit. The example is only one of four that could have been used. And if you see two unpaired cards with different suits, those stand for every combination of those exact ranks that are of different suits. The example is only one of twelve that could have been used.

So that you can more quickly determine whether the category is a pair, an unpaired combination of the same suit, or an unpaired combination of mixed suits, I have been consistent about which suits were used. Pairs always appear in a club-and-then-diamond arrangement. Unpaired same-suit hands always appear in a double-spade arrangement. And unpaired mixed-suit hands always appear in a heart-and-then-diamond arrangement.

How the Rankings Were Calculated

The ratings in my Official Hold 'em Rankings charts were formed by incorporating the percentage of showdown wins, my proprietary quick power ratings, with a "control" adjustment that deals with how well a hand actually plays in competition, how likely it is to be discarded, and how likely it is to win extra profit.

Although the mathematical adjustments made to the showdown rankings were mostly in keeping with fixed-limit games, rather than no-limit, the profitability of the hands is fairly similar between those hold 'em forms when other advice presented in this book is used. You'll find this to be a significant addition to hold 'em theory and statistical analysis.

And finally, here is my complete hold'em rankings chart.

CARO'S OFFICIAL HOLD 'EM RANKINGS

Rank	Main	Many	Few	
1	A-A	A-A	A-A	
2	K-K	K-K	K-K	5%
3	Q-Q	Q-Q	Q-Q	
4	J-J	J-J	J-J	
5	A-K suited	A-K suited	A-K suited	
6	10-10	A-Q suited	A-K mixed	
7	A-K mixed	10-10	10-10	
8	A-Q suited	A-K mixed	A-Q suited	
9	K-Q suited	K-Q suited	A-J suited	
10	A-J suited	A-J suited	A-10 suited	
11	A-10 suited	A-10 suited	A-Q mixed	
12	A-Q mixed	K-J suited	K-Q suited	
13	9-9	9-9	9-9	10%
14	K-J suited	K-Q mixed	K-J suited	
15	K-Q mixed	A-Q mixed	A-J mixed	
16	K-10 suited	Q-J suited	A-9 suited	
17	A-9 suited	K-10 suited	K-Q mixed	
18	A-J mixed	J-10 suited	8-8	

19	8-8	A-9 suited	A-10 mixed	
20	Q-J suited	Q-10 suited	K-J mixed	
21	K-J mixed	8-8	K-10 suited	
22	A-8 suited	A-J mixed	A-8 suited	**20%**
23	A-10 mixed	K-J mixed	A-5 suited	
24	Q-10 suited	A-8 suited	A-4 suited	
25	K-9 suited	Q-9 suited	Q-J suited	
26	J-10 suited	10-9 suited	K-9 suited	
27	A-5 suited	Q-J mixed	A-7 suited	
28	A-4 suited	K-9 suited	K-8 suited	
29	Q-J mixed	A-10 mixed	A-6 suited	
30	A-7 suited	K-10 mixed	A-3 suited	
31	K-8 suited	J-9 suited	A-2 suited	
32	K-10 mixed	A-5 suited	K-10 mixed	
33	Q-9 suited	A-4 suited	Q-J mixed	
34	A-3 suited	A-7 suited	K-7 suited	
35	A-6 suited	A-3 suited	Q-10 suited	**25%**
36	A-2 suited	J-10 mixed	A-5 mixed	
37	Q-10 mixed	K-8 suited	Q-10 mixed	
38	K-7 suited	Q-10 mixed	7-7	
39	7-7	A-6 suited	A-9 mixed	
40	J-9 suited	7-7	Q-9 suited	
41	10-9 suited	A-2 suited	A-4 mixed	
42	J-10 mixed	Q-8 suited	J-10 suited	
43	K-6 suited	K-7 suited	K-9 mixed	**33.3%**
44	K-9 mixed	9-8 suited	A-8 mixed	
45	Q-8 suited	10-8 suited	K-6 suited	
46	A-9 mixed	K-6 suited	A-3 mixed	
47	A-5 mixed	J-8 suited	Q-9 mixed	
48	K-5 suited	K-9 mixed	K-8 mixed	
49	A-4 mixed	K-5 suited	A-2 mixed	
50	K-4 suited	A-9 mixed	A-7 mixed	
51	Q-9 mixed	K-4 suited	A-6 mixed	
52	6-6	6-6	K-5 suited	
53	J-8 suited	K-3 suited	Q-8 suited	
54	A-8 mixed	Q-7 suited	J-10 mixed	

55	Q-7 suited	8-7 suited	K-4 suited
56	K-3 suited	J-9 mixed	K-7 mixed
57	A-3 mixed	K-2 suited	6-6
58	K-8 mixed	Q-9 mixed	J-9 suited
59	10-8 suited	9-7 suited	Q-7 suited
60	A-2 mixed	J-7 suited	K-3 suited
61	K-2 suited	A-5 mixed	Q-6 suited
62	J-9 mixed	10-9 mixed	K-6 mixed
63	9-8 suited	A-4 mixed	K-2 suited
64	Q-6 suited	A-8 mixed	Q-5 suited
65	A-7 mixed	Q-6 suited	J-9 mixed
66	K-7 mixed	10-7 suited	J-8 suited
67	Q-5 suited	Q-8 mixed	10-9 suited
68	J-7 suited	7-6 suited	K-5 mixed
69	Q-8 mixed	A-3 mixed	5-5
70	5-5	10-8 mixed	Q-4 suited
71	10-9 mixed	K-8 mixed	Q-8 mixed
72	A-6 mixed	Q-5 suited	K-4 mixed
73	Q-4 suited	5-5	Q-3 suited
74	K-6 mixed	A-2 mixed	J-7 suited
75	Q-3 suited	Q-4 suited	Q-7 mixed
76	10-7 suited	8-6 suited	K-3 mixed
77	K-5 mixed	Q-3 suited	J-8 mixed
78	Q-2 suited	K-7 mixed	K-2 mixed
79	9-7 suited	Q-2 suited	10-8 suited
80	J-8 mixed	4-4	10-9 mixed
81	8-7 suited	J-6 suited	Q-2 suited
82	10-8 mixed	J-8 mixed	J-6 suited
83	J-6 suited	10-6 suited	10-7 suited
84	K-4 mixed	A-7 mixed	J-5 suited
85	Q-7 mixed	J-5 suited	Q-6 mixed
86	4-4	9-6 suited	Q-5 mixed
87	J-5 suited	6-5 suited	9-8 suited
88	10-6 suited	K-6 mixed	J-7 mixed
89	J-4 suited	7-5 suited	4-4
90	K-3 mixed	J-4 suited	10-8 mixed

33.3%

50%

91	7-6 suited	K-5 mixed	J-4 suited
92	J-3 suited	5-4 suited	10-6 suited
93	K-2 mixed	J-3 suited	J-3 suited
94	8-6 suited	10-7 mixed	Q-4 mixed
95	J-7 mixed	8-5 suited	J-2 suited
96	9-6 suited	J-2 suited	9-7 suited
97	J-2 suited	Q-7 mixed	Q-3 mixed
98	10-7 mixed	A-6 mixed	10-7 mixed
99	Q-6 mixed	K-4 mixed	9-8 mixed
100	Q-5 mixed	9-8 mixed	Q-2 mixed
101	9-8 mixed	10-5 suited	J-6 mixed
102	10-5 suited	6-4 suited	10-5 suited
103	Q-4 mixed	J-7 mixed	9-6 suited
104	7-5 suited	9-5 suited	8-7 suited
105	10-4 suited	7-4 suited	J-5 mixed
106	6-5 suited	10-4 suited	10-4 suited
107	8-5 suited	8-7 mixed	3-3
108	9-5 suited	K-3 mixed	10-3 suited
109	10-3 suited	8-4 suited	10-6 mixed
110	Q-3 mixed	10-3 suited	J-4 mixed
111	3-3	Q-6 mixed	9-7 mixed
112	9-7 mixed	4-3 suited	8-6 suited
113	J-6 mixed	K-2 mixed	10-2 suited
114	Q-2 mixed	9-7 mixed	9-5 suited
115	8-7 mixed	Q-5 mixed	J-3 mixed
116	10-2 suited	3-3	7-6 suited
117	5-4 suited	9-4 suited	8-5 suited
118	10-6 mixed	5-3 suited	J-2 mixed
119	J-5 mixed	10-2 suited	2-2
120	9-4 suited	Q-4 mixed	9-4 suited
121	8-4 suited	7-3 suited	9-6 mixed
122	7-4 suited	6-3 suited	10-5 mixed
123	6-4 suited	9-3 suited	8-7 mixed
124	2-2	10-6 mixed	7-5 suited
125	9-3 suited	2-2	9-3 suited
126	J-4 mixed	7-6 mixed	10-4 mixed

75%

127	9-2 suited	Q-3 mixed	8-4 suited	
128	9-6 mixed	9-2 suited	10-3 mixed	
129	J-3 mixed	8-6 mixed	6-5 suited	75%
130	8-6 mixed	J-6 mixed	9-2 suited	
131	7-6 mixed	Q-2 mixed	10-2 mixed	
132	7-3 suited	J-5 mixed	9-5 mixed	
133	5-3 suited	6-2 suited	8-6 mixed	
134	J-2 mixed	8-3 suited	7-4 suited	
135	10-5 mixed	8-2 suited	7-6 mixed	100%
136	4-3 suited	5-2 suited	8-3 suited	
137	8-3 suited	9-6 mixed	6-4 suited	
138	6-3 suited	3-2 suited	8-5 mixed	
139	8-2 suited	4-2 suited	5-4 suited	
140	9-5 mixed	J-4 mixed	8-2 suited	
141	10-4 mixed	6-5 mixed	9-4 mixed	
142	8-5 mixed	8-5 mixed	7-3 suited	
143	6-2 suited	7-5 mixed	9-3 mixed	
144	10-3 mixed	7-2 suited	7-5 mixed	
145	6-5 mixed	J-3 mixed	9-2 mixed	
146	5-2 suited	5-4 mixed	6-3 suited	
147	7-5 mixed	10-5 mixed	8-4 mixed	
148	7-2 suited	9-5 mixed	5-3 suited	
149	10-2 mixed	J-2 mixed	7-2 suited	
150	4-2 suited	10-4 mixed	6-5 mixed	
151	3-2 suited	10-3 mixed	6-4 mixed	
152	5-4 mixed	6-4 mixed	5-2 suited	
153	9-4 mixed	8-4 mixed	6-2 suited	
154	8-4 mixed	7-4 mixed	4-3 suited	
155	6-4 mixed	9-4 mixed	7-4 mixed	
156	9-3 mixed	5-3 mixed	5-4 mixed	
157	7-4 mixed	10-2 mixed	8-3 mixed	
158	9-2 mixed	9-3 mixed	8-2 mixed	
159	5-3 mixed	9-2 mixed	4-2 suited	
160	8-3 mixed	6-3 mixed	6-3 mixed	
161	6-3 mixed	7-3 mixed	7-3 mixed	
162	7-3 mixed	4-3 mixed	3-2 suited	

163	8-2 mixed	5-2 mixed	5-3 mixed	
164	4-3 mixed	8-3 mixed	4-3 mixed	
165	5-2 mixed	8-2 mixed	7-2 mixed	
166	6-2 mixed	4-2 mixed	6-2 mixed	**100%**
167	7-2 mixed	6-2 mixed	5-2 mixed	
168	4-2 mixed	3-2 mixed	4-2 mixed	
169	3-2 mixed	7-2 mixed	3-2 mixed	

INTERESTING OBSERVATIONS FROM THE CHARTS

Here are some things you should consider when studying these charts:

1. When you're against few opponents (especially heads up), ranks are more important than suits. That's why A-Q of mixed suits ranks above K-Q suited in the "Few" column, but not in the "Many" column.

2. Some hands that you might instinctively think of as having more value in multiway pots than heads up, such as A♠ 2♠, actually rank higher on the "Few" list than on the "Many" list. Another peculiarity! This is because the ace by itself is much more valuable against just one opponent (or few opponents). Do you see how A-4 suited ranks 24th on the "Few" list, but 33rd on the "Many" list? I'll bet a lot of players would guess it would be the other way around.

3. The power of moderately high ranks is not as great heads-up or short-handed as many might suspect. Look at Q-J offsuit, for example. It ranks 27th on the "Many" list, but only 33rd on the "Few" list. What does this tell us? It tells us, among other things, that even though the Q-J combo isn't suited, thereby making it more difficult

to form a flush, the straight possibility is enough to make the hand more worthwhile against many players.

MORE ON THE "MAIN" COLUMN

Let's talk about the "Main" column, which is a compromise between the "Many" and "Few" columns. How can it be a compromise, you ask, when a pair of tens is shown as 6th in rank on the "Main" list, but 7th on both the "Many" and "Few" lists?

Simple. Notice that the 6th-ranking hands are different on those latter two lists, and neither one of those was quite as profitable on average as 10-10. Now, look at the 50th-ranking hands. On the "Many" line it's A-9 of mixed suits, and on the "Few" line it's A-7 of mixed suits. Your immediate conclusion might be, then, that the "Main" line would settle on a compromise and choose A-8 of mixed suits.

Well, guess what? This is not the case. The "Main" line shows K-4 suited. That's because factors similar to, but less obvious than the previous example of a pair of 10s are at work. Rest assured, the "Main" line really does choose the right compromise in expected profit between the other two lines.

You may occasionally want to browse forward to the charts in the next chapters to better understand some of the material. For example, you'll notice some things on the starting hand charts that will look like a mistake. You may even leap out of your chair screaming that there's a mistake because the ratings are illogical. For example, J-6 unsuited is listed just above Q-2 unsuited under the "Many" column.

J-6 UNSUITED VERSUS Q-2 UNSUITED

Maybe you're asking yourself, "How can that possibly be?" First of all, keep in mind that the exact order of these closely matched hands might not make much difference. The order might even be wrong and probably is for some very specific situations. But, even then, the mistake is trivial. The two hands are of almost equal value, but J-6 does come out on top using my formula.

Here are two reasons why Q-2 is not clearly superior, as you would guess at first glance:

1. A pair of queens or three queens is not much more likely to win than a pair of jacks or three jacks, but a pair of sixes or three sixes is relatively more likely to win than a pair of deuces or three deuces.

2. The J-6 is slightly more apt to combine with four board cards to form a straight. The reason is that with Q-2, both cards bump up against the ends of the straight spectrum—especially the deuce—giving less room to form a straight-making combo. I call this problem, being "dead-ended."

8-5 SUITED VERSUS 10-7 UNSUITED

What you're about to see may shock some hold 'em purists who have long believed that hands such as 8-5 suited must be light years more profitable than 10-7 of mixed suits. Surprise! You'll find the 10-7 ranking about equal with 8-5 suited against many players, and considerably above against a few. This is especially true heads up.

Actually, 8-5 is slightly better against many players and in some particularly loose games. Whether you're focusing on the "Many" or the "Few" columns, larger ranks of mixed suits, compared to lower ranks of the same suit, rate higher than you may have expected. This doesn't mean that old-fashioned thinking about suited connectors like 8-7 and 6-5 is wrong. It just means that in a whole lot of situations, ranks are more important than suits.

THE MEDIAN HOLD 'EM HAND

A cursory inspection of the charts would lead you to believe that the 85th ranking hand on any of the three lists—the midway point of the 168 possible hands—would be the median-ranked hand. If you look at the 85th hand on the "Main" list, it's Q♥ 7♦.

This isn't quite the correct median, however. So, let me explain this peculiarity. As we discussed earlier, the different categories of hands contain different numbers of combinations of cards that fit their definitions. Specifically, there are six combinations for any pair, four for any two suited ranks, and twelve for any two unsuited ranks, excluding pairs.

When this is taken into consideration, the median hold 'em starting hand, gauged by profitability, is approximately 8♠ 6♠, with 658 combinations ranking higher and 664 lower. It ranks 94th of the 169 categories.

OBSERVATIONS ABOUT ACES AND KINGS

1. Interestingly, A-6 offsuit is marginally more profitable in short-handed action than Q-8 suited. That's not too peculiar when you consider that aces and kings are very valuable by themselves short-handed, especially heads up.

2. A very revealing indication of the power of a single high card short-handed is that A-10 offsuit ranks 19th on the "Few" list, but 29th on the "Many" list. Remember, straight-making hopes for that particular hand are not high. In order to use both cards in a straight, you need K-Q-J. That's only one three-card combination that fits. With a hand like 8-7, though, there are four combinations that complete the straight: J-10-9, 10-9-6, 9-6-5, and 6-5-4. You can see that the A-10 relies heavily on winning with a best pair or sometimes with just an ace high. And those events are more likely to happen heads-up or against two opponents.

3. Find the least glamorous hand that includes a king on the "Few" list. That's right, it's K♥ 2♦ and it ranks 78th. But on the "Many" list, it ranks 113th. This should show conclusively that the power of a single high card is comparatively much greater short-handed.

OBSERVATIONS ABOUT K-Q SUITED

1. One hand that should stand out in your mind is K-Q suited. On the "Many" list, it ranks 9th and is well within the top 5% group. But on the "Few" list, it ranks 12th and falls just outside the 5% group. Interestingly, even K-J suited makes the 5% group on the "Many" list.

2. It's interesting to note how much difference in rank there is between 10-8 offsuit and 8-7 suited. As you'd expect and as the "Many" line shows, 8-7 suited is much more valuable than 10-8 of mixed suits in multiway pots. However, the "Few" line shows that the 10-8 of mixed suits is the better hand. This will be especially true heads up. The hands, however, are about even in the "Main" column. In fact, 10-8 offsuit shows up only one notch lower. In order to understand this, you've got to realize how higher ranks lead to higher pairs which make much more difference short-handed.

You also should understand that flushes you make with 8-7 suited (excluding straight flushes) are far from invulnerable. They get beat, especially in multiway pots. Most often they are beat when four, instead of three, of that suit end up on the board and another player has a higher-ranking card of that suit. Note, though, that similar comparisons of slightly lesser ranks do not show as much closeness. For instance, when you compare 8-6 offsuit with 6-5 suited, 6-5 suited is always better. That's because a simple pair of eights is very rarely much better than a pair of sixes, whereas in the previous example, a pair of tens does win significantly more often than a pair of sevens. Also, straights made with 10-8 are more likely to leave opponents with losing pairs (such as a pair of queens when the board includes Q-J-9), and that can mean winning extra bets.

3. Similarly, don't be unnerved because J-9 offsuit is listed above both J-8 suited and 10-9 suited on the "Few" list. In reality, these hands are almost identically profitable heads-up. Yes, there are many situations where the suited hands are better short-handed. But, in general, you should like or dislike these hands about equally.

OBSERVATIONS ABOUT EXTRA STRAIGHTS

You might wonder why 8-4 of mixed suits rates above 7-4 of mixed suits on the "Many" line. That's good thinking! You're right, there are slightly more ways to make a straight with 7-4, but that doesn't quite compensate for those rare times when the higher rank of the 8 matters. It's almost a tie, though, and when you're against a lot of opponents, 7-4 is better.

Whenever you feel the urge to improve your grasp of starting hands, study the previous rankings chart to see how values change when you're against many, rather than few, opponents. Then, look at the distribution of starting hands that follows. Although it deals only with the "Main" line, it gives you great insight into the actual probabilities of being dealt the hands you need.

HOLD 'EM STARTING HAND DISTRIBUTION CHART

I've structured the following distribution chart in according with my Main rankings, previously presented. The table you're about to examine lists the ranks in descending order and tells you what percentage of time you can expect to be dealt a hand ranking at least that high. It also provides the odds-to-1 against that happening.

HOLD 'EM STARTING HAND
DISTRIBUTION CHART
(BASED ON CARO'S "MAIN" RANKINGS)

Rank	Hand	Combinations Specific / All		Chances of Being Dealt This Hand or Better	Odds-to-1 Against Being Dealt This Hand or Better
1	A-A	6	6	0.45%	220.00
2	K-K	6	12	0.90%	109.50
3	Q-Q	6	18	1.36%	72.67
4	J-J	6	24	1.81%	54.25
5	A-K suited	4	28	2.11%	46.36
6	10-10	6	34	2.56%	38.00
7	A-K mixed	12	40	3.02%	32.15
8	A-Q suited	4	50	3.77%	25.52
9	K-Q suited	4	54	4.07%	23.56
10	A-J suited	4	58	4.37%	21.86
11	A-10 suited	4	62	4.68%	20.39
12	A-Q mixed	12	74	5.58%	16.92
13	9-9	6	80	6.03%	15.58
14	K-J suited	4	84	6.33%	14.79
15	K-Q mixed	12	96	7.24%	12.81
16	K-10 suited	4	100	7.54%	12.26
17	A-9 suited	4	104	7.84%	11.75
18	A-J mixed	12	116	8.75%	10.43
19	8-8	6	122	9.20%	9.87
20	Q-J suited	4	126	9.50%	9.52
21	K-J mixed	12	138	10.41%	8.61
22	A-8 suited	4	142	10.71%	8.34
23	A-10 mixed	12	154	11.61%	7.61
24	Q-10 suited	4	158	11.92%	7.39
25	K-9 suited	4	162	12.22%	7.19
26	J-10 suited	4	166	12.52%	6.99

27	A-5 suited	4	170	12.82%	6.80
28	A-4 suited	4	174	13.12%	6.62
29	Q-J mixed	12	186	14.03%	6.13
30	A-7 suited	4	190	14.33%	5.98
31	K-8 suited	4	194	14.63%	5.84
32	K-10 mixed	12	206	15.54%	5.44
33	Q-9 suited	4	210	15.84%	5.31
34	A-3 suited	4	214	16.14%	5.20
35	A-6 suited	4	218	16.44%	5.08
36	A-2 suited	4	222	16.74%	4.97
37	Q-10 mixed	12	234	17.65%	4.67
38	K-7 suited	4	238	17.95%	4.57
39	7-7	6	244	18.40%	4.43
40	J-9 suited	4	248	18.70%	4.35
41	10-9 suited	4	252	19.00%	4.26
42	J-10 mixed	12	264	19.91%	4.02
43	K-6 suited	4	268	20.21%	3.95
44	K-9 mixed	12	280	21.12%	3.74
45	Q-8 suited	4	284	21.42%	3.67
46	A-9 mixed	12	296	22.32%	3.48
47	A-5 mixed	12	308	23.23%	3.31
48	K-5 suited	4	312	23.53%	3.25
49	A-4 mixed	12	324	24.43%	3.09
50	K-4 suited	4	328	24.74%	3.04
51	Q-9 mixed	12	340	25.64%	2.90
52	6-6	6	346	26.09%	2.83
53	J-8 suited	4	350	26.40%	2.79
54	A-8 mixed	12	362	27.30%	2.66
55	Q-7 suited	4	366	27.60%	2.62
56	K-3 suited	4	370	27.90%	2.58
57	A-3 mixed	12	382	28.81%	2.47
58	K-8 mixed	12	394	29.71%	2.37
59	10-8 suited	4	398	30.02%	2.33
60	A-2 mixed	12	410	30.92%	2.23

61	K-2 suited	4	414	31.22%	2.20
62	J-9 mixed	12	426	32.13%	2.11
63	9-8 suited	4	430	32.43%	2.08
64	Q-6 suited	4	434	32.73%	2.06
65	A-7 mixed	12	446	33.63%	1.97
66	K-7 mixed	12	458	34.54%	1.90
67	Q-5 suited	4	462	34.84%	1.87
68	J-7 suited	4	466	35.14%	1.85
69	Q-8 mixed	12	478	36.05%	1.77
70	5-5	6	484	36.50%	1.74
71	10-9 mixed	12	496	37.41%	1.67
72	A-6 mixed	12	508	38.31%	1.61
73	Q-4 suited	4	512	38.61%	1.59
74	K-6 mixed	12	524	39.52%	1.53
75	Q-3 suited	4	528	39.82%	1.51
76	10-7 suited	4	532	40.12%	1.49
77	K-5 mixed	12	544	41.03%	1.44
78	Q-2 suited	4	548	41.33%	1.42
79	9-7 suited	4	552	41.63%	1.40
80	J-8 mixed	12	564	42.53%	1.35
81	8-7 suited	4	568	42.84%	1.33
82	10-8 mixed	12	580	43.74%	1.29
83	J-6 suited	4	584	44.04%	1.27
84	K-4 mixed	12	596	44.95%	1.22
85	Q-7 mixed	12	608	45.85%	1.18
86	4-4	6	614	46.30%	1.16
87	J-5 suited	4	618	46.61%	1.15
88	10-6 suited	4	622	46.91%	1.13
89	J-4 suited	4	626	47.21%	1.12
90	K-3 mixed	12	638	48.11%	1.08
91	7-6 suited	4	642	48.42%	1.07
92	J-3 suited	4	646	48.72%	1.05
93	K-2 mixed	12	658	49.62%	1.02
94	8-6 suited	4	662	49.92%	1.00

95	J-7 mixed	12	674	50.83%	0.97
96	9-6 suited	4	678	51.13%	0.96
97	J-2 suited	4	682	51.43%	0.94
98	10-7 mixed	12	694	52.34%	0.91
99	Q-6 mixed	12	706	53.24%	0.88
100	Q-5 mixed	12	718	54.15%	0.85
101	9-8 mixed	12	730	55.05%	0.82
102	10-5 suited	4	734	55.35%	0.81
103	Q-4 mixed	12	746	56.26%	0.78
104	7-5 suited	4	750	56.56%	0.77
105	10-4 suited	4	754	56.86%	0.76
106	6-5 suited	4	758	57.16%	0.75
107	8-5 suited	4	762	57.47%	0.74
108	9-5 suited	4	766	57.77%	0.73
109	10-3 suited	4	770	58.07%	0.72
110	Q-3 mixed	12	782	58.97%	0.70
111	3-3	6	788	59.43%	0.68
112	9-7 mixed	12	800	60.33%	0.66
113	J-6 mixed	12	812	61.24%	0.63
114	Q-2 mixed	12	824	62.14%	0.61
115	8-7 mixed	12	836	63.05%	0.59
116	10-2 suited	4	840	63.35%	0.58
117	5-4 suited	4	844	63.65%	0.57
118	10-6 mixed	12	856	64.56%	0.55
119	J-5 mixed	12	868	65.46%	0.53
120	9-4 suited	4	872	65.76%	0.52
121	8-4 suited	4	876	66.06%	0.51
122	7-4 suited	4	880	66.37%	0.51
123	6-4 suited	4	884	66.67%	0.50
124	2-2	6	890	67.12%	0.49
125	9-3 suited	4	894	67.42%	0.48
126	J-4 mixed	12	906	68.33%	0.46
127	9-2 suited	4	910	68.63%	0.46
128	9-6 mixed	12	922	69.53%	0.44

129	J-3 mixed	12	934	70.44%	0.42
130	8-6 mixed	12	946	71.34%	0.40
131	7-6 mixed	12	958	72.25%	0.38
132	7-3 suited	4	962	72.55%	0.38
133	5-3 suited	4	966	72.85%	0.37
134	J-2 mixed	12	978	73.76%	0.36
135	10-5 mixed	12	990	74.66%	0.34
136	4-3 suited	4	994	74.96%	0.33
137	8-3 suited	4	998	75.26%	0.33
138	6-3 suited	4	1002	75.57%	0.32
139	8-2 suited	4	1006	75.87%	0.32
140	9-5 mixed	12	1018	76.77%	0.30
141	10-4 mixed	12	1030	77.68%	0.29
142	8-5 mixed	12	1042	78.58%	0.27
143	6-2 suited	4	1046	78.88%	0.27
144	10-3 mixed	12	1058	79.79%	0.25
145	6-5 mixed	12	1070	80.69%	0.24
146	5-2 suited	4	1074	81.00%	0.23
147	7-5 mixed	12	1086	81.90%	0.22
148	7-2 suited	4	1090	82.20%	0.22
149	10-2 mixed	12	1102	83.11%	0.20
150	4-2 suited	4	1106	83.41%	0.20
151	3-2 suited	4	1110	83.71%	0.19
152	5-4 mixed	12	1122	84.62%	0.18
153	9-4 mixed	12	1134	85.52%	0.17
154	8-4 mixed	12	1146	86.43%	0.16
155	6-4 mixed	12	1158	87.33%	0.15
156	9-3 mixed	12	1170	88.24%	0.13
157	7-4 mixed	12	1182	89.14%	0.12
158	9-2 mixed	12	1194	90.05%	0.11
159	5-3 mixed	12	1206	90.95%	0.10
160	8-3 mixed	12	1218	91.86%	0.09
161	6-3 mixed	12	1230	92.76%	0.08
162	7-3 mixed	12	1242	93.67%	0.07

163	8-2 mixed	12	1254	94.57%	0.06
164	4-3 mixed	12	1266	95.48%	0.05
165	5-2 mixed	12	1278	96.38%	0.04
166	6-2 mixed	12	1290	97.29%	0.03
167	7-2 mixed	12	1302	98.19%	0.02
168	4-2 mixed	12	1314	99.10%	0.01
169	3-2 mixed	12	1326	100%	0.00

Note: The "All" combinations, "Likelihood," and "Odds-to-1 against" columns on this distribution chart give prospects for being deal that exact hand *or better.*

5 POST-FLOP CONCEPTS

THE ROAD TO PROFIT

Although most of your long-term profit will be made by deciding whether or not to play a hand from the get-go, how you respond to the flop will add to or subtract from your overall profits—and not in an insubstantial way. In fact, many players who would otherwise win, end up lifelong losers, simply because they mishandle their post-flop decisions.

It's often easier to gauge the value of starting hands by position before the flop than to estimate how strong a hand is when viewing the flop or beyond. Sometimes the strength of your hand relative to the flop is apparent, but often it's vague.

The problem is that we can easily calculate the odds of receiving your starting hand and compare this on a hierarchal scale to all other possible hands. After all, we know the exact identities of the cards remaining in the deck and what your absolute hand-value consists of. But on the flop, the turn, and the river, the deck essentially changes. The best hands are now relative to the board. Hands with previous high potential might be weak now. Hands that seemed really weak might be unbeatable. But since we don't know in advance what the board will be, we have no way of presenting easy-to-memorize statistics about how hands rank. That would require a separate set of rankings for every conceivable board in conjunction with every conceivable hand. In other words, this would be unmanageable and pretty much useless—you'd be buried by data. It's far better to proceed in accordance with general principals.

I can't stress enough that, once you've decided to play a hold 'em hand, the flop will usually disappoint you. There are 19,600 possible flops for each of the 1,326 starting hands. That means a total of 25,989,600 combinations of cards by the time you see that flop. Each of these combinations will be unique as to exact ranks and suits, although many will be logically identical. By logically identical, I mean that:

A♥ A♣ with a flop of 10♦ 9♦ 8♦ is the same as
A♠ A♦ with a flop of 10♣ 9♣ 8♣, but
K♣ Q♦ with a flop of 7♦ 4♦ 2♦ is *not* the same as
K♣ Q♦ with a flop of 7♣ 4♣ 2♣.

We can see that the two hands with a pair of aces are logically and functionally identical, because the aces are of different suits from the 10-9-8 flop. But the K-Q hands are logically and functionally different, because the suits of the 7-4-2 flop copy the suit of the queen in the first example and the king in the second. Therefore, you could make a queen-high flush and lose to a king-high flush in the first example, but not in the second.

What's important to understand is that you must know how to handle each flop, giving consideration to:

1. Whether it helped your hand;
2. How likely it is to help opposing hands; and

3. How the combined effects of the flop on your hand and opposing hands increased or decreased your prospects of profit.

One of the great mistakes made by too-loose hold 'em players is to continue to pursue the pot when it isn't profitable to do so. And one of the great mistakes made by too-tight players is to abandon the pot whenever the flop doesn't help their hand.

You need to keep in mind that, although the flop usually won't help you, it usually won't help an opponent, either. Keeping these thoughts in mind, here are some considerations to keep you on the road to profit.

PLAYING OVERCARDS

Don't move. Don't breathe. Stop everything you're doing. Please lend me your mind for a few minutes. If you play hold 'em, but haven't really mastered it yet, I want you to read this section. I'm going to start out with a little story.

THE BIGGER HAND

When I was very young, my grandpa used to fool little kids by asking them to play a guessing game. He couldn't trick me, though, and I was proud that he couldn't. In a few minutes, my grandpa will never be able to trick you, either—and we'll both be proud.

The way my grandpa used to trick those little kids was to show them a shiny new nickel. He'd tell kids that he was going to hide the nickel in one of his hands and that if they could guess which hand, they got to keep it. Grandpa would put his hands and the nickel behind his back. He'd take a couple seconds and bring both hands back in front of him for a kid to see. "Point to the hand

> with the nickel in it," Grandpa would command.
>
> Well, most of the time, one of those hands looked larger, because Grandpa wouldn't grasp as tightly and his knuckles extended further than the ones on his other hand. Grandpa's biggest looking hand was the one the poor kid usually chose. It was empty. It was an illusion.

THE HOLD 'EM ILLUSION

Here's the same illusion as it happens in hold 'em. If you're a serious player, you probably already realize that sometimes you can call a bet with nothing more than two unpaired cards that are higher than the flop. That happens when the pot is large and there aren't too many players contesting it. You're gambling that a card of one of your two ranks will come on the final two board cards, giving you a commanding pair that will win the pot. We have a term for this—calling with two overcards.

And that advice is correct. You should often (but certainly not always) call with two overcards in that circumstance; otherwise you'll be surrendering far too many pots to aggressive bettors.

You might wonder: If I am advising you to sometimes call on the flop with two overcards, shouldn't I advise you to also call with just one overcard if you have a straight draw? Maybe I should, because a single overcard and a straight draw, even an inside straight draw, is more powerful and profitable than two overcards.

However, there are things to know about straight draws that make them different from each other, depending on the exact cards and situation. Let's talk about it. When you play two overcards, you're hoping to catch one of six remaining cards of either one of the ranks. If you hold A-Q and the flop is 10-6-3, then you can connect for a commanding top pair by catching an ace or a queen. There are three of each remaining in the deck, a total of six cards. (Of course, you might also be supremely lucky and catch K-J, forming a straight.)

YOU

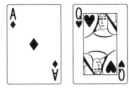

FLOP

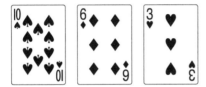

But if you have A-6 and the flop is 7-4-3, then you can catch any of three aces to make the biggest possible pair and any of four 5s to make a very powerful inside straight that's unlikely to be either beaten or tied. That's seven cards, instead of six, that can save you.

YOU

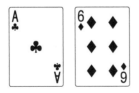

FLOP

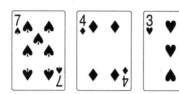

SINGLE OVERCARD WITH A BONUS VALUE

But it's even better than that for the single overcard and an inside straight draw. You have hope of pairing your smaller card and sometimes—not often, but sometimes—seeing that pair win in a showdown. With the A-6, you can pair that 6, in addition to catching an ace or a 5. Even though it probably won't be enough to win, it's at least an extra bonus, and the long-shot possibility has some value. With just the two overcards, the A-Q, you had just the six main chances and no extra ones, except the remote chance of catching perfectly for a two-card, fill-in straight. With the A-6, you have seven (count 'em, seven) main chances and three extra long-shot chances. Plus four of the main seven chances provide you with a powerful straight, not just a pair.

If you're beginning to think that you should play the single overcard with an inside straight draw more often than two overcards, you're right. Anytime you would even consider playing two overcards, you should be eager to play a single overcard and a smaller card providing an inside straight draw. And, of course, we're not even talking about a single overcard with another card that provides an open-end straight draw—that's much stronger still.

> *"If you're beginning to think that you should play the single overcard with an inside straight draw more often than two overcards, you're right."*

Now, there are a couple things to keep in mind. One is that not all overcards are equal. Aces rule, for sure. Another is that you can have both an overcard and an inside straight draw using just one card from your hand—for instance, if you hold A-2 and the flop is Q-J-10. As you see, the kicker can be small and outside the straight range, and you'll still have better prospects of drawing out on an opponent than you would if you held just two overcards.

YOU

FLOP

Also, keep in mind that a lower straight draw is usually more likely to hold up than a higher one. A higher straight is especially dangerous when you hold one card at the low end. Then someone can hold a single card to make the high end. For instance, if you have K-6 and the flop is 10-9-8, a 7 will provide a straight for you.

YOU

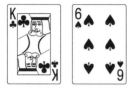

FLOP

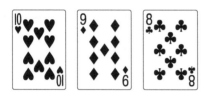

But wait! That's a dangerous straight, because, if that 7 appears, then anyone holding a single jack will beat you. But if you hold A-2 and the flop is 6-5-4, you are less worried about having your straight beat if a 3 appears. That's because an opponent is less likely to hold a 7 than a jack.

YOU

FLOP

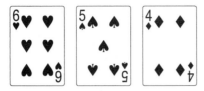

And, finally, having two high-ranking overcards *does* sometimes have an advantage over one high rank and a small card that provides an inside straight draw. If you hold A-Q and the flop is 7-6-3, that's arguably better in some situations— particularly for beginners who get in trouble when making second-best hands—than holding A-4. Why?

YOU

FLOP

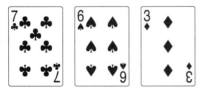

Didn't I already say that A-4 provides more ways to win? That's true, but what if it's a circumstance where an opponent very likely holds an ace? Then if one of the two remaining aces appears, you'll probably win with the queen kicker, but lose with the four kicker. Of course, if a queen hits, you'll have the best possible kicker, the ace. Put it all together and it's still usually more profitable to hold the A-4.

So, not all straights are equal, and in fact, the best card you can hold is an inside rank when both extreme ends of the straight are already present. This means a hand such as A-8, when the flop is 9-7-5. Visualize it again. You have A-8. The flop is 9-7-5. If any of four 6s flop, you'll make your straight, and it's unlikely that anyone would hold a 10-8 to beat you or even an 8 to tie.

YOU

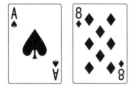

FLOP

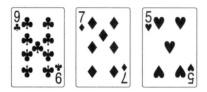

Also, keep in mind that high straights completed with a single card are more likely to be tied than low straights. That's because opponents are more likely to play high cards and, therefore, are more likely to hold the same high rank than the same low rank.

Remember, sometimes in hold 'em, you can choose to play a single overcard and a card that gives you an inside straight draw when two overcards wouldn't be strong enough. In fact, you should just about always play that single overcard and inside straight draw whenever calling with two overcards would be a close decision. (A rare exception may be when, if you connect, you'll hold the low end of a fairly high straight that can be easily beaten by a single high card.)

GRANDPA'S ILLUSION MAKES PLAYERS CHOOSE OVERCARDS

Strangely, though, many players prefer the two overcards. They see a single overcard as being too weak. And they see an inside straight draw as being too weak. They don't realize that the combined power can be considerably stronger than two overcards, because you have more chances of connecting, and the straight is more likely to hold up than an overcard.

The illusion of the two overcards being bigger than one overcard plus one small card providing an inside straight draw is the same illusion as when my grandpa let his knuckles bulge out to make the empty hand seem more inviting. The same thing happens in hold 'em, where you can choose which hands you play after the flop. Many players choose to play two overcards, but not to play one overcard and a small card that provides an inside straight draw.

That's the wrong hand to choose, and that's my grandpa's illusion. Don't let my grandpa fool you anymore. Sure, you can sometimes play just two overcards, and that hand will sometimes hide the nickel. But the hand that's more likely to hide the nickel is the one that doesn't look like it—one overcard with the inside straight draw. Choose to play that hand anytime two overcards would be a close decision.

BETTING WITH IMPUNITY

Betting with impunity is one of my favorite concepts. It means that you can bet for value without worrying about a raise from a weaker hand. This happens when you have a moderately strong hand and your opponents fear that you might have an even better one.

It's always easier to make a value bet if you know you're unlikely to be raised. For instance, you can use flush cards as a smokescreen to bet a strong or medium-strong pair or two small pair, especially when it seems unlikely that your opponent could have made the flush.

Let's look at an example:

It's no-limit. You enter the pot with a raise from one seat away from the dealer button position holding K♦ J♠. Specifically, the blinds are $10 and $20, everyone has folded so far, and you wager $45, slightly more than the minimum allowed (twice the size of the big blind). The player in the dealer position folds, the small blind adds $90 to the pot (making it $100 to play, since he already had entered a required $10 bet), and the big blind folds. You're now faced with a $55 raise. Should you call?

Normally, yes. The pot is now $165 (your $45, the small blind's $100, and the big blind's forfeited $20), so if you call $55, you're getting exactly 3 to 1 in money odds. (You divide 165 by 55 to get that answer.)

That's almost always good enough odds to call a bet heads-up in no-limit hold 'em games like this one (and absolutely good enough to call in limit games). So you call. Here comes the flop. It's A♠ K♥ Q♥. That's far from a desirable flop, even though you connected for your highest possible pair. You mostly worry about your opponent holding an ace, and also about K-Q, J-10, or two hearts with a good possibility of making a flush.

YOU

FLOP

Your opponent checks and you bet $150 into this $220 pot. Your opponent calls immediately. Even though you have a good chance of holding the better hand, you would have preferred that he'd folded. Had that happened, you would have added $120 profit to your pre-hand stack. You correctly surmise that the *average* profit you'll now earn—if any—from this head-to-head battle will be less than that $120.

The turn card is a seemingly inconsequential 2♣. Your opponent checks, and this time you decide to check along, although often you would bet.

Here's the river card: 4♥.

YOU

BOARD

Once more, your opponent checks and now you bet $250 into the $520 pot. You bet it instantly, in a show of confidence.

Why? It's because you've estimated that it's more likely that your opponent holds a queen (giving him a pair of queens), a king with a weak kicker (giving him an inferior pair of kings), or some smaller pocket pair, instead of him holding an ace or some other winning hand. You figure that he's already suspicious and prone toward calling, and if he merely calls your modest-sized bet, you're more likely to win than to lose and, thereby, earn more profit. But you're still worried about other hands he might beat you with, including one containing an ace or two hearts. What you really don't want is for him to raise, making you either fold without knowing if he was bluffing, or call a better hand in the vain hope that he is bluffing. If the river card had been 4♦, instead of that actual 4♥, you would not have bet. You would have had more fear of a raise.

But now, your opponent must be worried about the possibility that *you* made a heart flush. That's because you bet on the flop, when the two hearts showed, making it possible that you were wagering on the come. But you checked on the turn when another heart failed to appear. In your opponent's mind, this adds a meaningful likelihood that you hold two hearts. And when the third heart appears on the river, your opponent probably is going to give added respect to the possibility that you made a flush. Unless he holds the ace of hearts and a smaller heart, there's little chance he'll raise. Instead, he'll be content to just call—whether he has you beat or not—and see the showdown.

That's an example of betting with impunity: You have an opportunity to push your hand for maximum value with reduced fear of a raise.

Effective opportunities for betting with impunity can also occur before the final betting round when you're last to act. After you excercise such an opportunity to bet with impunity, whenever you're checked into on the next round, check along and accept a free card if you don't improve—and bet if you do improve.

WHEN TO BET SECOND PAIR ON THE FLOP

Betting second pair, means you're wagering when you hold a card that pairs the second-highest-ranking card on the board. Here are some of the key times you should tend to do it:

a. When you'd be betting into timid opponents.
b. When you have a big kicker.
c. When the top rank is small.
d. When your opponent is in the big blind or just called during first-round wagering when historically he raises when holding high cards.

PLAYING AGGRESSIVELY WHEN YOU'RE FIRST TO ACT

If there's one single place where I disagree with published contemporary poker theory, it's in the area of betting aggressively when you're first to act.

The most widely described situation is when you're heads up with a marginal hand and you must decide first. Should you bet? Well, that's easy. The answer is "sometimes," and it's very important that you understand it. If you think there's a yes or no answer, you're not living in the real poker universe where you often must vary decisions like this in order to be less predictable. But even so, which is better? Betting that marginal hand into a lone opponent when you're first to act? I think not!

> *"When you're heads up with a marginal hand and you must decide first: Should you bet? Well, that's easy. The answer is 'sometimes,' and it's very important that you understand it."*

The theory in favor of betting marginal hands says that you should sometimes bet hands when you act first that you wouldn't bet if you acted last. That's because, when you're last, you have the absolute chance of getting a free card by checking, but when you're first, you don't have this added benefit and betting has a proportionally greater value among your options. This reasoning is wholly true and unarguable. The question is: How much and how often is this really a benefit?

I'll skip the analysis and just get to the advice. I'm positive that you should check borderline hands in the first position heads-up much more often than most professional players do in practice. The truth is, you're at a disadvantage when you're first to act. So, all things being equal, your opponent has an edge when you have a borderline hand and must act first. This remains true whether you bet or whether you check. I believe you should check at least twice as often as you should bet, but there are exceptions that cry out for the bet.

You should especially bet any time you're against an opponent who seems to fold more often than is correct. And you should especially check (and then call) any time you're against an opponent who seems to bluff more often than is correct.

We're talking about a minor quibble I have with a few very thoughtful analysts who believe that betting from the first position heads-up with marginal hands is usually best. I believe just the opposite, based on careful analysis, but you can always define your opponents however you choose, and then either side of the argument becomes correct.

Although I've often advised that you should bet marginal hands quite liberally, you're much better off doing so when you're last to act. That's very important so I'll say it again. Bet marginal hands that have some already-made strength (usually a pair) more liberally if you're last to act. If you're first to act, usually check. If you have a speculative hand (often a try at a flush), usually check if you're last to act—just accept the free card. If you're first to act, sometimes bet, but usually check and *hope* to get a free card.

In summary, lean toward checking heads-up when you're first to act and hold a marginal hand.

PLAYING OPEN-END STRAIGHT DRAWS

Some of the tough decisions in hold 'em involve whether or not to call a bet on the flop when you have an open-end straight draw. Often, you should. But when it's close, you need to consider other things. Here are three:

1. Two Suited Cards on the Flop

If there are two suited cards on the flop, you're somewhat more likely to be beat by a flush, even if you make your straight. This can often turn a hand that would otherwise be slightly profitable—with three different suits flopping—into one that's clearly unprofitable.

In case you're wondering how often the flop will contain three different suits, it's 39.8 percent of the time. So, three out of five times, you'll see two or more cards of the same suit flop.

2. A Pair on the Flop

If there is a pair on the flop, you're somewhat more likely to be beat by a full house or four of a kind, even if you make your straight. This, too, can often turn a hand that would otherwise be slightly profitable into one that is clearly unprofitable.

3. High Ranked Kicker

Is your extra card high in rank? When a single card provides the open-end straight possibility (such as a flop of 9-7-6 when you hold K-8), the rank of that extra card is important. You want an additional chance of making a pair big enough to win if, for example, your opponent makes queens on the turn. Ace is best, of course. You won't often start with hands that give you the opportunity to flop a small straight attempt with an unrelated extra card, but when you do, the rank of the extra card should often be the deciding factor.

Whenever the decision about whether to call with an open-end straight attempt is close, you can use the three factors above—among others—to break the tie.

BETTING A FLUSH DRAW ON THE FLOP

Here's one of my favorite hold 'em plays that you can use quite often without opponents adapting. It's a well-known play, and many of your sophisticated opponents will use it quite often, too.

You have a flush draw on the flop—two of your suit in your hand, two on the board. You're last to act. Everyone checks to you. Bet. If it's a no-limit game, bet about half the pot size (or even smaller if it won't seem so suspicious that it invites a raise). Sometimes you'll win the pot immediately without a struggle, but even if you don't, you'll frequently have helped your cause.

Now, everyone is apt to check to you on the turn. Even aggressive players will usually check, because they're hoping you'll bet, so they can raise. If you make your flush, you just keep betting. If you miss, you check along and see the final card at no additional cost. The great thing is that you got a partially free card which could have cost double in common limit games where the pre-established size of bets increase after the flop. Yes, you paid to see it by betting on the flop, when the price was only half. The river card is also effectively free, because if you miss, you'll usually fold.

There's another twist to this tactic. You don't want to overuse it, because astute players may catch on and adapt, but one of the built-in tools of deception comes from mostly betting these flush draws when you have at least one card higher than the board. That way, you have additional chances of making top pair and continuing to bet on the turn.

When this happens, many opponents won't notice at the showdown that you were originally betting the flush draw. They sometimes just see the top pair and forget when you made it or how. This psychologically camouflages the fact that you're often betting flush draws on the come, hoping to get a free card.

FOUR SUITED CARDS ON THE BOARD

You should, of course, exercise caution when there are four cards of one suit on the board and you don't have a flush. But sometimes you should bet right into that board without a flush.

The best time to bet is when you have two pair, three-of-a-kind, or a straight against a lone sophisticated player who has checked into you. If there were raises before the flop and parts of the four-flush on the board are high cards, especially an ace, figure it's more likely that your opponent does *not* have a flush. He is more apt than usual to hold high cards, and those high cards are likely to match the ranks of the suited cards on the board. There are fewer likely ranks that will provide your opponent with a flush, and it's more likely than usual that he has a pair. Remember, opponents who are selective about their starting hands are more likely to form flushes when the suited cards on the board are *low* ranking.

"If there were raises before the flop and parts of the four-flush on the board are high cards, especially an ace, figure it's more likely that your opponent does not have a flush."

So, you should sometimes bet two pair right into four suited cards on the board. Not only can this be a profitable decision, the play will enhance your image.

Q & A: MEDIUM HANDS ON THE RIVER
QUESTION
Which of the following is not a legitimate reason to check a medium-strong hand on the final betting round?

a. Your opponent never bluffs.
b. Your opponent bluffs too often.
c. You have established a very loose image.
d. Your hand is about average in strength.

ANSWER
Remember the important word in this question is *not*. We're looking for the answer that is not a legitimate reason to check a hand on the last betting round.

The answer isn't A, and we'll discuss the reason shortly. In fact, the purpose of this question was disguised. I'm not interested in talking much about the right answer. I'm interested in is explaining why if your opponent never bluffs, that's a motivation to check. I'm guessing the advice won't seem intuitive to you.

The answer isn't B, either. This is the opposite of A, so you might have assumed that one of them must not be a motive to check. I mean, A was "Your opponent never bluffs" and B was "Your opponent bluffs too often." It's reasonable to assume that one of them would be a reason not to check. Actually, they are both reasons to check, as we'll see. The reason you often should check a medium-strong hand when your opponent bluffs too often is that bluffing too often is a mistake that you can take advantage of by calling. You will tend to make more money whenever you give opponents the opportunity to make key mistakes.

And that answer isn't D—your hand is about average in strength. Generally you should bet your strongest hands, bluff with your very weakest hands, and check your medium hands. All the exceptions we make to that basic concept as we consider more sophisticated situations are exactly that—exceptions. So, if your hand is about average in strength, that's often an excellent reason to check.

That answer is C. Having a loose image is not a good reason to check a medium-strong hand. When your image is loose, you can bet more of your hands for value than you could otherwise. Opponents are likely to call with even worse hands than usual. So, there's your answer.

But let's get back to the reason for the question. I want to talk about A. Why would you want to check if your opponent never bluffs? Makes no sense to you, right? Okay, let's look at it further…

CHECK BECAUSE HE NEVER BLUFFS: ABSURDITY OR POWERFUL TRUTH?

True story. It's 1981. The game is ace-to-five lowball, and we're at the Eldorado Club in Gardena, California. Owner George Anthony is playing. So is Bruce or Butch or Bosco—I can't remember his name. It started with a B; let's settle on Boris and be done with it. Boris was a hippie who showed up and played the big game for about a week, then vanished without a trace. Vanished without repaying my $500, too, but that's another story.

I'm in a pot with Boris. We each draw one card. Me, I make 9-8-4-3-A, a semi-strong hand that can often be bet for value. As I'm checking, I feel a rush of warm breath on my shoulder. I'm studying my opponent, so I don't bother to turn around. I'm hoping that this is pretty-woman breath and not pesty-male-poker-student breath. Boris turns over a pair of fives, losing the showdown.

Warm breath comes nearer. There is a gust in my ear, accompanied by a male mumble: "How come you checked that hand? Aren't you supposed to bet for value?"

"I checked because Boris never bluffs," I whispered.

"Never bluffs!" the student muttered. "That doesn't make any sense. How can some guy never bluffing keep you from value betting? How can you be scared of a guy who doesn't bluff?"

Well, can you guess how I feel about giving instruction at the table? I try to avoid it. So, I motioned the student away from the table, where I explained this...

INITIATIVE, CHECKING AND BLUFFING

In poker, when you check, you surrender your initiative and give it to your opponent. Checking can often give opponents opportunities to make mistakes. Never bluffing is a mistake! Correct strategy when competing against thinking opponents dictates that you must bluff a certain percent of the time for every situation. If an opponent bluffs that amount, you have a very tough decision about whether or not to call. Mathematically, in fact, it doesn't matter. Your profit expectation on each decision will be identical whether you call or fold.

If an opponent never bluffs, you gain the advantage of never having to call for fear that you're being bluffed. Remember, bluffing the correct percent of the time is part of the formula that would make a perfect opponent unbeatable. Bluffing correctly is profitable to him, relative to bluffing incorrectly. If a player never bluffs, he surrenders this profit. So, if an opponent never bluffs, it's correct to sometimes sacrifice a value bet and to check instead.

What if an opponent bluffs too much? Depends. If the opponent bluffs so often that you actually win more than half the time, obviously you should consider checking and calling. But even if your opponent errs by bluffing slightly too much, you might find a check more beneficial than a value bet. It's worth a lot of money if you keep this concept in mind.

So, yes, strange as it seems, you should consider the fact that an opponent never bluffs as a reason for you to check a medium-strong hand! This doesn't mean that you might not bet a medium-strong hand anyway if an opponent calls far too often, but the fact that he never bluffs weighs on the check-side of the decision. Think about it.

CALLING OR BETTING ON THE RIVER

KEEPING PLAYER'S HONEST:
THE STORY OF TOM, DICK, AND HARRY

"Somebody's got to keep him honest," Tom said, calling the bet. The next player to act raised. The original bettor reraised. And poor Tom folded.

"Betting is more a matter of feel than science," Dick once explained to me years ago in Gardena. I had folded before the draw. He had drawn two cards to queens with an ace kicker and made aces-up. I knew this for a fact, because he showed me. Because he didn't want other players at the table to hear us, his voice had been low and conspiratorial. He immediately was raised by a pleasant ninety-seven-year-old woman in a frayed pantsuit. Well, maybe not ninety-seven, but close enough. He called reluctantly. He lost. Poor Dick.

Another time we were playing hold 'em and young Harry said, "I'm going to fold. You've been bluffing too many times. I think this time you've got it." He threw his cards away proudly. The man he was addressing then said, "You shoulda called me, son," turning over a jack-high with a smirk. He had missed a straight. Poor Harry.

I'm not singling those three players out for ridicule. It just seems like these same mistakes are made by practically every Tom, Dick, and Harry you meet at the poker table. And because these mistakes are so common, I think we should examine them further.

TOM'S MISTAKE

How many times have you heard Tom's "Gotta keep 'em honest" line? Well, there's a bit of truth in it because if you never call with questionably strong hands, your opponents can bluff whenever they choose and beat your brains out. Now, I tend to be a guy who thinks getting your brains beat out is bad poker, so I advocate calling sometimes to "keep 'em honest." But when?

The simple answer is that you should call whenever you calculate that if you made the same call in the same situation a million times, you would show an overall profit.

That sounds obvious to experienced players, but it's important that you grasp the concept. You don't much care about whether you're going to make money by calling right now. In fact, most of the time, you'll lose money by calling. And that's how it should be, because, at least in limit poker, the rewards of winning the pot are always much greater than the cost of the call. Therefore, you're risking much less by calling than the reward you'll receive if you win. That means you can call and lose a whole lot of times for every rare time you call and win, and you'll still make money.

CATCH A BLUFF AND LOSE

So, sure, keep 'em honest at the river. You don't want to be bluffed very often in limit poker. But the weaker your hand, the less likely you should be to try to catch a bluff. There comes a point where your hand is so weak that you can catch an opponent bluffing and lose. And, of course, if your hand is relatively strong, but not strong enough to catch most "legitimate" bets, you might unexpectedly beat opponents who are too exuberant in their value betting. So, even when you think you're trying to catch a bluff, the stronger your hand is, the more likely you are to win.

This is even more important when you're in a situation like Tom's. Tom made the mistake of trying to catch a bluff without considering how many players remained to act behind him. One of the simple techniques I teach is to decide in advance when you're the cop and when you're not the cop. You're the cop—and in a position to keep opponents "honest"—when you're heads-up or when you're last to act and nobody has called. Hey, when nobody else calls, we're all counting on you! Otherwise we don't get to see if the bettor is bluffing, and that can drive us crazy, right?

But even if you're in the last position and everyone else has passed, you still shouldn't call all the time, and the stronger your hand is, the more likely you should be to call. Everyone knows that, but did you know that you often need a stronger hand to call in the last seat after everyone has passed than you would if you were heads up?

How come? It's because most opponents are less likely to bluff into many opponents than against just one opponent.

Not only is this how most opponents play, they are correct in playing that way. Yes, the pot is usually bigger when there are more players. That means there's more to win by bluffing and more to win by calling. But the success rate for a bluff is greatly reduced against many opponents. What happens in practice is that potential callers at the river, when there are many of them, do not adequately take into account how significantly the possibility of overcalls diminishes the value of a call. This lack of correct handicapping is true whether it applies to the original call or the overcall.

YOU MUST CALL MOST OF THE TIME

If a single player calls only 50 percent of the time, then, with weak hands, it's always a good idea to bluff in limit games and to bet less than the size of the pot in no-limit games. Remember, the pot might be five times the size of the bet in a limit game. So, if you lose your bet half the time and win the pot half the time, your profit is enormous. You lose $100 on one failed bluff; you win $500 on another bluff that works. That's plus $400 on two attempts, or an average gain of $200 on a $100 bet—a 300 percent return on investment or a 200 percent gain. It's what skilled players live for.

But what if there are two opponents that can call. What if they are oblivious to the fact that they should be more careful with their calls when there are many opponents in the pot? What if they continue to call half the time? Now, half the time that the bluffer survives the first opponent, he loses because the second opponent calls. That comes out to only a 25 percent chance of success—still enough to merit a bet, especially since the pot he's shooting at is likely to be larger when there are many players.

What if there are four potential callers? Then there's only a 6.25 percent chance (50 percent times 50 percent times 50 percent times 50 percent) that the bluff will succeed against opponents that won't adapt. The odds are then 15 to 1 against success, and the bluff is unprofitable unless the pot is at least 15 times as large as the wager. And it gets worse if there are more players.

Also, it gets worse because most opponents call more than half the time. Heads-up, they better, otherwise they're likely to get bluffed out of their bankrolls. Another important point about overcalling is that it takes a much stronger hand to justify an overcall than a call itself. Suppose the pot is $100. If you're the last caller and it costs $10, you're getting 10 to 1 odds and you'll break even winning just one out of 11 times. But if there's already been a call and you're the overcaller, you're facing a $110 pot, getting 11 to 1 odds. Unfortunately, if you only think you have the same chance of winning as the first caller, you're only going to win the pot half the time that you beat the original bettor. That means the pot you're going after is theoretically only half as large—$55. So, you're investing $10 to win $55. You need to have a hand strong enough to beat the bettor one out of six-and-a-half times to break even.

Trust me, there's a lot of difference between a hand that will win once in 11 times and one that will win once in six-and-a-half times. The lesson learned: You need a hand that is much stronger to overcall than to call, even though the pot is bigger when you overcall.

There is another factor. Players don't correctly adjust to the additional strength they require to overcall. Therefore you need to be more cautious than you theoretically should be when you make that first call with players waiting to act behind you. This was Tom's mistake. It might have been better had he raised with his medium-strong hand to prevent calls behind. This is a powerful tactic that you should occasionally choose when you think there's a reasonable chance that you're facing a bluff and many opponents could overcall with mediocre hands if you merely call.

"You need a hand that is much stronger to overcall than to call, even though the pot is bigger when you overcall..."

The next time you're at the hold 'em table, remember that the art of calling bets isn't about keeping players honest. Tom forgot that.

DICK'S MISTAKE

Dick's mistake was thinking that you should just bet at whim—whenever you feel like it. In fact, there is great science that governs when you should bet and when you shouldn't. Here are just four of dozens of major factors that guide you wisely toward the right decision:

1. Often, you shouldn't bet a strong hand if your opponent bluffs too much. You'll sometimes make more money checking and letting him try to bluff when he holds a weak hand.

2. The more liberally your opponent calls, the more medium-strong hands you should bet for value.

3. If a player is threatening to call, you should bet all medium-strong hands. When you see this, the player is trying to prevent your bet. That means he's weak and looking for a cheap showdown, but will often call reluctantly if you bet.

4. You should not bet medium-strong hands into very tight players. You won't get called by weak hands that you can beat and are only likely to get called or raised when you hold the worst hand.

When Dick said betting was more a matter of feel than science, he was just plain wrong.

HARRY'S MISTAKE

Harry's mistake is very common. He thinks opponents keep careful track of what they've done recently and that if they've been bluffing a lot, you can "time" them and figure they're not bluffing this time. Sure, there's a good chance that the player will have a strong hand this time, but that's usually so regardless of previous actions. Players who bluff too much are always profitable to call unless you have a specific reason, usually a tell, to believe they almost certainly aren't bluffing right now.

Actually, some players will back away from a pattern of bluffing, fearing that they're going to the well once too often, but others will keep trying the same trick as long as it's successful. The best advice, if you're in doubt, is to call or fold in accordance with your opponent's demonstrated frequency of bluffing.

When you hold questionable hands against opponents who have bet and who bluff too much historically, keep calling. When you hold questionable hands against opponents who have bet and who don't bluff much historically, keep folding. Don't try to time your opponents. Harry didn't know that.

KEY POINTS

So, we've learned:

1. An overcall must be done with a much stronger hand than a call.
2. If opponents waiting to act behind you are oblivious to point #1 above, a first call must be done with a stronger hand than would otherwise be profitable.

3. A first call when others are waiting to act should indicate more strength than a call with nobody to act behind you, assuming the pots are the same size.

4. In practice, it's less profitable to bluff two players than one player, and even less profitable to bluff three or more players. In fact, on average, all attempts to bluff four or more players, throughout the history of poker, have been massively unprofitable.

5. Sometimes it's better to raise than to call with a medium-strong hand with players to act behind you.

SIX MORE RIVER CONCEPTS
1. Most Players Are Afraid to Raise With a Weak Hand on the Last Round

But they would willingly call a pot only half that size with a very marginal hand, hoping the opponent was bluffing. Well, using limit hold 'em as an example, a raise costs no more in relative size than a call would if the pot were half as big. In fact, if your hand is absolutely hopeless and you think your opponent may be bluffing, a raise is often the best choice! It's scary, and it will lose money most of the time, but it earns profit overall.

I very often use this play with broken straights and flushes, when my opponent may be bluffing and a call is unlikely to win even if he is. Don't do this regularly, but look for the rare opportunities when it might work. You might argue that winning a pot in this manner doesn't qualify as a little extra edge—it's a big one. True, but it isn't often going to be successful. On average, trying this play at the right times will only add a small amount to your bankroll. It's just another tiny edge, but all these tiny edges added together make for significant profit.

2. Be Careful About Raising in the Middle Position

If you're in the middle on the final betting round, only raise with extremely strong hands (and not always) and with weak hands when you're bluffing. Most semi-powerful hands tend to make more long-range profit if you either call (usually) or fold (occasionally).

The reason for this is not obvious and goes beyond the scope of this discussion, but analysis shows again and again that this very common raise—when you're in the middle of two opponents on the final betting round—is seldom your best choice when you hold a fairly strong, but not extraordinarily strong, hand.

3. If You're Averaging a Big Profit Per Play Calling on the River...

Then you're probably not calling enough. Unless you're making all that profit on tells or by calling opponents who bluff too much, you want to see yourself break a little better than even (or settle for exactly even) by calling on the river on a per-call average.

You could easily be the world champion of "profit-per-call" by only calling when you're absolutely sure you'll win. But then you'd lose money on all the other times you didn't defend against a bet because you weren't positive of victory. In hold 'em you only need to win once in a while to break even by calling on the last betting round. If the pot is $100 and it costs $10 to call your only opponent, you only need to win once out of eleven times to break even. If you wait until you're the favorite to win, your average call will seem to be worth a lot. But you'll actually be losing significant money overall by wasting profitable opportunities to call more frequently.

4. Overcalling on the River

You need a substantially stronger hand to overcall on the river than you would to make the first call. If you think you have just as good a chance of winning as the opponent who made the first call, that often isn't enough! Let's again assume the pot is $100 and it costs $10 to call. Against a single opponent, you should call if you'll win at least one time in eleven. But if another opponent calls first, the pot is now $110. It still costs $10 to call, so now you only need to win once in twelve times. But this is much harder to do, because even if you beat the original better, you still have to beat the first caller. And you'll only beat the first caller about half the time. That means, to justify an overcall, you need a hand that has almost twice as good a chance of beating the bettor as you would if you were the only opponent.

Many professionals ignore this concept and overcall too frequently. There are other theoretical factors we should consider—like how everything we've just discussed influences the first caller's strategy—but we'll leave the concept the way it's stated for the sake of simplicity.

5. What to Do Against a River Bet When You're Trapped in the Middle

I wasn't overstating the case when I identified the tactic of raising from a middle position on the final betting round as usually unprofitable. You should typically just call with most hands that seem strong enough to raise. Save your raises for your very strongest hands. Research has shown that you'll make more money just calling with powerful, but not cinch, hands.

The exception is when you think there's a strong chance that the bettor is bluffing and you have an opportunity to drive out a potential winning caller who is waiting to act. So, a key secret on the river—particularly in limit hold 'em games—is to avoid raising in the middle and seeking an extra call from the bettor unless you have overwhelming strength. If you raise with lesser-quality hands, make sure you have some other motive in mind.

6. Betting Weak Hands into Other Hands that Seem Weak

Don't wait for the showdown. You will often win a whole pot that you might only win half the time by checking and learning who's weakest in a showdown. And you might have the best hand and lose the whole pot if you check and your opponent bluffs.

6 BLUFFING CONCEPTS

Suppose you're playing hold 'em, which probably isn't stretching your imagination much since you're reading this book. You hold K♠ J♠ in the $100 big blind. Everyone folds, except the player on the button, who raises $175. (Did I forget to tell you we're playing no-limit in this example?) The player in the small blind folds.

You decide to call and that makes the pot $400, including the forfeited $50 small blind. Note that folding is also a legitimate option here, depending on how selective and dangerous the raiser is. I see players—even professionals—make similar raises quite frequently and that's just plain wrong. However, a reraise is almost never correct, barring a powerful tell indicating that the raiser is weak.

You have an ideal calling hand—if you decide to call at all. You'll be acting first for all future betting rounds, which isn't conducive to going on the attack. And, by just calling, you get to see the flop and leave your opponent guessing about whether you have high-ranking cards or low ones. So, I'm glad you decided not to raise in this situation.

Now that you called, the flop comes 6♠ 7♠ 4♥. Many players almost automatically bet when faced with this scenario, believing they might take the pot right now without a fight, but that even if they get called, they have an excellent chance of making a flush or catching a winning pair with the two overcards. I agree that it's a good decision to bet against many players in this circumstance, but "automatic" isn't the proper way to look at it.

This time, you decide to check, and that's perfectly okay.

How can both choices be okay? Let me wander away from this hand for just a minute to drive home a point. Winning hold 'em (or winning at *any* form of poker) isn't about whether you bet, fold, call, or raise in debatable situations. *Most* situations will be debatable, and anyone who tries to prescribe a hard set of standards about "which hands to bet when" is leading you astray.

But while most situations are open to interpretation, some are clear. So, my teaching is about giving you clear reasons to fold, clear reasons to raise, clear reasons to call, and clear reasons to check—*when* those decisions are clear. If you stick to that and use my other advice to break ties on the majority of decisions that are debatable, you're likely to succeed at hold 'em. It's just that simple.

CHECKING OR BLUFFING: WHICH IS CORRECT?

Now back to the game. To refresh your memory, you hold K♠ J♠, the flop is 6♠ 7♠ 4♥ and you've decided to check, even though betting would also be a strong decision. Your opponent also checks. The next board card is 6♣. That's a pair on the board, but no help for you and probably no help for your opponent, either.

Again you check. And again he checks. The river card is a 2♦. Now what?

YOU

BOARD

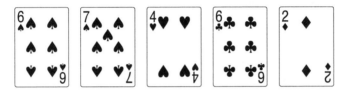

Let me save you the time and give you the answer. You should usually check. If you "bluff" in this situation and take the pot, guess what? You probably didn't bluff—you only think you did. Your hand doesn't require a bluff attempt, because it has a good chance of actually being best with K-J high. It isn't weak enough to require a bluff. The main reason you might occasionally bet is to prevent your opponent from bluffing and taking the pot.

I'm guessing there's a good chance that you're opponent either holds an ace or K-Q, if he has you beat. If he's a savvy player, he's likely to call with an ace, unless you risk a large-enough bet. Of course, it's remotely possible that he'll call with an even worse hand than yours, in which case you weren't bluffing, you were value betting and didn't realize it.

One of the concepts in play here is that you should bet hands, hoping for a call when you perceive that you have significant advantages, and you should bluff when your hands are very weak. Whenever you hands seem about average for the situation, you should check, unless observations about this exact situation dictate otherwise. Your hand is about average. So, usually check.

Now what would happen if you held much weaker cards. Say you called with 9♥ 8♥ (which I don't usually recommend for that $175 raise) and you both checked to the river. Now you should more strongly consider bluffing. It's very unlikely that you'll win in a showdown, so you have more motive for bluffing. But it's still a tough decision whether to bluff or not.

WHOM TO BLUFF: CONSERVATIVE OR AGGRESSIVE PLAYERS

So, let me ask you: Which type of player do you think is easiest to bluff—one who plays conservatively or one who plays liberally? Okay, that wasn't a hard question. Conservative players are easier to bluff, right? And if you keep that in mind throughout your hold 'em adventures, you'll avoid the common mistake of trying to bluff players who call too frequently. You should almost never do that—not occasionally, not even once a week. Repeating: If you're against an opponent who calls too often, you should almost never bluff. If you follow that one simple rule, you'll avoid a leak in your bankroll that is suffered by even some world-class pros.

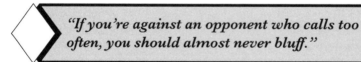

> *"If you're against an opponent who calls too often, you should almost never bluff."*

Beyond that, and at the core of my teaching about bluffing, is this simple surprising fact: Most opponents call too frequently, and as a consequence you need extraordinary reasons to bluff. If you promise to keep that in mind, we're ready to continue with our bluffing lessons.

ARE BLUFFS REALLY PROFITABLE?

Some of you will think the following concept is strange: In the long run, most players will lose a lot of ground on their bluffs—for their whole hold 'em careers.

Wait! How can that be? It can be and it is. I'll tell you why.

Like I said, most of your opponents will call too often. Since they call your bets when you have true strength, you earn chips you would not earn if they called less often. But, they don't just call more than they should when you hold strong hands. They call more than they should when you try to bluff, too.

Does this mean you can't win with a bluff? Of course, it doesn't mean that. There are times when you can bluff and win, but you need to make sure the times are *right*. In fact, you don't just need to find the right times, you need to find the right opponents. There's an art to the bluff, and many top pros are quite skilled in that art.

Not just you, but a few of the best pros, too—though they may not know it—lose chips in the long run through their bluffs. What I just said will help a great deal, and I'll say it once more. Some pros, too, if you count all their bluffs and add them up, lose chips for their entire playing career.

Why? Once more, they get called too much. You might ask: "Don't some pros win a lot on their bluffs?" Yes, they do, but they also lose on their bluffs, but in a strange way. For their bluffs to work, they need to seem tight to their opponents. If they seem too tight, they don't earn the calls they would have earned if they didn't seem so tight.

But here's an interesting fact: You can earn more through calling bluffers than through your bluffs! The reason is that your opponents call too often and many bet too often. So, you should strike them where they're weak.

"Here's an interesting fact: You can earn more through calling bluffers than through your bluffs!"

Just so there's no doubt, though, let me say this one more time. You can bluff now and then and make it pay off. But, most times you'll earn more if you lure your opponents into a calling mode—which is where they want to be, by the way—and save your bluffs for those rare times when they make the most sense.

BLUFF MISSION 1

Concentrate on the player to your left. Watch every hand he or she plays and study the gestures. Remember to listen for voice tells. Don't try to draw conclusions! Drawing conclusions is a mistake. Observation is the key. Usually the major conclusions will come to you effortlessly. Eventually, try to find an opportunity to bluff that player. Keep these things in mind:

1. Most players are easier to bluff after they've come from behind and have just gotten even, especially if forfeiting the money they've already wagered in the current pot will not put them behind again.

2. Most players are easier to bluff after you've made some friendly gesture. If you've shared a joke or let the player share your hand while he's out of a pot, it could be a good time to bluff. If you've accepted coffee from or bought coffee for this opponent, it could be a good time to bluff.

3. Most players are easier to bluff when they're conspicuously looking at you or at their chips. They're subtly trying to discourage your bet.

4. You can get away with a large share of bluffs if you bet decisively while a player is reaching for his chips as if to call. That's because the player is usually just trying to prevent your bet.

5. It's much easier for your bluff to succeed if you make a sizable bet in a no-limit or pot-limit game than if you are confined to betting a fixed limit.

Next time you're at the table, try the experiment. You have two hours to run two bluffs against your target to your left.

FOLLOW-UP

Don't worry if your bluffs failed. In limit poker, because the pots can be many times the size of the bet, your bluffs can fail most of the time and still be profitable. The point is, you became very familiar with one player and you learned things about him that would otherwise have escaped you. You tried to bluff, and whether or not you succeeded, you took that action with a better understanding of your opponent's behavior. You might have gotten unlucky and targeted an opponent who was difficult to bluff. That doesn't matter, either. The value is in having accomplished the mission and knowing how to apply this type of observation to your future games.

BLUFF MISSION 2

In the same game, simply try to focus on two players at the same time. Pick these players at will, but don't include the one who figured in your bluff exercise.

FOLLOW-UP

Answer these questions about the two players you focused on:

1. Which player was more conservative?
2. Which player had the better emotional control?
3. Which player would be easier overall to bluff?
4. Did either player seem to dominate the other?

That's all. The main reason for this mission is to teach you to focus on one thing at a time. In this case, comparing two players. You can learn to be conscious of other things going on at the same time, but this should happen automatically. When you try to monitor many things, you usually fail. You'd be surprised how many more things you will be aware of when you concentrate on one mission at the poker table. It's magic.

FANCY PLAY SYNDROME

Before we move on, I want to discuss **FPS**—that's **Fancy Play Syndrome**, the bankroll-eating poker disease that devastates one-and-a-half million players each year. The symptoms are easy to spot. The afflicted player will usually choose the most creative play, rather than the most profitable one. That's because he wants to impress his opponents with his cleverness.

> I was once playing poker at the same table as a guy I was trying to teach to be a winner. Everyone at the table knew each other. And everyone knew I was teaching this guy—let's call him Joe—to play poker. I believe Joe had the potential skill to earn a profit, even in that tough game.

> Joe suffered from the worst case of FPS I've ever seen. I watched aghast as he tried, and failed, to bluff me three times consecutively. After the third time, he sighed and said, "I was sure you wouldn't call me that time. You should expect me to have a big hand sooner or later."
>
> "I do expect you to have one sooner or later," I teased. "And when that happens, I'll fold."

When you have an opponent demoralized in a poker game, always be friendly. Teasing is all right, but mean-spirited sarcasm will work against you. The trick is to make sure your opponents know you're someone to be feared without making them angry. Make them think twice before they target you in the future. You should be the one with the psychological leverage, not them. So, keep your opponents in awe of you, whenever possible.

In fact, on that day, my psychological warfare worked in my favor and my student began playing a very predictable game against me, thereby making himself easier to beat. But against everyone else, he was determined to put on a show. He was dealt two big hands back to back. He raised with neither hand, managing to win a meager amount from hands with which he should have scored big. He then put in maximum raises with a strong, but not great hand, and got bluffed out on the river by an astute opponent.

Hold 'em is a game where you're only rarely able to impress opponents. Much of your profit comes from making the most profitable and most obvious decisions consistently over a long period of time. If you do that, you'll impress your opponents. You'll impress them with the realization that you have their money.

KEEPING THINGS SIMPLE

I'm going to explain a similar but powerful concept: Don't choose sophisticated strategies when simpler ones are better. And there's something we need to talk about that's also closely related. In order to understand how silly some poker advice gets, you need to understand how today's scientists have reinterpreted one of the concepts that William of Ockham, a 14th century English philosopher, popularized. Well, maybe you don't need to understand him. He might have slept with goats, for all I know.

I'm talking about Occam's Razor. It has come to mean that when there are competing theories that can explain an event, the simplest one is usually better. That's important, and I'll repeat it: When there are two or more ways you can explain why something happened, the explanation that's simpler is more likely to be right.

Let's say you see a carton of milk that stayed on the kitchen counter overnight. The milk is supposed to be in the refrigerator, but it isn't. As far as you know, you've been alone in the house. Now, you could theorize that some unknown enemy broke into your house, drank some milk, then poisoned it and left it on the kitchen counter hoping you'll drink it and die. Or you could reason that you probably forgot to put the milk back in the refrigerator.

Either is possible. But, guess what? You and I are both gamblers at heart, and you know which way we're going to bet—that you forgot to put the milk back in the refrigerator, right?

Anything is possible, but the simpler answer is better. It's Occam's Razor—you shave away all the unnecessary complexities and make the most obvious explanation the favorite.

Now, what does this have to do with bluffing at hold 'em? Well, I just read some advice from a serious poker player, posted on the Internet, saying that in a pot-limit hold 'em game, you should come into a pot with 8-7 suited behind two callers and a raiser. He says that the raiser probably holds a big pair, so if the flop almost completely misses you, showing an ace and two other cards and no one-card out for a straight or flush, call the player who holds that big pair. The theory is that this surprise call on the flop with *nothing* will make the bettor sure that you have *something* and put you in a position to steal the pot with a well-timed bluff sometime on the next two betting rounds.

Anything wrong with this? Plenty!

This is an example of creative play. I teach variations of this myself, and it belongs in your poker arsenal. But, it's a play that you should use only rarely. Here's where Occam's Razor comes in. You can take any poker situation, add complexities, argue how players will respond until they're just right to fit your conclusion, and make practically any bizarre decision seem like the most logical. Any bluff can be justified.

But, it remains that the simplest conclusion is that you shouldn't play that 8-7 suited at all most of the time and that, when you do, you should check or fold willingly when you miss and the original raiser bets into the flop. There's no long-range bluffing profit here. The simplest choice of strategy is usually the best. Exceptions are exceptions for a reason.

And, here's another example. Many experts advise players to bet on the flop in hold 'em with an inside straight draw. Some call this a semi-bluff. Had this been presented as a rare exception, it would have been profitable advice. But, by using more-complex arguments to make it the main tactic, the experts are violating Occam's Razor and ignoring the obvious explanation of what you should do—check.

The reason I'm telling you this is, once you become skilled at hold 'em, it's easy to justify doing the unusual. But the most obvious decision is usually correct. You should make occasional exceptions to keep observant opponents off-guard and to earn extra profit.

But, if you stray too often from what are the simplest and most obvious decisions, you're sure to sacrifice profit. Remember Occam's Razor next time someone justifies a poker decision with a complex argument when a simpler argument leads to a different decision. Complex is sometimes right, but usually it isn't.

OLD AND PROFITABLE WISDOM ABOUT BLUFFING

All around us, everywhere in poker, survive ancient adages. Like what? Well, like: "Don't count your chips while you're sitting at the table." That one even made its way into Kenny Rogers' song, "The Gambler."

"You gotta know when to hold 'em; you gotta know when to fold 'em." Same song. Frankly, Kenny, we need to talk about this. As an advocate of poker integrity, I sometimes worry about opponents who know when to hold 'em and know when to fold 'em. But, hey, I understand what you meant, brother. And all you head football coaches out there, go paste that message on your refrigerator where you won't forget. Put it right beside the one that says, "Never check the scoreboard until after fourth quarter."

What? Oh, you think it makes sense to check that football scoreboard? Me too. And I think it makes sense to count your chips at the table. It gives me an idea whether I'm winning or losing. Besides, if you don't count your chips at the table, you might not get to count 'em at all "when the dealing's done"—if you know what I mean, guy.

Sometimes, I adjust my strategy according to my chip count. If I'm winning more than two buy-ins, I figure players are intimidated and will fall victim to marginally aggressive bets and raises. The more I'm losing, the more likely I am to be restrictive in my hand selection. That's because opponents are not intimidated, but, rather, inspired; and they will tend to play better and less predictably against me. When that happens, I often cancel those borderline bets that win money when I have my opponents under my spell.

The more I'm losing, the fewer borderline plays I make. The more I'm winning, the more borderline plays I make. So, yeah, I count my chips. But this gets worse, Kenny. I often count everyone else's chips while they're sitting at the table. It's a hard habit to break, but I'm trying. I know that, on average, most players who are losing are harder to bluff, because they're desperate to get lucky and get even. And players who are winning substantially are often harder to bluff, because they think they're gambling with "free money." The players easiest to bluff are usually the ones who are just about even. So, it pays to count chips.

CAN YOU BLUFF A BLUFFER?

There's another poker adage I know you've heard: "You can't bluff a bluffer." Familiar, right? And folks will argue about this one. Some think it makes sense, and some think you really can bluff a bluffer. Those who think it makes sense contend that bluffers believe others act the same way they do, so every bet is suspect. Those who think it doesn't make sense contend that frequent bluffers are easy victims of bluffs, because they envision that their opponents are more timid than they actually are. Bluffers think opponents are afraid to call *and* afraid to bluff. This attitude makes them less likely to call, according to the argument.

What's the truth here?

If you're a break-even player now, and you haven't been applying what follows, then, poof!—you're suddenly a winner. If you were a marginal winner who hasn't been applying my advice, then, poof!—you're a *big* winner now. If you're a small loser who hasn't been abiding by the following advice, then, poof!—I just made you a winner. If you're a huge loser who hasn't been using the advice that follows, then, poof!—get a job.

THE SECRET TO HANDLING BLUFFERS

Okay, we're ready. The adage is right. You usually should not bluff a bluffer. Let's say it's just you and your opponent on the river. You have a very weak hand that will almost surely lose in a showdown; and you have no clear idea what the opponent is holding. He goes first; he checks.

This is the time, right now, that you must ask yourself one of the most profitable questions in poker: Is my opponent a frequent bluffer? Ask, because if he is, my friends, you must abandon all thoughts of bluffing. Here's why.

Just to make it simple, we'll say there were ten possible hands your opponent could hold. Of these ten, two are very strong, which he would have bet, and three are very weak, which he would have bluffed with. Assume, for the simplicity of this example, that he would never check-raise or bet the marginal hands. We can see that he would bet with legitimate strength twice, but would bluff three times. The other five times he would check.

It's easy to see that in this situation, faced with a bet, you should always call with any hand strong enough to beat a bluff, because for every five bets, on three of them, your opponent will be bluffing. Fine. But in this case, your opponent didn't bet, and you don't hold a hand strong enough to guarantee a win against a bluff.

So, the question is, after your opponent checks, should you try to win the pot by bluffing? Using the same example, the answer is no. You must never try to bluff. Because, when given the opportunity, this opponent always bluffs, we can conclude that the only thing that remains after his check are hands he'll feel comfortable calling with.

Don't make the mistake of thinking there are still ten hands he could hold, two great, three terrible, and five in-between. You should figure that once the player checks, he holds a reasonably strong hand. If he's like most frequent bluffers, having abandoned his opportunity to bluff, he now intends to call. That means, if you bluff, you will lose. This type of player cannot be holding a worse hand, simply because he would have bluffed with it. In this extreme example, you will get called and you will lose every time you try to bluff.

The strange thing is, this "extreme" example isn't very extreme. This is precisely what happens in real life, in real hold 'em games, against real opponents. Opponents who bluff too much should generally not be bet into after they check. Just check along and limit your loss.

> *"Opponents who bluff too much should generally not be bet into after they check."*

ACTING FIRST AGAINST A FREQUENT BLUFFER

But what if you're first to act, instead of last? It turns out that you usually should still be reluctant to bet into a frequent bluffer for a very simple reason. This player bluffs too often. That's his weakness. This means when he bets into you, you will usually call. If you had a strong enough hand, you would check and call if he bet, allowing him to destroy himself with too much bluffing.

But you don't have a strong enough hand. You have a hopeless hand, and you're first to act. My advice? Check. Just give up on the pot, unless you think your opponent is unusually likely to throw away his hand right now.

But what can you possibly gain by checking? You'll lose the

pot, sure. But you might accomplish something that is quite valuable to your long-range success. You might let his bluff succeed! Think about it. We're talking about you holding a totally hopeless hand here, one that can't win in a showdown. Let's say that you figure it's borderline at best whether a bluff is worthwhile. Given that definition, a bluff theoretically is worth nothing to you in the long-run (you'll win a few times, you'll lose many times, and overall you'll show no profit).

A POWERFUL BLUFFING TACTIC

Well, if you gain nothing long-term by bluffing, then wouldn't you prefer a tactic that gains something? Good choice. This is where you can take advantage of your opponent and pad your purse or your wallet. Since you know he bluffs too often, you're going to be calling him every chance you get with reasonable hands. That means he might wise up and stop over-bluffing. You don't want that to happen. So, the best way to condition him to continue his bad habit is to reward him. We can do this for free, simply by checking and letting him have the pot. Why for free? It's because we already estimated that bluffing would not be profitable and was break-even at best.

"Don't bluff a bluffer" is excellent advice, but not for the reasons usually stated.

BLUFFING STRATEGY IN LOOSE GAMES

Obviously, opponents call too much in loose games— otherwise these wouldn't be loose games. That's the main mistake opponents make in these games. You should expect this key mistake to hurt you when you try to bluff, because clearly, you don't want to be called. But in loose games you should expect to be called. Sure, everyone knows that, but you'd be surprised how many serious players bump their head against poker's wall by trying to bluff anyway.

The secret is to never bluff in loose games unless you have a specific reason on a particular hand against a particular player. In tighter games, you can bluff once in a while at random, but in loose games, you must resolve never to bluff without a major motive.

Q & A: BLUFFING ON THE RIVER
QUESTION

Playing in a typical limit poker game, what is the maximum number of players you should try to bluff on the last round of betting?

a. One
b. Two
c. Three
d. The more, the better

ANSWER

B. It's usually a mistake to bluff three or more opponents on the last betting round. Mathematically and theoretically, what I just said is nonsense. At least, it's nonsense if you're thinking about a hypothetical game in which everyone is trying to play correctly. In that case, you should attempt a bluff more rarely against many opponents than against a single opponent, but you should try to bluff many opponents at least some of the time.

That makes sense. But here's the truth that we touched on earlier. Typical players don't correctly adjust their calling decisions based on the number of opponents. They seem to consider their hand in isolation and make their decision on the basis of its strength. While they usually adjust somewhat to the fact that other opponents might overcall, they don't adjust nearly enough. In some case, they may not adjust at all. Here's what happens in that case…

Let's say it's exactly 50 percent likely that each opponent will call. The pot is $100, and it costs you $20 to bluff. Mathematically, it looks like this:

One opponent. Bluff attempt is worth $40. You would gain $80 on two tries.

Two opponents. Bluff attempt is worth $10. You would gain $40 on four tries.

Three opponents. Bluff attempt costs $5. You would lose $40 on eight tries.

Four opponents. Bluff attempt costs $12.50. You would lose $200 on sixteen tries.

FOR THE MATHEMATICALLY INCLINED ONLY

Your chance of succeeding with the bluff is just a matter of calculating 50 percent (0.5) to the power of the number of opponents. Divide this answer into one, and you get the number of attempts required, on average, for each successful bluff. Begin with $100 as your profit on the one time you will win. Subtract $20 for each attempt you do not win, which is all but one. Divide that result by the total attempts. This is the profit or loss, on average, per bluff.

Example for two opponents: 0.5 to the 2nd power is 0.25, then 1 divided by 0.25 yields 4 attempts for each win. Start with $100 profit for the one win. Subtract 3 times $20 = $60 for the three failed attempts. Total is $40 profit. Divide by four tries. Answer is $10 per bluff attempt.

I'm not suggesting that this is a good real-life model of how players actually react to a potential bluff. Certainly, a single opponent doesn't fold half the time. I'm just simplifying and saying that, in general, typical opponents pay too little attention to the number of potential callers. So, to a great degree, real poker does follow the logic presented.

What does it mean? Well, sometimes it's okay to run a rare bluff against many opponents. The chemistry may be right. The cards may dictate that the early opponents must fold, and you should only worry about the last one. Or they may dictate that if you get past the first opponent you'll win the pot. Also, some opponents choose not to be embarrassed. So, if the first players pass, some players are less likely to risk that how-dumb-can-you-be look from those who already folded. Better, they may think, to just follow along and not risk the criticism. In spite of those cautions, it is still true that most players tend to call largely on the strength of their hands, without giving enough regard to the number of opponents.

And because of this phenomenon, you should seldom attempt to bluff more than two opponents on the last betting round.

7 IMAGE, PSYCHOLOGY, & MANIPULATION

INTRODUCTION

I put a lot of emphasis on poker psychology. Sure, I'm the guy responsible for a lot of those poker statistics out there. When two-time world champion Doyle Brunson's poker bible, *Super/System-A Course In Power Poker*, was in the planning, I sat in a room for weeks—with just a pen, a notepad, and a calculator—calculating the 50 tables for the statistics section. There were no personal computers back then in 1976. It was the first time such elaborate poker statistics were ever presented correctly—thousands of them. I was obsessed with getting it right.

And though I've spent too much of my life programming computers and designing artificial intelligence for poker, that isn't where the money grows! It *doesn't* grow from statistics and or computer analysis.

The money in poker comes mostly from the way you handle people, read them, manipulate them, and relate to them. It's about image, psychology and manipulation. Image is how you perceive opponents and they perceive you. Psychology is the art form through which you understand what makes an opponent tick in the various situations that occur at the poker table. And manipulation is how you exploit the other two factors—image and psychology—to extract the maximum amount possible in the game of poker.

As the old adage goes, "Poker is not a game of cards played by people, but a game of people played with cards."

That's why I have devoted so much energy to studying and writing about **poker tells**—the body language that often lets you know when an opponent is bluffing and when he isn't. That's why I talk so much about the image you should take to the poker table to extract the most profit. Image is at the core of all the potential profit you'll earn at hold 'em. How your opponents see you will largely determine how much money they will *give* you. That's so important that I'll say it again. The way your opponents see you determines how much money they will give you.

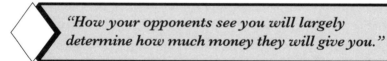

"How your opponents see you will largely determine how much money they will give you."

THE ROAD TO PROFITS

Before you jump to the conclusion that just sitting at the poker table with the right image will make you rich, let me explain. You still need strategic information. You need to know, in general, when to raise, play a hand, bet, fold, check—and much more. Then, and only then, can you get more out of the game by adding psychological warfare. Without the basic strategy concepts integral to hold 'em, you'll just be a losing player. A conspicuous image could even cause you to be a bigger losing player.

So, don't be fooled. I don't want you to apply psychology before the basics. I want you to apply the basics and *then* use psychology. How important is psychology at poker? Well, once you've mastered the basics and a little more, you can probably win consistently against weak to average opponents.

But now we get to the really important stuff. Once you've mastered the basics and a little beyond *and* you're making a reasonable profit because you always play your best game and maintain good discipline—once you're at that point, what's next?

Well, next *isn't* to sit down and study every nuance of the game. Technical analysis of why it's slightly better to raise than to call in a specific situation against undefined opponents will not help you that much. It might add pennies to your profit, but that isn't worth the time at this point.

Right now you want to figure out how you can dramatically increase your profit. Doing that starts with your image.

IMAGE

Let me remind you that the key to walking away with bigger wins is not how many pots you win, but the *size* of the pots you win. Your end of day profits come down to how much you win overall. To maximize this, you want to adopt an image that opponents feel comfortable paying off. That's right, your opponents are more comfortable surrendering their chips to some personalities than to others. Certain players who think they know the most about poker are very off-target with their images. They actually tempt opponents to play better against them.

This is exactly what you don't want to happen. You don't want to seem as if every decision you make is well calculated and designed to do damage to your opponent. What? Yes, that's right. Your decisions should be well calculated and designed to do damage, but they shouldn't *seem* so.

Some of you know that I often advocate the wild image. This image includes a lot of advertising, especially when you first sit down in a game. I have experimented with many different images—even for months at a time—but I can tell you that nothing will bolster your profit so much as a playful, unpredictable image.

This image confuses opponents and causes them to play poorly. But because you're playful, they don't mind giving you their money as much as they mind giving it to others. It makes losing to you as painless as possible. I don't use the wild image all the time, and it might not be right for you. If it's not, there are other ways to establish yourself as the force to be reckoned with at the table.

TURNING IMAGE INTO PROFIT

When evaluating the importance of poker concepts, there is one that I rate very highly. That concept deals with the image you present at the poker table and how much it affects what you can expect to win.

Could I be more specific? Sure. I believe that finding and conveying the right image is so important that thousands of players who are capable of making a life-long profit are, instead, broke and miserable. In other venues, you keep hearing me stress again and again that you need the right kind of image to win big at poker.

Here are six elements that should comprise that image:

1. Friendliness

This is incredibly important. Many players think that they can intimidate or irritate their opponents into handing over their stacks of chips. They think they can win just by presenting themselves as angry and rude. While this demeanor may occasionally lure a call, the overall effect is to win less money. Yes, you might sometimes put an opponent on emotional tilt, and, I guess, that is a rational argument in favor of being unfriendly and intimidating.

But, in general, you'll make more money by being friendly instead. When you are mean-spirited, when you criticize your opponents, when you snarl and snicker, when you badger and berate, you're making your opponents feel uncomfortable. They will not enjoy losing to you. Just remember: You'll earn a lot more if your opponents enjoy playing with you. That way losing won't bother them as much.

So, be friendly. Make the poker experience rewarding for your opponents. If they don't mind losing to you, they're more likely to hand over their money and enter pots against you when you have the edge They're also more likely to come back and offer you another chance at their money on the days that follow.

Casinos are in the business of making profit. To maximize their potential, they don't aggravate their customers into making wagers. Instead, they lure them into making wagers by creating a pleasant experience for gamblers—so that their customers don't feel the pain of losing as much as they might otherwise.

As a poker player intent on making a profit, you should treat *your* customers the same way.

2. Playfulness

You need to go one step beyond just being friendly. It's also important to seem playful. Act as if you're enjoying the poker experience, too. Show that you don't mind losing pots to your opponents. Laugh and giggle and have a good time. It's easy to do if you know you're going to end up with the money eventually.

3. Recklessness

This is what I mean when I talk about my favorite wild image. Although the image may not be one that you're personally comfortable presenting, you should at least let your play suggest recklessness.

What does this mean? It means that you should seem to not care about money and seem willing to throw your chips into the fray at the slightest provocation. The benefits of this are twofold: First, you will get many more callers when you have the best hand; second, you won't have to worry about being bluffed as often. Because players fear that money means nothing to you, they will hesitate to try a bluff and you'll actually be able to make more quality laydowns than you might otherwise.

Additionally, if you appear sufficiently reckless to your opponents, you won't have to face as many raises and check raises. Opponents will tend to fall in line and call with their weak hands while frequently failing to raise with their stronger hands. In other words, adding recklessness to your image can turn otherwise competent opponents into perfect opponents—that is, they're loose and timid—they call too much, and they don't punish you with a raise when they have the best of it.

Remember, though, that recklessness is an image, not a fact. You must establish this image by playing only a few selected pots that seem bizarre to your opponents. Then, you must convince those opponents by your banter and your mannerisms that this is something you do all the time, even though it isn't. Establishing recklessness without being reckless is an art form, but it's worth the effort.

4. Confidence

Your opponents are intimidated by your confidence. So, you should tend to make all your actions crisp and assertive. Let your opponents wonder what you know that they don't. When confidence is coupled with the other elements that go into the right winning image, your opponents become completely bewildered and very easy to beat.

5. Luckiness

There is nothing that scares typical opponents more than the thought that you might be lucky. That's why you should never complain about your bad luck at the table. If you do complain, opponents won't give you the sympathy you're seeking. Instead, they'll just think, "Hey, there's someone even unluckier than I am. Maybe I can beat him." And they'll be inspired and play better against you.

So, it's important to make opponents think that you're lucky. Emphasize the fortunate things that happen to you. You might simply tell your opponents how lucky you are. I do. Many players like to present themselves as unlucky. Then they brag about being able to overcome misfortune through skillful play. Most opponents are not intimidated by these boasts. What they instinctively fear is that you're lucky, and you should bury your ego and make them think that luck is why you win.

We'll look at this concept more closely in "Luck and Psychology," later in this chapter.

6. Unpredictability

This final element is one that is best illustrated with a little story.

You're thirsty. Cautiously, you sneak up to a soda vending machine, put money into its slot and down slides a can of Coke. Amazing! What's so surprising about that? Nothing, really, and that's the point. Barring a malfunction, your next confrontation with a vending machine will be awfully predictable. Don't give it enough money, you get silence. Give it the right amount, you get your Coke. People don't waste much

> time "playing" vending machines. They have better things to do.
>
> Now take your typical slot machine. Feed it five quarters and who knows what could happen? This mystery, this unpredictability is what makes so many lose so much while maintaining their good spirits.

It's time to talk about poker. When you sit down to play, you're exactly like a slot machine, aren't you? Do me a favor, just say yes. Okay, don't say yes, but you'll be sorry. You'll be missing a great truth about poker. That truth is this: If you conduct yourself as a slot machine, you'll win more, if you conduct yourself as a vending machine, you'll win less.

You must make opponents bet more on impulse than they normally would. You do that by taking advantage of their human tendency to wager more carelessly at worse odds when they see the outcome as suspenseful.

That's why I spend so much energy convincing students to polish their table images. A correct image is a friendly image. If opponents don't have fun losing to you, you're surrendering one of the great psychological advantages in poker. That's one secret of a slot machine. It never threatens you. A hostile image at a poker table is a very destructive thing.

A second secret of a slot machine is that its image is unpredictable. If I devised a slot machine that had only a two percent edge, you'd suppose it would be popular. But what if every single time you wagered a dollar, it returned 98 cents? Nobody would play after they realized this. But if I extracted the same two percent edge by sometimes returning $2, $5, $25, $100, or $10,000 and sometimes nothing, I'd get action. It's the issue of predictability versus unpredictability.

You, too, must be perceived as totally unpredictable when you play hold 'em. If your opponents occasionally (but very rarely) see you playing hands no one else would play, if they see you bluffing when no one else would bluff and betting when no one else would bet, then this will make the right kind of impression.

Once that impression is made, it won't fade quickly. Then you can play the best solid strategy you know. Your slot-machine image will fill your opponents' heads with hope. And they'll lose more to you than they will to anyone else.

CARO'S FUN PRINCIPAL: THEY COME

Always remember that your hold 'em opponents came to gamble. They came for the excitement. They came to feel their pulses race in the face of an unpredictable fate. Some of them drove all the way from Ventura to play hold 'em in Gardena. Some of them drove all the way from Panama to play in Las Vegas. But, wherever they drove from, they didn't go to all the trouble just to be bored. They didn't come hoping to throw hands away.

Your opponents crave the unexpected. If you learn to understand that principle, you'll be a better player. You'll probably be a better person, too, but that's another topic.

Your opponents drove fast, locked their cars, walked briskly across the parking lot, put their names on a waiting list, paced the lobby until that name was called and finally sat in your game. They expect something in return for their effort and they don't want to be bored.

When you play a very predictable game—when you act like a vending machine—you spoil their fun. Sure, you can play a routine strategy against average opponents and still win. But you won't win much. In order to achieve maximum gain, you must encourage your opponents to bet more money on impulse than they normally would.

In Summary

You've learned that it's possible for a human being to play better poker than a vending machine. Who else would tell you that?

Unpredictability is a key ingredient in your winning image. Put all six ingredients together and you'll have a powerful winning edge every time you play poker.

YOUR IMAGE MAY MATTER MORE THAN YOU THINK

Usually, image matters more than a solid game plan. Sure, you can play solid poker, but it you ignore how you are perceived at the poker table—your image—your profits will suffer. In fact, you might barely be able to win much money, if at all.

Here are eight image factors to consider.

1. First Impressions

There is no one in the whole world who doesn't form quick impressions of others. Even though rationally we acknowledge that it's better to arrive at opinions about others based on evidence, we seldom have time to do this. Therefore, other people's images give us clues about what to expect, and unless our first impressions are proven to be wrong we act in accordance with these images.

Poker opponents do the same thing, and they can be easily manipulated by your image. The really good thing is that opponents will marry their early impressions. They are not likely to reevaluate without solid information to the contrary. So, when you show them some strange plays early, these will stick in their mind. The rest is simply maintaining an image consistent with those plays.

I like to confuse opponents. I know they came to the game with a bias toward calling. I always try to capitalize on this weakness. If I play a very loose game, I can get even more calls from these opponents and win extra money on my better hands. Unfortunately, if I play a very loose game, I will lose money overall. So, the solution is to play a moderately tight and selective game while making my opponents think I am playing loose and undisciplined. I usually am able to accomplish this. And I do it by showing a few bizarre plays early and using other psychological tricks to stay in that image thereafter.

If a player always looks like he's concentrating and trying to make a well-considered decision, opponents will sense that he isn't a player they should gamble against. This player will win more small pots than he should but get bluffed out of pots often and unexpectedly. The image of this "concentrating" player will become his undoing.

2. Don't Be a Victim

We not only use our images to our own advantage, we can sometimes be victims of other people's images. In poker, you should make sure you are reacting to the way opponents play, not to the way their images suggest they play.

Picture this:

> A young woman sits in your game. She is wearing lots of jewelry. She is laughing as her boyfriend leaves her to go to a ballgame.
>
> "See ya later, sweetie," he says. "Take these guy's money, okay?"
>
> She says, "I'll try. Anyway, you have a good time and I will, too."
>
> She is really erratic in the way she pushes chips into the pot. It's like she doesn't care. She giggles, too. In one of the early pots, she even wins with Q-8 from an early position (a hold 'em starting hand you know better than to play), and she is giddy.

You create a mental file on her—someone's rich girlfriend here to have fun, out of her element. Fine.

Time goes on. Twenty minutes. An hour. Three hours. Her personality hasn't changed. But, wait. She's winning! What? Think back. Is she really playing just as frivolously as her first hands suggested? Or is she playing sensibly, while her image leads you to believe she is playing frivolously?

Be warned. You too can be unduly influenced by opposing images. Try to judge opponents by the way they play, not by the way their images suggest they play.

3. Pushing Players Around

Your profit comes from pushing opponents in the direction your image suggests. If your image is wild, playful, and frivolous, you must push opponents toward calling. If your image is solid (not usually the best image), you should push opponents toward folding, so you can bluff more.

If you study opponents carefully, you can create a dynamic, fun-to-play-against, not-painful-to-lose-against image that still leaves room for you to bluff when the occasion merits. Usually (see the final point), despite your loose and unpredictable image that wins calls from most opponents, you can bluff opponents who pride themselves on being too smart to be conned by you.

4. You Might Be in the Wrong Game

In most limit poker games, you'll win more with a "call image" than with a "bluff image." If you find yourself in a game where a bluff image works better, fine, but you can probably find a more profitable game somewhere else.

5. No Regard for Money?

As I've told you, I'm an advocate of the "wild image." The more players perceive you as carefree with little regard for money, the more they will call you. Remember: You must couple this type of image with kindness! If you seem mean spirited, your opponents may still call on the last betting round, but they'll choose better hands to play against you in the future and, in general, they'll become tougher opponents. Always make losing as painless as possible for your opponents.

6. Be Comfortable with Your Image

You don't need to use the wild image. Make sure you're comfortable with whatever image you decide to use. You can get a lot of the wild-image benefits just by seeming deceptive and by exaggerating your betting movements. Making bets extra crisp draws attention to yourself and makes you appear livelier, even if you don't have the wild personality to go with it. You don't need to put yourself on stage. Just make sure you're never a non-entity.

7. Stop that Bluff

A tight image does more than allow you to bluff. It also invites bluffs! This means you must call more often if you choose that image. A loose image does more than win extra calls. It also intimidates opponents and makes them less likely to bluff! Players seldom select wild or loose opponents as bluffing targets.

8. Bluff the Smart Ones

As I've said, you can *still* bluff with a wild image. You need to be very selective, though. Target those who think they are too smart for your image. If these opponents think they can see right through your advertising, you can bluff them.

"A loose image does more than win extra calls. It also intimidates opponents and makes them less likely to bluff!"

THE IMPORTANCE OF NOT GOING QUIET

Whatever image you use to make yourself known to the table, to show that you're willing to gamble and you're not just there to eek out the profits from suckers, there's one thing you can't afford to let happen: You can't afford to go quiet.

What does that mean? It means that sometimes you will work very hard to establish an image. You will advertise, you will get opponents laughing, playing bad, ready to mail their money straight across the table and into your stacks. Now, all you need is to play some decent cards.

But what if the decent cards don't come? The fact is, once you've set your image, you can now sit back and play conservatively and, usually, the money will just start coming your way. You don't have to keep advertising. You just need to maintain your playful image through carefully calculated table talk. Players won't even notice that you've stopped playing your frivolous game and have gotten serious about profit taking. Unless….

Unless what? Unless you go quiet. It means that you can't find a profitable hand to play after you've set your image. The cards don't come. Ideally, you'd like to pick up some big hands right now. That will make all the psychological elements work. Maybe you've just raised with 10-6 offsuit and giggled while losing the pot (or winning the pot). You've made two or three similar plays. Now you pick up A-K and play it the same way as 10-6. Then Q-Q. Now J-J and A-Q suited.

You win most of these pots. People pay you off. Each win is worth much more than it would have been if you hadn't bothered to set your image. Often, these hands don't win. But most of the time you don't have to show the loser, and players think you just played another 10-6, so you actually get advertising value for playing tight!

But what if you don't get any cards to play at all? Well, you can't just sit there. Then your plot becomes obvious and everyone sees through it. You need to stay active. You might be able to sit for twenty minutes, but if thirty minutes approaches and you haven't been able to splash any chips out there, you've gone quiet. It's a horrible thing to happen to an image.

Usually, it's worth entering a pot with a substandard hand or two just to avoid going quiet. You may want to call with K-10 offsuit against a semi-early raiser, even though this is a bad percentage play. You may want to raise with J-9 suited. Just pick a couple of hands that aren't horribly unprofitable and do something.

You won't always be able to escape going quiet, but all that advertising money you've invested is worth protecting if you can. Sometimes throwing a few more chips out there at a small disadvantage is all it takes to keep opponents from realizing you've shifted gears and are now playing dead serious.

IMAGE, LOSING AND AGGRESSION

There is a bit of contrary advice I need to talk to you about. As I said before, when players see you losing, they often become inspired. They play better. All your most aggressive plays designed to extract every penny of profit may now actually cost you money.

When this occurs, you need to back off.

So, wasn't it contradictory advice to say that you should avoid going quiet? No! When you're conspicuously losing, you often should abandon your most aggressive plays. But when you're in danger of going quiet at a time when your opponents are bewildered by your play and ready to throw extra chips your way, you need to do something to make sure they don't think you've evaporated. Those are different concepts.

By avoiding going quiet, you are trying to keep the psychological advantage that you have worked hard to establish. When you've been losing for a long period, you no longer have that advantage, so you might as well go quiet or even quit.

MY FORMULA FOR MAINTAINING A PROFITABLE IMAGE

Here it is, simple as simple can be.

1. I first set the image.

2. I sit back, play much more selectively, and let the good cards win for me.

3. If the good cards don't come, I try to salvage what I can of my image by reluctantly, and selectively, playing a few substandard hands so nobody notices that I'm basically waiting for superior cards.

4. Most important: I try never to go quiet.

PSYCHOLOGY

Here's one of the most important concepts in poker: Opponents *want* to call. Because most hold 'em opponents come to games looking for reasons to call, you should think of them as shoppers who are ready to spend their money. When you have a strong hand, think of that hand as a product that you're seeking to sell.

> *"Here's one of the most important concepts in poker: Opponents want to call. Because..."*

Now, here's the secret. You will earn a lot more money in the long run if you make opponents want to call you when they are having trouble deciding whether to fold. Sure, if they have reasonable hands, they will call no matter what. That's their nature. But if they have substandard hands, they may or may not call. Getting these players holding substandard hands to call you—and knowing they would not call other players with those same losing hands—is part of the magic of world class play. Just think how much more money you can earn if you can get two such extra calls every hour!

No, don't just nod. Really think about it. Experts talk about the rarest and most skillful players earning two big bets an hour in profit. Some say two small bets an hour is more reasonable. Let's middle it and say that in a $10/$20 hold 'em game, it's $30 an hour and in a $75/$150 game, it's $225.

That's an excellent achievement, and you need to be extremely capable in many facets of poker to achieve this. Additionally, you need the cooperation of weak opponents. But, listen. That $30 or $225 an hour is their target, the number that top pros strive (and often fail) to achieve after years of practice and study. And here I am flat out telling you that you can get that much, and maybe more, just in extra calls alone.

But, you are only likely to win calls if you have established the right image and advertised correctly. Advertising in poker is simply the art of convincing opponents to call you with very weak hands because they believe you are apt to be bluffing. So the trick is to bluff a lot less often than these opponents believe you do. (This doesn't mean you can't ever bluff successfully, however.)

> *"Advertising in poker is simply the art of convincing opponents to call you with very weak hands because they believe you are apt to be bluffing."*

Advertising effectively can earn you money. Advertising ineffectively—just for show—can actually *cost* you money. But let's examine how to induce calls so that you can increase your profits.

SIX ADVERTISING TIPS TO MAKE MONEY

Advertising in poker leads to profits. Following are six effective ways to use your image to increase the bottom line.

1. Make it Realistic

Try to make opponents think you are just playing a carefree game when you advertise. If you appear to be advertising, your strategy may backfire, and if it looks out of character, you may even seem ridiculous. I see top pros try to advertise by playing squeaky tight, then, on rare occasions, coming down with a weak hand and making sure every one sees it. But that "Did you see this?" strategy just looks phony. Few are conned by it.

It is far better to be playful in your demeanor whether you're in a pot or not. You should be willing to gamble frivolously with break-even hands. You should be a joy to lose to, and joyful when you lose. The attitude I strive for is, "I just don't care." Opponents are much more willing to buy that attitude and not think that they are being conned.

2. Be Fun to Lose to

As I've just said, your opponents are less likely to think you're conning them if you're a joy to lose to and you don't seem to mind losing. But, beyond that, they will be much more willing to part with their money if you don't add psychological punishment to their defeats. Be a gracious winner *and* loser. If opponents play a poor hand, you can advertise by convincing them you sometimes play the same way (and you've been lucky doing so).

Instead of criticizing a hand that beats me, which is a mistake some pros make, I often say, "Wow! I didn't think you had that. Believe it or not, I won twice with that same hand yesterday. I don't always play it, but I'm surprised it's winning so often. Maybe it's the hand of the month!" Laugh and have fun. Think about how different this attitude is from one that makes your opponents uncomfortable about playing poorly. When you ridicule opponents for poor play, they play better in the future, because they don't want to suffer that same ridicule again. So, what have you accomplished?

Also, think about how many extra weak calls you might win from this opponent in the future, just because you've shown you won't be critical of bad play and simply because he likes you!

That's right! Opponents will give you extra calls with borderline hands simply because they like you! But this will only happen if they also think that you are not painful to lose to and that you gamble, too.

3. Blatant Plays

If you continue to talk about strange plays that you made—but call them *good* plays—opponents tend to believe you. After all, they've already seen you make these plays.

I get tremendous mileage out of one or two very blatant plays. I like to spread hopeless hands. I want them to be so absurd that players will remember them and giggle with me. If I just play a lot of semi-weak hands, that's not advertising. That's just doing what they do. And they won't notice.

I've actually done this: I was the big blind at a no-limit table and got in free with 3♥ 2♥. The flop added two more hearts, so I had a flush draw. Nobody bet until the river. The final board was 7♣ K♥ 4♥ 9♦ 9♠. Someone made a very small bet on the river. Two other remaining players folded, leaving just me. I called! The bettor showed K♦ J♥—a pair of kings. I quickly spread my hand for all to see—a hand that couldn't possibly beat anything! "I thought you had me beat, but you just never know," I laughed, leaving everyone scratching their heads. You see, that was very cheap advertising. It was a tiny bet. And I knew my advertisement was getting a maximum audience, because all eyes were glued to the showdown. And, yes, it turned out to be a very profitable session.

When you master the art of being playful, you can fold and describe ridiculous hands that you "almost won" and opponents will think you really had them, because they saw one or two equally silly plays with their own eyes. Let me stress again, when you master techniques like this and present them just right, it's an art form. You risk seeming forced and phony unless you practice. But, it's worth the effort. At best, you can make a single advertising play and make opponents think you're playing frivolously all the time. At worst, you've lost an insignificant amount. When it works, it often means many bonus calls that build your bankroll.

4. Don't Claim that You Bluff a Lot
Claim that you don't bluff as much as "everyone says." This has the same effect and is more believable.

5. Be Careful When You Advertise
Your advertising dollar may be wholly or partially wasted if:

a. Not everyone is paying attention.
b. Your game is temporarily short-handed.
c. You're not going to stay long.
d. Your game may break.
e. The game is very loose and seems crazy enough that your advertising may not add that much extra profit.

In these cases, I don't bother to advertise.

6. Tournament Advertising Tips

a. Don't advertise if your table will break soon.
b. Do advertise, if at all, just before the limits increase.

When you do that, you're paying a reduced rate for advertising that will bring you "sales" at an increased price.

PROFITING FROM ADVERTISING

Advertising is creative art. You need to practice. The perfect accomplishment is to get opponents to start talking about your plays so that you don't have to mention them yourself. When this happens, you can profit greatly. Repeating: You should bluff and advertise much less often than opponents believe you do.

THE PSYCHOLOGY OF INDUCING CALLS

I'll say it again and I'll keep stressing this important concept. Players want to call. And you can help them achieve that goal with some well-timed and well-executed psychological ploys. Let's look at five of them.

1. Exploiting the Urge to Call: The Great Reflex

Opponents have a calling reflex. This is an almost-automatic response to anything seen, heard, or imagined. Most opponents want to call, and if you give them a reason, they will. In fact, it's very much like facing down a rattlesnake in the dessert. If you want that critter to strike, just get its attention. Reach forward, clap your hands, kick up some dust, run, stick out your tongue. Anything! That rattler is predisposed to bite. If you don't want to be bitten, freeze, or back off slowly.

The same goes for poker opponents. If you want to be called, do *anything*. Any move you make will tempt an opponent to call. Let me tell you why. Most of your opponents have come for the thrill of playing poker. They did not come to throw hands at the muck, one hand and then the next, for the whole night. The thrill of poker dictates that most opponents will have a bias toward calling and against folding. You must grasp that truth: Most of them *want* to call. That's what they came for. They have an urge to play pots and call bets. Don't let that truth out of your head.

So what makes your opponents think that they should call right now? Lots of things might make them think that they should call. They have the urge, you know. And one thing that seems to make them aim their chips at the pot for sure is if you move.

That's right, just move. Shift your weight in your seat. Wow, you win a call. Thump the felt in front of you with your cards. Cool, you get called. Play with your stacks of chips. Yes, that works, too. Now you get it. The more you move, the more you get called. It's the law.

When an opponent starts to fold, try to see if you still can win that call. Just barge in and try to break his train of thought. He'll probably stop and think it through once more from the start, and this time you might get called. This technique has proved its worth in gold to me. As your opponent starts to fold his hand, you should spill your stacks of chips in front of you, clear your throat, bounce in your chair, or do some weird things that will make your opponent pause. Once you win that pause, you have won a brand new chance at the call that you seek.

I don't care if you win that call or don't win that call. It doesn't cost you a single penny to try. And when it works, that's a whole bet that you can add to your stack. It's real cash, and you can spend it. So, you should try hard to earn it. It's worth the effort. It's a free roll, and you might get the opponent to reevaluate, start thinking all over again, and make the call.

Does this strategy always work? No. If your opponent has a very weak hand, nothing you do is likely to win the call. And if your opponent has a reasonably strong hand, doing nothing—although it won't increase the probability of a call—isn't likely to prevent the call. But there's a whole herd of hands in the middle where your opponents can be easily influenced by what you do. And that's where the profit is. When you want a call, do something. Do anything. Do it fast.

True, almost everyone gains when weak opponents call more than they should. But, if you go out of your way to exploit their weakness, you can potentially win much more than anyone else. Conversely, if you go against the grain, swim upstream, sail into the wind—pick one—and decide you want to condition opponents to not call, you might succeed. In that case, if you don't want a call, your best bet is to do nothing.

2. Words Are Not Cheap

Opponents are susceptible to simple words. For example, "I don't think I'm bluffing this time." Even though you're denying that you're probably bluffing, you're putting doubt in their head, and they'll call. Compose your own words to suit your personality, your opponent's personality, and the situation.

If you just blurt, "Call me, I'm bluffing," that's not as good as the more subtle statement that I suggested above. It's too blatant, and your opponent is likely to feel conned and instinctively think, "Oh, sure!" With the "I don't think I'm bluffing this time" wording, though, he's likely just to feel bewildered. You're telling him you're not bluffing. But, at the same time, by adding "this time" you are subtly implying that lots of times you do bluff. It makes opponents suspicious. It wins calls. It works.

3. Either/Or Talk Works Wonders

Suppose you hold A♣ 10♦ and as you face the final round of betting, the board looks like this: A♠ K♠ 6♦ 6♥ J♠. Bet. Then just say, "I guess I actually made this royal flush, but maybe I missed everything completely," and you'll force your opponent's thinking into either/or mode. Either you made a great hand or you're bluffing. This gives you the luxury of betting a medium hand for value without fearing a raise.

Being able to bet without fearing a raise is very important. I call this "Betting with impunity." When you can do that, you can profitably make many daring wagers where you otherwise would have had to check. I use this often in hold 'em games. Suppose I have the second highest pair and an ace kicker against an aggressive opponent. Now the river card is a third heart. "You're not going to believe this," I say. "I might have called all the way with 9-6. They might even have been spades. I'm not going to tell you what suit my cards are, either. I might be bluffing." Remember, you should only do this if you've established a playful image; otherwise it might seem like taunting.

Faced with this confusing either/or talk, your opponent is not likely to risk a raise. Either you have that flush or you're bluffing with garbage. You'll usually just get a call without having to fear a raise.

What's wrong with a raise? Can't you just throw your second-highest pair away against a raise? No! If you did that routinely, your opponents eventually would figure out that they just need to raise you on the river to win most of the time. Correct strategy dictates that you call most of the time when you're raised on the river, even with hands that are not wonderful. You'll usually lose with this call, but the pot is large enough that you only need to win once in a while to make these calls worthwhile. So, you usually have to call a raise, and it's worth going to the effort to talk your opponent out of raising if he does hold the better hand.

Another amazing thing about this either/or, bluffing-or-big-hand talk is that it will get very weak hands to call. After all, they can gamble that you missed the flush. The fact that you actually have the second-highest pair with an ace kicker doesn't occur to your opponents, because you've made them use up their limited thinking time pondering whether you made the flush or you didn't. Either/or.

4. Earning Profit From More Calls

We've already learned that you need to be fun to play with. If opponents enjoy playing with you, you'll earn maximum calls from opponents who won't find calling you and losing painful. Once you establish that image, you can earn a lot of extra money betting medium hands and being called by very weak hands. You will, in fact, make money with hands other players can't even bet profitably.

5. And if Opponents Don't Call Much?

Despite everything you'll try, some opponents simply won't call much. Against them, bluff more often and don't bet medium-strong hands aggressively.

GETTING A CALL: A REAL-LIFE STORY

One night I managed to get called for $150 by an opponent holding an 8-high on the river in a $75/$150 limit hold 'em game! The opponent, a pleasant but boisterous man of about fifty-years-old had been drinking, but even so, this story illustrates the psychological power of a players' tendency to call. It happened like this...

Before the flop, I called with 8♥ 8♦ in a middle position with no one else having entered the pot. I like to vary my strategy in this circumstance—sometimes raising, sometimes calling, and even rarely folding when I have a strong-acting player waiting to act. But this time I decided to call.

The man I eventually coaxed into making the call on the river with 8♣ 3♣ accepted a free ride in the big blind. There were no other players active. The flop comes K♣ 6♥ 6♣, giving the opponent a flush draw, which would become an apparent likelihood the second time he checked and called. He checked. I bet.

He called. The turn card is another king. He checked. I bet. He called. The river card is an offsuit 5, so the board is now K♣ 6♥ 6♣ K♠ 5♦ with no flush possible. Remember: My opponent holds 8♣ 3♣ as I'll soon discover for certain.

He checked. I bet. As he starts to fold, he says, "What do you have?" I hesitate and answer, "I have a good hand" in a tone intended to be doubted. I figure, maybe I can get an ace or even a queen to call. It's worth a try. Then I add, "I have a pair of eights."—the truth, which would get me a 20-minute suspension in some tournaments that have the ridiculous no-telling-the-truth-about-your-hand rule.

"You don't have a pair of eights," he declares, spreading his 8♣ 3♣ face-up on the table. He is in the process of folding, of course. Many people would just show their eights here to prove he was wrong. After all, he isn't going to call with an 8-high nothing. Is he? Well, I sense opportunity. "Either that or I have 7-4 suited, "I muse. He hesitates, and I set the psychological trap by feigning slight desperation. "I'm just kidding," I bluster. "I've got that beat really bad… I think."

You need to understand that I don't really expect to win this call, but the feeling is like having some big ol' marlin on the line that is too much for your tackle. You're probably not going to land it, but it's worth a try. "Either I have a pair of eights or I have 7-4 and you'll win," I declare, trying to bring his decision into focus as he begins to fold again.

But you can't just leave a statement floating like that or the opponent will think he's being conned and will fold. This is all in the tone of voice and the timing. I ask, "Which do you think it is? I've been playing poker for a long time and I don't usually bet 7-4 in this situation,

I'll tell you that!" Now, he perceives that I'm trying to talk him out of the call, not into it. This is key to proper psychology here.

He begins to fold for a third time. But I interrupt his action with, "You don't want to be calling with that hand. That's a terrible hold 'em hand." Again he ponders. Finally, again, he decides to fold. But I interrupt this action by throwing a $5 chip across the table and saying, "Let's not slow up the game," although this whole interaction has only taken, perhaps, thirty seconds. "I'll give you that chip if you'll throw your hand away."

He immediately declines the chip and calls $150. Perhaps those who think of hold 'em as a purely tactical, chess-like game where psychology plays only a secondary role should ponder that true story.

LUCK AND PSYCHOLOGY

I don't allow my students to be superstitious. Each hand is based on a nearly random shuffle of cards, favoring no one in particular. No matter what has happened in the past, the next deal always means a brand new start for you. The cards don't remember who won the last hand nor do they conspire to favor certain players or aggravate others.

But streaks do exist. I can use powerful computer algorithms to deal cards for billions of hands. Then what? Well, then you can look at those hands and see things that will amaze you! You'll suffer a hundred hands in a row without winning a pot. You'll win with three full houses in a row. You name it, you'll see it.

But this is all natural. This is what's *supposed* to happen. This is the way it should be. Streaks are normal, not something to be surprised about. If you flip a coin twenty times and it comes out tails, tails, tails, heads, tails, tails, heads, tails, heads, heads, heads, heads, heads, heads, tails, heads, tails, tails, tails, heads— that's nothing amazing. There were six heads in a row, but so what? If the sequence came heads, tails, heads, tails, heads, tails, heads, tails, heads, tails, heads, tails, heads, tails, heads, tails, heads, tails, heads, tails, that's peculiar. Each sequence is equally rare—just over a million to one against, in fact—but sequences with recognizable patterns suggest that something might be interfering with random events. There might be a bias. Not necessarily, but maybe. There may also be a bias when you see long streaks, but probably not. Always remember that streaks are natural, something you need to learn to live through. If you don't, you will be unprepared to win at poker.

Luck has influence. But the longer you play poker, the weaker its influence. And the big secret is that the more you act as if forces other than fair and random distribution of cards determine your fate, the worse you'll do. If the game is honest, there are no mysterious forces to fear.

But your opponents will fall victim to the illusion of luck. And that's good. You just need to figure out how to take advantage, and I'm here to help you.

USING THE ILLUSION OF LUCK TO WIN MONEY

I have witnessed the longest streak in poker history. So, nothing you tell me about good luck or bad luck is going to impress me. I saw a woman in the 1970s go years as a "card rack." But there's nothing supernatural about this. Luck just happens. There is no force behind it except the power of probability and "probability storms" that have the illusion of supernatural power. Trust probability to do the right thing. Eventually, it will.

The woman was named Sumi. There is no doubt

that she got much better than average cards in key situations for two years running. That doesn't mean she got big hands all the time, but clearly she had so many unusually big hands in key situations that she came to believe that this was the norm. She also tended to risk an extra raise very frequently.

This magic combination of super-aggressive play, her obvious expectation that good cards would come, and the fact that they did come in a history-making streak, meant that she had tremendous power over her opponents. This was the single event that did most to convince me how powerful a weapon good luck can be in the minds of opponents.

This is why I have often stated that it's much better to declare that you're lucky than to let opponents know that you're running bad. If opponents truly believe you're lucky, you can actually see the fear in their eyes.

TEN FACTORS YOU SHOULD CONSIDER ABOUT LUCK

1. Luck is the Most Powerful Element of Profit

But not *your* luck. It's everyone's luck—yours and your opponents'—that influence the way players will react. You can tap into their reactions to luck to make profit. But don't trick yourself into thinking that luck is earning the money for you. You're earning the money because you understand the absurdity of putting faith in luck. And your opponents are losing the money because they do not understand this.

2. Luck Isn't Necessarily Fair

Your luck is not guaranteed to break even, not in your lifetime. And there is no guarantee that cards will break even either. The trick is to do better with your luck than others would do with the same luck. Life isn't fair. We've talked about some people spending years in hospitals. Some even get struck by lightening. Others stumble upon unforeseen riches. Poker isn't fair, either. Don't expect it to be.

But if you have skill and you make each decision matter, you'll probably win even without your "fair share" of luck. And, in truth, it's extremely probable that the cards will break pretty close to even for you over the years.

Even in life itself, things don't break even. Some people waste away in hospitals and other prance down pretty paths. In poker, it's possible for two break-even hold 'em players to sit in the same $75/$150 game for a year. One might win $150,000. One might lose $150,000. It will be all dumb luck, but which one do you think will be giving the lessons? Which one will be taking the lessons?

3. Even if the Cards Do Break Even, Other Elements May Not

Some of these other elements are:

a. Whether you are able to find the best games.

b. The size of the games you're playing when you get your best and biggest cards.

c. Getting backing for games beyond your bankroll. Although I've always tended to play my own money, I've seen many world-class players get their start this way.

d. Being in the right place when the "producer" comes to town to unload $10 million.

4. Good Luck Influences Players

Players lose by calling more often with weak hands when you seem lucky, because they can't believe what they're seeing. You might think it should be just the opposite, but it isn't. There's not as much discredit in being beat by someone on a winning streak, so the weak calls won't be scrutinized if they lose. Also, when you seem lucky, opponents lose by not betting or raising frequently enough with winning hands, because they're intimidated.

If you think opponents stay out of your way when they think you're running good, you need to reexamine this. You need to make continual value bets and raises when you're conspicuously lucky. Opponents will call more often with weaker hands. They will also be less likely to maximize their advantage by raising when they have quality hands. Both these factors play heavily in your favor and dictate that you should go into high gear and bet and raise with small advantages when you've been lucky.

You've probably heard that so-and-so "knows how to play a rush." Well, now you know what that means. Nothing more.

5. Players Tend to Call More on Winning and Losing Streaks

On a winning streak players feel that luck is with them and they should stretch their calling to take advantage. On a losing streak, they just don't care. This means you should value bet medium-strong hands more often against opponents who are conspicuously lucky or conspicuously unlucky. One caution here: Be careful about betting into players who have been lucky and don't fear you. Although they'll call more often with weak hands, they'll also make your value bets less profitable because they're more apt to raise when they have you beat, maximizing their advantage.

> *"Be careful about betting into players who have been lucky and don't fear you."*

6. Streaks Can Only Be Seen in the Rear-View Mirror

In hold 'em, as in life, there are always impressive things that have already happened. They never have *any* influence on what the next random cards or events will be. You can only see these streaks in the rear-view mirror.

7. Bet More Liberally When Winning; Less Liberally When Losing

When you're winning, most opponents are too intimidated to try tricky responses to your bets. They'll usually call when weak and often won't raise when strong. That's exactly the style of opponent from which you'll extract the most profit.

But when you're losing, opponents are inspired. They play better against you. They raise for value when you least expect it. For this reason, value bets simply don't work as well—and often don't work at all—when you're losing.

8. Players Who Complain About Bad Luck Seldom Bluff

Seldom call opponents who've taken the trouble to point out their misfortune. Bad-luck losers would rather just show their bad hands and ask, "See what I mean?"

In hold 'em, a player might start with 7♠ 6♠ and miss a flush on the river. Normally, he'll often try to bluff. But if he's been complaining that he "never makes a flush," he's much less likely to bluff at the moment. He's more apt to show the hand without wagering and say, "I just missed another one" in an attempt to gain sympathy. That's why you can fold more securely when such an opponent does bet. You're less likely to catch a bluff, so you have less motive to call.

9. Never Complain About Bad Luck

Opponents won't be sympathetic. They'll be inspired. And they'll play better. Simply deny that you're experiencing bad luck. That's the road to profit.

10. Luck Isn't Only in the Cards

If you're a regular player, you probably will get about your expected allotment of flushes this year. But you might not get them at the right times, and they might not win. There is more bankroll fluctuation attributed to the key situations you encounter than to the simple strength of the hands you're dealt.

But, the biggest luck factor in poker is whether you happen upon the best games and whether you are there on the few really great times when players come to unload bushels of money. It also depends on just how lucky you'll be in those rare games, even if you are fortunate enough to get a seat. Also, if you jump around between limits, it matters whether you win your best pots in smaller limits or in bigger limits. Because of these layers of luck, poker is more volatile than many assume. Over time, your results will be more influenced by fluctuations in game conditions than by fluctuations in cards.

MANIPULATION

You've set a good image and you've got your psychology working. Now it's time to put all the pieces together and manipulate the pieces into profits.

The first thing to realize is that no opponent is immune to psychological manipulation. As H. L. Mencken said, "No one ever went broke underestimating the taste of the people." (Actually, he said "American people," but I don't see why people in the United States should be singled out in this regard.) And no pro poker player ever went broke underestimating the common sense of his opponents.

Most opponents, even experienced ones who should know better, are easily bewildered by psychological ploys designed to make them think that you play hands you don't. You should be aware, though, that if you're not really as talented psychologically as you think you are, your actions risk providing more value to observant opponents than you gain through manipulation.

In other words, make sure you're actually in command and not just providing tells. Against the very best opponents, it may be better to forego manipulative actions in order to be less easily read.

SEVEN WAYS TO MANIPULATE OPPONENTS

You're ready to turn knowledge into power. Let's look at seven ways to manipulate your opponents.

1. Make Them Back Off

Get opponents to worry about what *you're* going to do next. You can do this by making unusual plays that stick in their minds or by making all bets sudden and decisive. This latter trick, which is a good compromise for those who feel uncomfortable "being onstage," works very well to limit opponents' tendencies to bet or raise with small advantages. When you can get strong opponents to stop doing that—because they're worried about *you*—you've taken them off their best game and diminished their profit.

2. You're the One

Try to become the one force to be reckoned with at your table. You know you've achieved this when you often see players sneak a peek in your direction before betting, raising, or calling.

3. A Better Image

If opponents think that you're dangerous, but that you know what you're doing, you've gained psychological leverage. But, you gain much more psychological leverage if your opponents think you're dangerous and you don't know what you're doing. Opponents predictably run for cover and hold their fire against a "loose cannon."

You need to put your ego aside and allow your opponents to think you are playing poorly or are just lucky. I'm often telling my opponents how badly I play—that I'm just having fun— to help them falsely conclude the one or two bizarre plays I make are indicative of my overall game plan. I even say, "Don't criticize me or tell anyone else I play like this. It would ruin my reputation! I'll play better on request, but then I might take your chips."

This psychology usually leads to me taking their chips anyway, and it has another great benefit. It empowers opponents to play poorly. If I can do it, they think, why can't they do it, too? Of course, in truth, I'm *not* doing it. I'm only splashing a few ridiculous hands for show, and the rest is all talk.

If I'm asking them not to be critical of my play, they believe I'm not likely to be critical of theirs. And that means they can get into the action by playing substandard hands without embarrassment, which, deep in their souls, is really what most of them came to the casino to do.

4. Raising Blind

One of my favorite hold 'em tactics is to raise the blinds, or just raise from a late position without looking at my cards. The maneuver makes it look like you don't care much about money and causes opponents to think twice before they attack you. They become predictable and you become the force to be reckoned with. And, actually, you're not sacrificing much profit, since you would have raised with many hands anyway, and the substandard ones are not huge underdogs.

If the small blind has the habit of almost always raising my big blind heads up, I will frequently reraise without looking. How much of a disadvantage is this to me? Not much at all. Since my opponent habitually raises, his hand is almost random from my point of view. Theoretically, I am almost raising a random hand with another random hand, and I will have a positional advantage, being last to act, through all remaining betting rounds. This reraise without looking provides large psychological returns for a little cost.

5. A Daring Reraise

When a fairly aggressive opponent check-raises me on an early betting round, I often raise again with hands that would normally take slightly the worst of it. This makes me seem more bewildering in the future, and the cost is minimal. It's likely that if I don't have the best hand, I'll be checked to on the next round, and—if I'm still trailing—I might even recover the "lost" bet by checking and seeing a free card.

6. Select Your Audience

Tend to select weak opponents for advertising plays. Your stronger opponents tend not to realize that they are being excluded from the "giveaway" money, and they call unprofitably on future hands.

7. When to Advertise

Tend to advertise when opponents seem to have weak hands. You'll still get full psychological value, and you often stumble into a winning hand!

LETTING OPPONENTS HANG THEMSELVES

In thinking back over all the poker I've played, there is one single signature trait to my game plan that stands out clearly: I choose tactics that give select opponents a chance to hang themselves.

Sure, sometimes I do a lot of betting with marginal hands and occasionally with silly, hopeless hands while I'm trying to impress opponents by building my "wild image." My ambition is to be called more frequently when I have strong hands later, because I know that most opponents' main weakness is that they call too often. I want to help them exaggerate this weakness and call even more often against me specifically, so that I win even more money than I would otherwise. As we've discussed, I do this by choosing a friendly, frivolous, wild image that makes them suspicious of me.

But I reserve most of my daring bets and showboat plays for opponents who call too often when they have weak hands, but are unlikely to maximize their edge by raising when they have slightly superior hands. That category of "timid caller" should be attacked with a barrage of bets whenever you hold medium-strong or better hands. This keeps you in control of the game, and you win extra money from their weak calls. You should also bet silly hands into these players once in a while—just for show. It conditions them to keep calling.

Playing Aggressive, Unpredictable Opponents

But what should you do about the opponents who are less easily manipulated, show pride, are aggressive, are less predictable, raise unexpectedly and bet with weak hands in an attempt to control the game?

Those are the opponents I let hang themselves.

When I have medium-strong hands or very-strong hands, I will let them do the betting. If they're pushing a weak hand or bluffing, I don't want to chase away my profit with a raise. If

I'm first to act, I will check and give them an opportunity to bet. Sometimes I'll check to their betting round after betting round. Even if they don't bite the first time, I'll give them another chance.

And I ask myself a single question before I employ this let-him-hang-himself strategy. Is this opponent a liberal caller who is predictable? If the answer is yes, I will usually bet my semi-strong hands, because my biggest profit will come from weak calls and additionally, I don't fear unexpected value raises from hands that might be slightly better than my own. But if the answer is no—this player isn't a liberal caller who is predictable—then I'm going to give this player some rope.

He can tie his own noose. I check, he bets, I just call. I check, he bets, I just call. Like a musical rhythm. It works, it keeps working, over and over. Sometimes it's a bluff when he bets, sometimes a weak hand, sometimes a value bet that I just call with a stronger hand. Over and over, the same rhythm. I check, he bets, I just call. It works.

And that's the signature of my style of poker. Whenever I can, I let opponents hang themselves. It's a powerful weapon in limit and no-limit games.

Limit Hanging Example

Let me give you an example for a limit hold 'em game:

The blinds are $200 and $400 and I'm fourth to act. The first three players have already folded when I look down at my cards and see K♦ K♠. Sometimes it's okay to lay a trap by just calling with this hand, but that's risky. I'm more likely to just call with aces than with kings for a very powerful reason.

With aces, I don't have much fear of a disaster on the flop. My pair of aces will still be competitive no matter what. Of course, if the flop shows a pair of jacks without an ace, I'm going to worry about someone holding a third jack that will crush my pair of aces. Or in addition to trips, someone might flop two

IMAGE, PSYCHOLOGY, & MANIPULATION

pair, a straight, a flush, a full house, or even four of a kind. But all these worries are relatively small. I'm almost always going to survive the flop with aces. So just calling with aces in order to set a trap is a valid option, although—in truth—I choose to raise most of the time.

But right now I don't have aces; I have kings. It's also a valid option in this early-to-middle position to just call with kings, setting a trap. But you should do that much less frequently. Quite often, by just calling you'll invite an ace with a small kicker into the pot. If you do that and the flop shows an ace, you're likely to lose when by raising you could have chased away that inferior ace-containing hand and won. That's why I raise the vast majority of opportunities with kings—and that's exactly what I do now. The betting on this round is by fixed $400 increments, so I raise the big blind, putting in $800.

Everyone folds except the player on the button (dealer position), who I know to be an erratic, aggressive player who tries to dominate the game. He reraises to $1,200. The blinds fold. Now what?

Well, I'll tell you "now what." Now I must decide whether to cap the raising by making it $1,600 or just call. "Capping" is the term used to mean that you're entering the final permitted raise. Often, you aren't allowed to raise beyond the fourth bet, although some casinos allow a fifth bet and some have no limits on the number of raises whatsoever when the action is down to heads-up. Here there is a cap, and if I reraise, we'll have reached it.

But wait! Here's an aggressive player that I've seen attack with weak and medium-strength hands quite frequently. Additionally, he likes to bluff his way out of trouble. It's tempting to tax him another $400 right now, and I'll often do that, but in this case I decide to hand him the rope. I just call. The pot is now $3,000, consisting of our $1,200 each and the $600 in surrendered blinds ($400 big and $200 small).

Here comes the flop. It's K♣ 2♥ 2♣. It couldn't be much better for me than this dominating full house.

YOU

FLOP

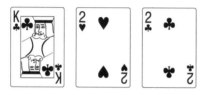

I could bet and hope for a call or possibly lure a desperate raise if my aggressive opponent tries to steal. Or he could have held the remaining king and have a legitimate call. There's a long-shot chance he could hold a deuce if he was flat-out trying to leverage the pot without much of a hand with his first-round reraise. Or he might hold a pocket pair and be able to call. Perhaps he even stumbled into a flush draw. Or maybe he began with a pair of aces. All I know is, I have the best hand, barring the highly unlikely possibility that he holds two deuces, giving him four of a kind.

So, I want to make the most money possible from my good fortune. When I consider my aggressive but intelligent opponent's penchant for taking control and think about the strong likelihood that he might fold the hand if I bet, I decide to check and let him have the stage.

He bets $400. I could raise, but there are so few hands that he could have bet from strength relative to those he might be bluffing with that I don't want to risk having him fold early. I just call.

The next card is the Q♦.

TURN

Again I check. The fixed betting limit has now increased to $800 and, sure enough, he bets it. Here's where you could make a good case for completing a check-raise tactic, but I don't. If he's bluffing, I'll probably lose him right there. It will be an incomplete hanging. And if he has a legitimate betting hand that he'll call my raise with, most likely I'll be no better off than if I simply call now and check-raise on the river. So, that's what I do. I call the $800. The pot has now grown to $5,400, awaiting the final round of $800 wagers.

The river card is a 7♦.

RIVER

Actually, I would have been happier if a club had fallen on the chance that he had a flush draw and connected. Also, a higher-ranking card would have been nice, perhaps pairing him and making him more comfortable betting. But, hold 'em is sometimes complex, and even that latter happening might work against me, instead of in my favor.

Suppose he's been bluffing all along with J-3 and a jack falls on the river. If I check, hoping he'll continue bluffing, he may decide that the pair of jacks without a significant kicker isn't strong enough to bet, but perfect for seeing the showdown. In that case, I would have made more money had he missed completely (which he, in fact, did) and continued to bluff.

I won't analyze this hand to death, but I want you to understand that there are more things than you might suspect that can be considered before making a hold 'em decision. And, although you probably won't have time to examine them all before making your choice, it pays to try to consider as many as possible.

Once more I decide to check, reasoning that there's a good chance my opponent has been trying to buy this pot and he should be given one last opportunity. He bets. Now I raise, because there's no sense being deceptive now with no more betting rounds on the horizon. He folds immediately. As I suspected, this was probably a power-play bluff from the beginning. And if I hadn't given him the opportunity, I wouldn't be raking in this $7,800 pot, netting a $3,800 profit.

Things won't always work out this well when you use this tactic. But, on average, you'll often make a larger profit by checking and calling than by either betting, or checking and raising. The lesson is that there are many times against aggressive opponents when you should surrender the lead when you hold big hands, letting them have the rope with which to hang themselves.

No-Limit Hanging

I will use this letting-my-opponent-hang-himself tactic repeatedly against a no-limit opponent who has too much spirit, too. Let's say my opponent has $4,000 in chips left. The pot is $3,000. I hold an unbeatable hand. This is the final round of betting and my opponent checks to me. What should I do? Clearly I must make some bet, because I can't lose. But it's no-limit, so how much?

If it's a liberal caller who's predictable, I will often bet $4,000—all my opponent has in front of him. I will then use body language and sometimes chatter to try to ensure I get the call. Sometimes I will bet less, but I'm happiest when I can justify betting the whole $4,000.

There's a mathematical concept at play here. My opponent needs to be at least twice as likely to call $2,000 as $4,000 or else I should bet the maximum $4,000 or some other sum. Remember, I have the best hand. I cannot be beat. So now it's just a matter of how much I can earn.

If I replay this same hand forever and get called 25 percent of the time when I bet $4,000, each bet is worth $1,000. That's because 75 percent of the time I do not get called. One in four times I win $4,000 (excluding the possibility of a tie). Three in four times I win nothing. My net gain is $4,000 for four tries, which is $1,000 a try. In order to average $1,000 a try by betting $2,000, I need to be called twice as often—50 percent of the time.

If a $2,000 bet will get called 60 percent of the time and a $4,000 bet will get called 25 percent of the time, then I'm losing $200 by betting the whole $4,000 that my opponent has in front of him. You can use a simple formula. Just multiply the size of the bet times the chance of a call. So, $4,000 at a 25 percent chance of a call is 4,000 x .25 or 1,000. And $2,000 at 60 percent chance of a call is 2,000 x .6 or 1,200. What if you bet $1,800 and estimated that you would be called 75 percent of the time? That's 1,800 x .75 or $1,350, superior to either the $4,000 or the $2,000 bet.

GAUGING THE BEST BET

You need to gauge in no-limit hold 'em how likely your opponent is to call various size bets? And that's one of the reasons that the no-limit game is much more complex than limit, where the size of each bet is predetermined by the rules. You can simplify no-limit by just moving all-in whenever you have a significant advantage, but in doing so you're really sacrificing profit. That's because an all-in bet may not be mathematically the best bet, only the easiest bet.

The same goes for the conventional practice of routinely betting the size of the pot. The most profitable size for a bet is usually around the size of the pot—sometimes less, sometimes more—and depends on your opponents. My analysis shows that the ideal bet size for most hands against most opponents averages less than the size of the pot, despite the common wisdom that the pot should be the most normal bet size.

Anyway, back to the point. It's no-limit, I hold an unbeatable hand, and my opponent has $4,000 and has checked to me on the final betting round. The pot is about $2,000. He's an unpredictable fellow who often plays a lively game. How much should I bet?

Frequently, I'm going to bet about $1,000. Why? It's because I think there's a good chance that this player has a fairly weak hand and he isn't an extremely loose caller. He's unpredictable and aggressive. I need to give him some rope to hang himself. A $1,000 bet might do just that. Now, forget what I previously said about the size of the bet needing to relate mathematically to the likelihood of a call. That would mean a $1,000 bet would need to be called four times as often as a $4,000 bet. Against this type of player, it doesn't matter.

But let's analyze this a little more.

Analyzing the Hanging

While this list could be longer, some of the important things that can happen now are:

1. My opponent might have a weak hand and call hoping I'm bluffing.
2. My opponent might have a weak hand and will fold.
3. My opponent might have a strong or semi-strong hand that he sandbagged and will raise.
4. My opponent might have a semi-strong hand that he sandbagged and will decide to just call at the last second, meaning I probably could have made more money by betting higher.
5. My opponent may have a hopeless hand and decide he has a good chance of bluffing by using his remaining $3,000 that I didn't bet.

Numbers 1 and 5 clearly work in my favor. If I know that my opponent has a strong or even a semi-strong hand, I should probably bet the maximum $4,000 and not risk making less, but I don't know that. So, I'm giving my opponent a chance to make a small call, hoping I'm bluffing with a weak hand with which he might not have called a larger bet.

Additionally, I'm giving him a chance to hang himself with some semi-strong hands with which he might not have called $4,000, but will use to raise. And most importantly, I'm giving him a chance to hang himself with a desperate raise of his last $3,000 with a garbage hand with which he couldn't even have called the $1,000, if that were all the money he had. That last possibility, the biggest of all hangings, is the one that makes this $1,000 underbet profitable.

Once you understand how this tactic works, you'll be able to use it again and again for pure hold 'em profit.

PSYCHOLOGICAL DEFENSE AGAINST LOSING

One of the big mistakes you can make is to slump in your seat and seem defeated when you're losing. This just encourages opponents who are ready to take advantage of your misery. They'll play better against you, because you've made yourself a target—someone they have increased hopes of beating.

Of course, the fact that you're losing, in itself, inspires your opponents. But don't make it worse. Continue to act confidently, laugh, make your moves animated and assured. This will make your opponents less likely to leverage all their advantages against you. If you can keep them from betting or raising just one time when they have an advantage, you've earned something. And you're more likely to do that if you convey optimism, rather than surrender emotionally.

SHOULD YOU SHOW YOUR HANDS IN POKER?

I'll start out, as I sometimes can't keep myself from doing, with a little story to set the stage for the concepts involved in this section.

KENNY VERSUS PAULA

"I never show my hand unless you pay to see it," fast-action young Kenny tells Paula, throwing his hand almost hostilely facedown into the discards.

Poker Paula had just folded, surrendering the pot to Kenny, and politely requested, "Let me see what you had."

Was Kenny's reaction appropriate? Not if he wanted to impress Paula with his poker prowess, charm her, date her, marry her, chew on her earlobes, or whatever. But what if all he wanted was to extract

> the most money from her in the future? Then was his
> resolve not to show his hand profitable?

To give you the right answer, I'd need to understand more about Kenny's style of play, how skillful he is. Does he dominate Paula at poker, or does she dominate him, or neither? It all matters, you see.

And what kind of hand did Kenny bet? Was it a strong hand and, by not showing, did he want to instill doubt so that she might call next time? Was it a bluff that he didn't want to show because that would make him more vulnerable to calls in the future? Kenny might have furthered his cause by not showing—but probably not, for reasons we're about to discuss. And one thing's for sure, his statement about never showing his hand unless paid is wrong-headed. And now we'll discover why.

My Strategy for Showing Hands

I always show my hand when asked. Why? It's because a big chunk of my game plan consists of making opponents feel comfortable playing against me. If I don't want to show a hand, I'll often try to mix it in the muck as soon as my opponent folds. That way, it would be pointless for my opponent to request to see the hand. It has already vanished. (Some professionals recommend that you hold your winning cards until the dealer pushes you the chips, but I don't do this every time, and I've never encountered a problem.)

When is it right to show poker hands? There are lots of times that you can gain psychological leverage over an opponent by showing a hand. In general, you should consider doing so whenever you can steer an opponent into a mode of behavior that's most likely to help you in the future. I'll explain that in a minute.

But, there are other reasons to show a hand. One of my

favorite plays in poker goes like this. It's just me and another player on the river. My opponent has bet. I'm studying him, trying to decide whether to call or fold. I'm looking for tells, but the darn guy just won't give me any clues whatsoever. Now, I could accept this happenstance as my fate and just randomly decide whether or not to call.

But I don't. Instead, I turn my cards face-up on the table and ask, "What would you do with this hand?" This unexpected action sometimes triggers the reaction I'm seeking. Often, my opponent has bet a borderline hand, and neither of us has a firm grasp on who holds the winning cards. It's hard to read an opponent who's in doubt about whether he wants a call or doesn't want one.

So, I make certain he knows what he wants. I spread my cards face-up and ask him what he would do if he were in my place? And you know what? I'm not really as interested in his answer as in how his body reacts (although his answer can provide clues, too). Keep in mind that a player who's bluffing is likely to remain unmoving and do nothing to trigger a call. That advice is straight from *Caro's Book of Poker Tells—The Body Language of Poker*. Also, in the book is the corollary: A player who has you beat will usually be more animated.

If I show my hand and my opponent becomes less animated, I figure he now realizes I have him beat. He may have previously been betting for value, but now he's essentially bluffing, because he can see with his own eyes that my hand is better than his.

Additionally, I will try to pick up a tell from what he says to me. Players who know they have the best hand are not under stress. Their choice of wording will seem natural. Players who know they can't win if you call are under stress. They will struggle with their words, and what they say often will sound unnatural, strained, and less precise.

A FORMULA FOR SHOWING HANDS

Are there best-profit formulas for when to show hands? Sure. Here's mine:

1. When Opponents Ask

Repeating: I always show hands when asked. Although I sometimes may be showing cards I don't want to reveal, complying with the request usually helps to keep my opponents in good spirits, promotes harmony, and averts hostility.

This is precisely what you should do if you seek to extract the most profit from opponents. Anything you do that makes opponents take the game more seriously works against you. And hostility makes them take the game more seriously. As I've stressed throughout this section, promoting fun and good humor gives permission to opponents to continue being carefree gamblers who don't mind losing to you as much and are not needlessly inspired to play their best game.

2. Opponents Who Call Too Often

I try to show weak hands or bluffs when my opponent's main weakness is that he calls too often. I sometimes bet weak hands into opponents who call too much. Yes, it's true that you don't get away with many bluffs when your opponents call too often, and that fact makes bluffing unprofitable. But I sometimes bet weak hands anyway.

How come? It's because I take advantage of opportunities when I know, usually through a tell, that my opponent has lost interest in a hand. Let's say all the cards are dealt and it looks like my opponent has missed a flush. Fine. So have I. We both have nothing, but one of us will win the showdown. I almost always bet in this situation. In limit poker games, this is strategically the best decision, because rather than win half the time in these showdowns among equally weak hands, I'll win almost all the time by betting.

Of course, there's risk. My opponent may not have the weak hand I'm expecting. But in general, this weak-hand-versus-weak hand bet is one of the most profitable in poker. What happens after your loose opponent folds? If he's good natured and you can show your hand playfully without upsetting him, you should. You want to exploit his weakness of calling too often by giving him reason to call even more often in the future. You won't be encouraging him to call in similar situations where he has nothing (he still won't), but you will be encouraging him to call your legitimately strong hands with even more losing hands than he would otherwise.

You should seldom sacrifice an opportunity to show weak hands against too-loose opponents. Also, anytime you make a weak call because you were trying to catch a loose opponent bluffing, make sure you show the failed hand. The more you can do to make your opponent think you play weak hands, the more he'll call in the future.

Now, I've heard the argument that loose players call by nature, so you don't have to do anything to encourage the mistake. That's false. Loose players have their cutoffs, just like tight players do. Loose players will expand their boundaries and call even more against you specifically if you can convince them that you're the one they should make exceptions for. A great deal of my profit in poker can be accounted for by the fact that loose players call me much more often than they call other opponents.

3. Opponents Who Are Too Tight

I try to show strong hands against opponents who are too tight. Yes, despite the fact that I often employ a "wild" image in a hold 'em game—an image that encourages lots of calls—I do bluff. But I pick my targets. The target is typically a tight player who prides himself on not being gullible. This type of player thinks he can see through my "act" designed to make weak, loose players call. Okay, so I bluff him occasionally, but I seldom show these bluffs when they succeed. Instead, I show the strong hands when I bet legitimately and he folded. That makes him proud of his decision and determined to repeat the behavior in the future, giving me another opportunity to bluff.

Sometimes, I'll only flash the hand to the tight player (unless others request to see it, too). Showing my strong hand encourages the too-tight player to remain bluffable in the future. Now, you might think that occasionally showing a strong hand harms my chances of getting calls from the loose players. That's not how it works.

What unconsciously registers in the loose players' minds is the ratio of strong hands I've shown versus weak hands. When they're faced with a call, they believe that there's a very good chance they can win a big pot for the price of a much smaller call, because they've seen with their own eyes that a great deal of the hands I've shown are weak or hopeless. That fact that I've shown some strong hands doesn't do much to discourage their calls.

In general, show weak hands when you're against loose players and strong hands when you're against tight players. And don't worry much about the opposite-type players seeing the hands. They're paying less attention and are not as likely to be impressed by the exposure when they're not involved in the pot.

4. Heads-Up

When I'm heads-up in the course of a poker hand, I sometimes show some of my cards in an effort to see how an opponent will react. This is usually legal (however, check with the house rules first so you don't foul your hand!) and doesn't interfere with the decisions of other players since only two of you are involved. Remember the example we discussed previously in Kenny versus Paula. It's a powerful one: A player has bet into me and I can't decide whether or not to call. So, I show my cards face up and ask what he would do. Suddenly my opponent knows for certain whether he wants me to call or not, and this often provides the tell I need to make the right decision.

5. Opponents Who Get Antagonized

I don't show a hand if it will antagonize an opponent. If my action is not likely to be taken in good spirit—especially when I show a bluff—I don't do it. My main goal in a game is to promote goodwill and make opponents enjoy playing against me. If you make opponents your enemies, they'll try harder and play better against you. (The reverse is sometimes true of players who lose emotional control temporarily when they're angry, but that's not the general rule. And even when true, it's better to keep the atmosphere friendly for the sake of your other opponents, because there's more profit in happy games.)

When Kenny told Poker Paula, "I never show my hand unless you pay to see it," he was creating a hostile poker environment and losing potential profit. He should have realized that showing cards is just another optional weapon in your poker arsenal. It's an option you can use correctly or incorrectly.

And now that you know the correct way, the rest is up to you.

MANIPULATING WITH TALK

I remember playing a short-handed hold 'em game at the Commerce Casino near Los Angeles. I had flopped an ace-high flush. My conversation as my opponent started to bet and then hesitated was playful and went something like this: "Don't you be betting that hand into me. What if I have a flush? Oh, you are betting? I might be trying for the biggest flush in the history of poker. I might already have it. I might have a pair of sixes. Nope, it's a pair of jacks. Anyway I call."

Sounds like babble, right? But it isn't. Every word, my inflection, my tone of voice, my brief pauses for reaction, everything was carefully gauged to elicit a tell and to put me in a position to manipulate the action and get the most profit.

No, I don't expect everyone to be able to duplicate what I do. You don't need to completely master the psychology of poker conversation to be rewarded. You just need to understand the basic truth. Not the specifics of what to say, but why it's important to say the right things.

There are three basic concepts to keep in mind; don't annoy your opponents, pick the right time to talk, and say the right things. Let's look at them.

THREE CONCEPTS OF MANIPULATING WITH TALK
1. Don't Annoy Your Opponents

Many people hear about my reputation for using hardcore psychology and manipulation at poker and assume that I talk a lot at the table. They're wrong.

Some players are annoying to play against because they're always babbling, whether they're in a hand or out. Many opponents resent this incessant chatter. The unwelcome talk demands their attention and makes it difficult to ponder things that are not poker. You see, your opponents often wish to evaporate within their own thoughts. Then time passes for them. They sometimes wish to brood over bad losses. Time passes. They sometimes wish to escape poker hell when the cards are making everyone else happy. So, they daydream. And time passes.

What you shouldn't do, what you must never do, is deny your opponents the chance to escape into their own minds. You want happy opponents who are willing to lose their money to you without feeling the same pain they feel losing to more strident opponents. The less it hurts them to lose money to you, the more money they will lose to you. That is something I keep constantly in mind when I'm playing poker. It's so important that I'm going to repeat it. The less it bothers your opponents to lose money specifically to you, the more money they will give you.

> *"The less it bothers your opponents to lose money specifically to you, the more money they will give you."*

2. The Right Time to Talk

There are times when everyone is friendly and engaged in conversation. I often join in. But when they're not in a hand, I try not to bother them. What's important is to talk to them when they *are* involved in a hand. That's when they're not daydreaming and I have their full attention. It's also when they don't mind being talked to. In fact, they welcome it, because unconsciously they think they're gaining information. They are, but it's the information you want to provide—usually false—that will coax them toward choosing the action you desire.

In my game at the Commerce Casino, I suggested to my opponent that I might have had all kinds of different hands. But as I suggested each one, I watched my opponent's reaction. Since I'd flopped the nut flush, this wasn't an attempt to determine if I had my opponent beat; it was an attempt to determine how I should play the hand. Let's say my opponent held a pair of tens. Some opponents would have given me a clue to the approximate strength of their hand by showing false concern when I suggested I might have a pair of sixes, but not looking at all worried if I said I had a pair of jacks. This is instinctively how many players behave—looking concerned when they have you beat and looking unconcerned when they're worried. Most opponents go out of their way to act weak when they're strong and strong when they're weak.

But nothing happened as I rambled. The equality of reactions, no matter what I said, indicated to me that my opponent didn't have much of anything and thus, didn't care about exactly what I held. He just wanted me to throw my hand away and hoped that any mention of any strength was a lie on my part. He actually had a jack and an 8 offsuit, neither card pairing the flop. He paired eights on the turn and could use his jack for a flush after the final river card (a fourth heart on the board), checking and calling on both streets. In this case, the information was worthwhile. By determining that he was weak or bluffing, I just called, rather than raised, on the flop. Had I raised, he most likely would have folded immediately and I would not have made $400 additional. But although the value of this type of babbling is significant if used correctly, this example exaggerates the profit.

Sometimes the knowledge you gain is worth nothing, and sometimes it works against you, because you lose a hand you wouldn't have played or would have played differently. But on balance, the information you gain translates to profit.

3. Say the Right Things

Very often by simply talking and saying the right things, you'll see something that will provide a clue as to the strength of an opponent's hand. But you shouldn't speak for no reason at all. I very often see players trying to work this verbal magic on their own, and they say the wrong things at the wrong times. It's pure luck whether they talk someone into a call they're seeking or out of that call. Of course, in general, they're more likely to talk them into it, because players are looking for rationalizations for calling and usually anything you say raises suspicions and is better than nothing if you want to be called. However, some words are much better than others, and I always try to say the things that are most likely to get the result I'm seeking.

But I don't just talk for the fun of it. When I'm not in a hand, I'm usually quiet. I'm confident that when I leave the poker table to cash out, nobody ever says, "Doesn't he ever shut up?" like they do with undisciplined blabbermouths. And nobody says, "I'm sure glad he left. Now we can play poker in peace." The reason nobody feels that way about me, despite my sometimes animated and vocal behavior while playing, is that I'm always sensitive to what fits the situation and what doesn't.

It matters a great deal how you conduct yourself at the table. There seem to be a lot of players who believe that psychology doesn't matter much, because opponents are almost always going to make decisions based on their cards. That's wrong. Most players are going to make decisions based on *you!* I know that's controversial, but it's the truth. Very few hands "play themselves." Most involve borderline decisions that make it unclear to an opponent what he should do. Because most of these decisions are precariously balanced, it doesn't take much to push those decisions in the direction you desire. It's just a matter of knowing what you want to accomplish and saying the right thing.

USED CAR SALESMAN

Used car salesmen know that what they say and how they say it influences people. Advertising people know it. Everyone knows it as they try to persuade others around them. Saying the right words at the right time in the right way makes all the difference in the world. So why don't poker players know it?

VALUE OF TALK

How much is saying the right stuff worth? Hard to say. If you're a slight winning player making $1 an hour, then if you could move to $20 an hour by saying the right thing, that would increase your earnings 20 times. But that's a silly way to look at it. To me, talking is so important to the game style I play, that I believe it triples my earnings compared to playing the same way in silence. However, if I couldn't talk, I wouldn't play the same way; it just wouldn't be the most-profitable solution. I'd have to abandon a lot of my "exploratory" hands where I see the flop in order to manipulate my way out of trouble. It's hard to know exactly how much mastery of this phase of poker psychology is worth, but it's worth a lot.

A POWERFUL TIP TO GET A CALL

There exists a magic word that will get opponents to bet weak hands into you or to outright bluff. Use it often when you are strong and would rather have your opponent bet than check.

The magic word is "might." Warn them that "I *might* call you." The reason this works so well is that almost nobody can see through to the con. If you say, "Go ahead and bet," an opponent might be suspicious and lose his nerve. If you say nothing, an opponent might decide not to risk a bet. But if you say you "might" call, the natural response is mentally to finish the statement with "or you might not call." Most players will jump at this opportunity to take a chance if they only "might" get called. Your subsequent raise will be wholly unexpected.

Q & A: YOUR POKER IMAGE
QUESTION

Which of the following statements about your image at the poker table is false?

a. The image you present while playing poker can mean extra profit, but it isn't as important as maintaining an intense level of concentration.

b. It's harder to bluff if you have a lively, aggressive, and bewildering image.

c. Almost all opponents can be manipulated by your image, even ones who pride themselves on their ability to ignore it.

d. Some players have a natural image that works in their favor without careful planning.

ANSWER

Now that you're familiar with some central concepts I teach about image, you won't be so surprised by the answer. Consider this a quick refresher course in what you've learned. Remember, we're looking for an answer that's false.

The false answer isn't B, because it is harder to bluff if you have a live, aggressive, and bewildering image. But I believe that's usually a sacrifice worth making. Most of your opponents share one thing in common: They didn't come to the poker game hoping to throw hands away. They came to the game hoping for excitement, hoping to be able to win pots. Although the true profit in poker comes from making correct decisions, and a decision to throw a hand away is just as meaningful as a decision to call or raise, most of your opponents don't react that way emotionally. They want to call.

And because your opponents want to call, because they came to call, it is already difficult to employ a bluffing strategy with the hopes of making money in the long run. Sure, you can be very selective and find good opportunities to bluff, but you're swimming upstream against the current. The current carries opponents toward calling.

So when you additionally choose a table image that makes opponents think you're loose and unpredictable—a lively player—you are making them suspicious and even more likely to call. That's okay. In return for having to be even more selective about bluffing, you get more calls when you hold good hands, and on balance, that usually works in your favor. You're really taking advantage of your opponents' main weakness, which is calling too much.

So, your lively, aggressive, and bewildering image does make it harder for you to bluff.

And the false answer isn't C. Indeed, almost every opponent can be manipulated by your image. I rejoice in manipulating opponents who think they're too smart, too alert, or too savvy to be manipulated. Often, the manipulation is not on a conscious level. These players often call in borderline situations and give you extra money because they unconsciously know you are a tricky and carefree player. Sometimes when they have expressed, through words or body language, that they are above being fooled by you, you can actually bluff them more easily. Just go out of your way to seem to be eliciting a call and these rare, smug opponents are likely to fold. In any case, most of them can be manipulated by your image, just like everyone else.

The false answer isn't D, either. Some players actually do have a natural image that works in their favor. I knew a woman who had a particularly ditzy personality but played fairly tight poker. She would get called at an amazing rate. As far as I know, she wasn't trying to establish this image, it was just her nature. And it worked in her favor. There are many players with natural images that invite calls, as well as a few whose dispositions invite folds. Your table image matters, whether it's deliberate or not.

The false answer is A: *The image you present while playing poker can mean extra profit, but it isn't as important as maintaining an intense level of concentration.* That's really, really false. First, while an intense level of concentration sometimes can be a good thing, it won't usually add much to your overall profit. Being generally alert will get most of the money. That extra concentration certainly adds something, but it may detract from your ability to play long sessions. You might burn out early.

I recommend that you concentrate as much as is comfortable, focus on the right things rather than everything, and keep portraying that playful, lively and confusing image. Sure, extra concentration helps, but beyond a certain point it's nowhere near as valuable as projecting the right image.

8 TREATING HOLD 'EM AS A BUSINESS

It's okay to play hold 'em frivolously. It's a great game. There is no reason that people can't enjoy hold 'em casually without having to carefully crunch its statistics and critique its tactics. But if you've reached the stage that you'd like to play hold 'em seriously and you're ready to make some money, you need to treat it like a business by understanding powerful concepts that apply to all forms of poker. It's okay if playing poker *is* fun, as long as you aren't playing *for* fun.

As pure recreation and entertainment, hold 'em is one of the most fascinating games ever devised. And perfectly reasonable people—many of them doctors, lawyers, and stock brokers—may be too busy managing the success of their professions to invest the time needed to master the game. These people may want to hear a few tips, but mostly they just want to play hold 'em, not devote their lives to it. Poker is fun for these people; it is not a business.

But for you, it's probably more than that. If you're ready to take poker seriously and play with the intention of making money, then you need to think of it as being your business. And the good news—it can still be fun.

SIX FOUNDATIONS OF A SUCCESSFUL POKER BUSINESS

Every business has a basis on which to build. Following are the six foundations of a successful business.

1. Treat Hold 'em as a Business

Step number one: It's time to think of poker differently than you've thought before. These seven concepts, each attached to the other, will get you in the right frame of mind.

a. Just knowing poker isn't enough; you need to play seriously…

b. Playing poker seriously isn't enough; you need to play poker ample hours to earn a living…

c. Playing poker seriously ample hours to earn a living isn't enough; you need to play in the right places…

d. Playing poker seriously ample hours to earn a living in the right places isn't enough; you need to play at the right times…

e. Playing poker seriously ample hours to earn a living in the right places at the right times isn't enough; you need to play against the right people…

f. Playing poker seriously ample hours to earn a living in the right places at the right times against the right people isn't enough; you need to play your best game all the time…

g. Playing poker seriously ample hours to earn a living in the right places at the right times against the right people *and* playing your best game all the time *is* enough—*if* you keep records!

2. Keep Records

Records aren't just for your accountant or for your taxes. You need to keep them to analyze what works. Which games are better for you? Which limits? Which opponents? Which casinos? Which hours? Use these statistics just as a good baseball manager would to make strategic decisions like when to bunt, when to steal bases, when to use a left-handed pitcher.

Additionally, when you have records, you can't con yourself about how well you're doing. You must face reality, and that can motivate you to improve and stay focused.

And never destroy your records. It's okay to declare a new campaign and start fresh, but keep those old records for reference. In fact, starting over with a new campaign isn't a bad idea. The past is the past, and presumably you've learned new things, decided on better strategies, and maybe determined to apply new discipline from this point onward. Fine. Then there's no reason you can't declare your brand new campaign, the "New you," just like a baseball team begins a new season. And you don't even need to wait for the last season to end, if it will please you psychologically to begin anew right now. You can even give this campaign a name. Call it "Hold 'em Shock and Awe" or whatever makes you happy.

But wait!

Before you begin that new campaign, make sure you do not destroy your old records. I made this mistake when I first started out, and I wish I had all my early records now to contrast them to my current experiences.

Keep very detailed records. They will help you.

3. Choose the Right Location

Remember, you're thinking of a poker game as your business. In order to succeed you need to do business in the right location. In poker, you get to choose the location where you'll do business every time you play. Choosing the right location—

meaning the right game—is so important that it doesn't just determine how much you win. It often determines *if* you win. And once you're in a game, deciding correctly whether to stay or quit is critical.

> *"Choosing the right location—meaning the right game—is so important that it doesn't just determine how much you win."*

Suppose you want to open a restaurant. You've heard the old adage, "The three keys to retail business success are location, location, and location." Perhaps that's a little overstated, because there are many other factors to consider and things to do when establishing a restaurant or setting up a successful retail store. But, location is often the most important, because if customers can't find you and visit you easily, they will usually shop elsewhere. The point is, you want to do business where you have access to the best customers, so you can make the most money.

Poker is the same way. And, in poker, your weakest opponents are your best customers. If you're a serious player or a professional, when you take a seat in a poker game, you're setting up shop. You've opened for business. Suppose you had to buy a license to sit in that one seat at that one table for years to come. Then you'd have to hope you'd chosen a good casino and that the players who challenged you day after day would be easy to beat (good customers) and that the game would be the limits you want.

Fortunately, it doesn't work like that. There's no license required, and you don't need to build or lease a seat at a table, freezing you to a single location. One of the great things about poker as a business is that you get to choose your best location every time you play! It's like opening your restaurant in what you perceive to be the best location, but three superior restaurants suddenly open around you, under-pricing your meals and taking your business. Wouldn't you like to just plop down your restaurant somewhere else tomorrow, and keep the profits flowing?

Well, that's almost exactly how it works with poker. If there are better games elsewhere, you move. You do business at a new location. Sometimes changing seats to get a positional advantage on an opponent is valuable by itself. In other words, you might not need to move your poker business to another table or to a casino clear across town. You might simply decide to use the storefront next door (an adjoining seat at the poker table).

And since location is the key to your poker profit, you better take advantage of this amazing opportunity. You'd be surprised how many knowledgeable players fail to use the concept of location to their advantage.

4. Time is Money

Here's one of the most important concepts about the business of poker. In poker, it isn't money you should be thinking about. Money takes care of itself if you play correctly. What matters most is time.

If you're a fairly good player making two minimum bets per hour, whenever you make a mistake costing you two bets, that's a whole hour you need to make up. Each time you play poorly for a session, you might need to invest days undoing the damage. Think of poker as an exercise in accumulating the most "good" hours possible. Each time you stray from your best game or spend time in the wrong game, those are hours wasted.

5. Treat Your Regular Opponents Like Business Clients

Treat other players nicely. They are your customers; they supply your profit—especially the weak opponents. Learn their habits. Also, keep track of their results, just as many successful businesses keep track of their customers' purchases on a database. They want to know who bought how much, just as you should want to know who supplied you the most profit. You don't only want to know how much they bought; you want to know which products they like. Does their money come your way through their generous calls or through their penchant to surrender pots? Do you profit from them mostly because they lack emotional control from the first hand or because they only play poorly when they're losing.

And who are the profit suppliers in poker? They're simply the biggest losers. Maybe (rarely) there's a particular opponent who is not a big loser but who is especially profitable for you. That's because, maybe you can bluff him or he's intimidated by you or he furnishes you profit some other way. But usually the biggest losers overall are also you're best customers, so you should try to identify who they are and play against them whenever possible.

6. Keep an Adequate Bankroll

If you don't have an adequate bankroll, you're likely to go broke. This is an absolute mathematical truth. And it is the main reason why most skilled, emotionally stable players fail at their "poker business." Spending needed parts of an accumulating bankroll (because you think a long losing streak seems unlikely) is a diagram for doom.

Most winning players go broke. Wait! Did you hear what I said? I said, most *winning* players go broke. Even medium- and big-limit world-class players go broke as well. The reason is that they may start with $5,000, win $100,000 in four months, spend

$80,000, and lose back $25,000. Then what? Then they're broke despite having won $80,000. These are big winners with big problems. I'll say it again: Keep an adequate bankroll.

FOCUS ON YOUR BUSINESS

Pay close attention to the following seven concepts. These concepts are essential if you are to make your business a profitable venture.

1. Stick to Your Game Plan

If you decide not to play A-10 in hold 'em from an early position every time you encounter it, you chose right most of the time. But sometimes, under the pressure of the moment, you'll decide wrong. This can't happen if you divide yourself into two people—one gives commands and stays home; the other follows orders and goes out to play hold 'em. If you want to change your game plan, you need to go home for permission. Then you can't make the wrong choice, because—under the stress of misfortune—you have no choice.

You need to give yourself some flexibility to adapt to conditions. You might want to play that A-10 against an opponent who clearly is entering pots with inferior hands or one that you can easily outplay. But, unless those pre-specified conditions arise, you won't play A-10 early. You must obey the commands you gave yourself before you left home and locked your door behind you.

2. Focus on Poker

Sometimes things at poker or away from poker look so gloomy that seemingly nothing could make it worse and you feel as if "it doesn't matter" right now. But there will come a time when it will matter. Play for that time.

3. Focus on Decisions, Not on Luck

Whether you win or lose is none of your business!

I sometimes seat a student on the floor and have him or her cut out pictures from magazines representing eight to 10 players in a game. Then I have the student deal hold 'em starting hands one at a time and decide which player to give them to. The student must try to remember who was left out of good hands recently and be fair about the hand distributions. After awhile, this task gets very tiring. Then I ask, "Is this the job you want in poker?" Of course, the answer is "no." Seeing that the hands are fairly distributed isn't a job you want to have. Let someone else or some other random force do it. You just stick to your job, making the right decisions at the poker table.

4. Make Certain Your Bankroll Stays Big Enough

This point is so important, I'm going to repeat it again— keep an adequate bankroll. Most people underestimate the size they need for comfort. They tend to spend portions prematurely that they think are excessive. Remember the earlier example, I gave? This often means they can start with, say, $3,000, win $17,000, spend $10,000 they think is unnecessary, lose $10,000 and end up flat broke and begging. Everyone views them as losers. But, actually, we've just looked at an example of a $7,000 win and a player who should have expanded his bankroll from $3,000 to $10,000 had he not spent the profit. You'd be surprised how many players fail because they spend their winnings excessively.

Keep in mind that you don't need an adequate bankroll when you first begin. It's perfectly acceptable to play with what you have, hoping to get jumpstarted. Often, you'll fail and you'll have to gather another starting bankroll and start again. Despite what others may tell you, there's nothing wrong with starting out under-funded. But when you succeed in building a bankroll beyond what you can easily replace from real-world finances, that's when you need to protect it. That's when you don't want to spend parts of it. Eventually, your bankroll will grow so large that you can begin to take profits for your own use. But don't do that prematurely.

Here's the deal: If you're in the automobile repair business, you'll need to buy a lot of equipment. If you want to go on a vacation—or even if you need money to pay your rent—you probably won't sell your set of wrenches or your hydraulic jacks. If you do, you'll be out of business. It's the same with your hold 'em bankroll. That's your equipment. It's the equivalent of the tools you need to do your job, and you've got to think of it as separate from your other resources.

5. Important Decisions Versus Important Consequences

Understanding this non-obvious concept can help you save your poker career and your bankroll. Sometimes, things that will have important consequences cannot be influenced by your actions and that's when you should spend your time, instead, pondering important decisions—the ones you *can* influence. Luck has important consequences, but you can't do anything about it, so there are never important decisions involving pure luck. Spend your time deciding something else. If choosing one door at random means you die and choosing the other door means you live, you shouldn't waste any time choosing a door. Instead, you should use your mental energy making a decision that might help you if you survive. The first type of choice has important consequences—life and death, in this case. But it is not an important decision. Just choose a door and be done with it.

Once you grasp this concept, you'll stop fretting over whether you're getting your fair share of luck and concentrate on making quality tactical decisions at the table. And your bankroll will have the best chance of growing.

6. Leave the Game if You Suspect Cheating

It isn't necessary that you're right about the occurrence of cheating (and you usually won't be). The mere fact that you'll be wasting your mental resources worrying about cheating instead of making quality decisions is enough to cause you to play worse. Leave.

7. Don't Let Impatience Dictate Bad Play

Most people play unprofitable hands simply because they hate waiting for the next deal. If players received new starting hands as soon as they folded, most would demonstrate much greater discipline. The trick is to learn the art of *feeling bad* when the winds of probability are blowing the wrong way during the hand. Don't worry about whether luck is on your side; just strive to have probability on your side. Once you motivate yourself to despise being in a pot with wind in your face, rather than at your back, you'll feel good about folding. When you decide not to play bad hands that would otherwise need to fight the winds of probability, just envision that you're sitting out a storm under shelter. You'll feel good about waiting.

WHAT'S THE RIGHT LIMIT FOR YOU?

You're a hold 'em player, right? You want to mix it up, go to war, splash chips, and maybe bet the ranch like in those Old West movies. I understand. Me too. But there's something about the stakes you play for that often affects your fate more powerfully than your poker skills.

PLAYING POKER FOR FUN

Yes, you can play poker for matchsticks or bottle caps, for pebbles or rubber bands. In fact, you can play for free by agreeing to give back the rubber bands you win when you're done playing. Personally, I believe that the winner should be allowed to keep at least half the rubber bands, but that's just me.

Anyway, you can play poker for free. But you can't play free poker for fun. Sooner or later you realize that the really motivating idea behind poker is money. Without money, it scarcely matters whether you bluff or not, or whether you get away with it or not. It's free, but not fun.

There are other situations that ruin the concept of poker when you least expect it. I've played in tournaments where the players with the most money at the end of a given time period are declared the winners and collect the prizes. What does this mean to those who have few chips as the end approaches? It means they might as well gamble up and hope to get lucky. There's no such thing as a bad hand anymore. The same concept is true when you play poker for free, because the only really apparent reward is winning the pot and gloating. Every time you win a pot, you gain one gloat. Simple.

True, you should be able to gloat if you end up with the most rubber bands, but nobody cares. Playing for free is good for learning the procedures, but it takes the fun out of poker. And it can be the wrong kind of practice once you begin to understand strategy, because your opponents aren't trying to make rational decisions, and they almost never can be bluffed.

Advice: Don't play for free if you're already comfortable playing for affordable money.

PLAYING POKER FOR TINY STAKES

Tiny stakes matter. They may not matter much, but it's not the same as playing for free. If you play penny ante with a five-cent maximum bet, you might get lucky and win $3.45. But this might take many hours of time. Or you might lose $2. It turns out that the difference between winning the $3.45 and losing the $2 isn't enough to motivate most people to play well. And that's a very important concept.

The result is that few people play their best poker when the stakes are tiny and insignificant. This is why skillful players who sit down in a $5 limit game while waiting for a seat in a $100 limit game seldom show an overall profit.. The result just doesn't seem to matter to them (even though it should). They figure they can lose badly and overcome the setback in a single hand once they are provided a seat at their intended limit.

This is why Bill Gates might not be able to play winning poker at any customary limits. There may not be any games where the stakes are enough to motivate him. The legendary twice-world champion and Hall of Famer, Doyle Brunson, jokes about the time Bill Gates was playing $3/$6 at the Mirage. Gates sent a copy of Brunson's poker bible, *Super/System-A Course in Power Poker* over to Doyle's $3,000/$6,000 game for a requested signature.

But instead of acting honored by the request, Doyle good-naturedly needled Gates, refusing to sign a book for anyone with billions of dollars who was afraid to come over and gamble with the big boys. I know what Doyle's motive was. He was trying to tease Gates into his game, and it might have worked. Not that time, though.

But there's another point here. Bill Gates *already* was sort of playing poker for $3,000/$6,000 right then! How come? Because there's no conceptual difference to Bill Gates—richest dude alive—between playing $3/$6 and $3,000/$6,000. Both stakes are meaningless. It's sort of like you were playing in a game where you got $10,000 in chips for a penny and someone needled you for being unwilling to play in an adjoining game where they were playing ten chips for a penny.

No matter what the outcome, the result would have no bearing on your life. And as a result, you might not play any more seriously at $3,000/$6,000 than at $3/$6.

Advice: Don't play for tiny stakes unless you're a very poor player who would lose meaningfully more money by playing larger. If you care about mastering the game, you'll probably improve faster by playing for stakes that are large enough to make you feel a little bad if you lose. Bill Gates can't do that.

PLAYING POKER FOR LOW LIMITS

This is almost the same discussion as the previous one, except the effects of playing at this limit can be more destructive. These are not tiny limits, but *low* limits.

Here's the scary thing about low limits. They only seem too low to matter in the short term. Overall, they can devastate bankrolls. Players who refuse to gear down and play serious poker at these limits can become lifelong losers. Some players will discipline themselves enough to win consistently at a stake that doesn't really challenge them, but it's a tough trick for most players.

Advice: Unless you're willing to take the smaller games seriously, seldom play poker for limits that are several levels below what you like to comfortably play. Just avoid them. Psychologically, these limits don't seem to amount to much while you're "warming up" for a bigger game or when no larger limit is available, but collectively they do matter. And if you choose to play or are forced to play all the time at a level that doesn't provide a chance of losing enough to be slightly painful, you might never be an overall winner. It depends on your temperament, though. The best method is to play as good as you can at every limit, but that isn't possible for many people, hard as they may try.

PLAYING POKER FOR HIGH LIMITS

Big secret. Almost nobody is a favorite to beat poker at a limit that seems uncomfortably high. This is one reason why those occasional forays from $20/$40 into $100/$200 seldom succeed for players who have been making a stable income.

The danger is at least fourfold:

1. You're more likely to talk yourself out of continuing to play a hand on the early betting rounds when it's slightly profitable than you would in a smaller game. It's too frightening taking that risk.
2. You're likely to sacrifice profitable opportunities by not playing a lot of starting hands that you would play at the limit you're accustomed to.
3. You are much more likely to be bluffed.
4. You may not feel free to advertise and mix it up as you would in lower limits, allowing your opponents to control you, instead of you controlling them. In effect, you're playing a much-too-predictable game.

So, in the same way that playing too small can be damaging to your bankroll, so can playing too large. In fact that's the reason many otherwise skillful players lose their entire bankrolls. I've seen bankrolls accumulated over years of discipline evaporate in a single night when serious players have impetuously jumped into hold 'em games above their comfort level.

PLAYING POKER FOR THE RIGHT LIMITS

You need to decide, in accordance with what I've just said, what limits seem right for you. Then you should only play higher if an extraordinary opportunity arises, and you should only play significantly lower if you can maintain your discipline and make decisions as if they matter.

Additionally, you need to remember:

1. The larger your bankroll grows, the more you should seek to defend it by playing for stakes that can do less damage proportionately.
2. As limits rise, the quality of your opponents usually

improves. This means it may sometimes be more profitable to play a level just below the one where you're pushing your risk-tolerance near the danger zone. You'll probably make more money against weaker opponents at a level you feel comfortable splashing chips when you need to.

3. You should avoid playing in games where your lifestyle might change in a single session. In limit hold 'em, I rarely play above $200/$400 limits, and often at $75/$150, $100/$200, or $150/$300. Sure, you'll see me occasionally play $1,000/$2,000, but that's not where I feel most comfortable or have the greatest control over my opponents. For no-limit hold 'em, I'll seldom play when the big blind is greater than $200, and typically, I choose smaller games. Once in a while, I may even go beyond this, but I've grown out of the phase in my life were I craved spectacular wins and enjoyed the thrill of trying to avoid devastating losses. Nowadays, I play poker to have fun and feel comfortable. But, you're right, this new philosophy makes me want to play less often. It's a lot less exciting than it used to be. Yet, I realize that the true excitement in winning at hold 'em—or any form of hold 'em—comes from making a meaningful profit over time.

To sum it up, I'm advising you to play hold 'em for stakes that matter to you. But avoid playing for stakes that frighten you. If you're a capable player, I believe that finding the right limit for you will go a long way toward keeping your bankroll healthy.

ESSENTIAL BANKROLL CONCEPTS

I'm going to answer one of poker's most perplexing questions: How big should one's bankroll be to play specified limits? In the past, I've made the following point about bankrolls, and they all remain true today beyond question: It is up to you to determine how much security you require and how much risk you'll tolerate. The more you risk, the more likely you are to achieve sudden success, and the more likely you are to go broke in the attempt. At the same time, you should never criticize a person for taking "too much" risk, so long as that person understands the risk being taken and has the best of it.

> *"The more you risk, the more likely you are to achieve sudden success, and the more likely you are to go broke in the attempt."*

Anyone who claims that you must follow precise mathematically formulated guidelines to protect your bankroll, probably doesn't have a clue about how other real-world factors outside of poker, plus your own tolerance for risk, affect this decision. (Despite this, I'm about to unveil bankroll requirements based on my own sophisticated formula that will work wonders for most players.)

Mathematical formulae designed to protect your bankroll are not especially useful. Notably, the Kelly Criterion—which can be used to calculate the percentage of bankroll you should risk in accordance with your advantage—is not easily adapted to poker. That's because it's difficult to determine what your advantage is for a given poker session in the same way that you can determine your advantage for a single wager.

Common mathematical methods don't consider the reality that small bankrolls are easily replaced and are not worth protecting in the same way that large bankrolls are. That's a powerful concept that not many players realize.

You need to keep your bankroll, and if you didn't know before today, you will know why after you study the chart that follows. Because you need a specific amount to play a given limit, you not only can be demoted to a lower limit by losing money from your bankroll, you also can be demoted by spending it.

The minimum mathematically proper bankroll to play at a given limit is one buy-in. However, as your bankroll grows, you should be less and less reckless.

Not everyone needs a bankroll. Casual players don't. I recommend that most serious players, especially professionals, keep an expanding bankroll to be used for poker and for nothing else. But some players—those who have comfortable assets or who play only occasionally—have no real reason to maintain a bankroll. They can simply choose to play when they want, using whatever money they want. Still, it might be helpful for them to estimate a portion of their assets they can afford to risk at poker and imagine they have that bankroll. Then, they can choose their appropriate limit in accordance with my Recommended Bankroll Requirements.

RECOMMENDED BANKROLL REQUIREMENTS

Keep in mind my general philosophy, which I stress with my students over and over again: Nobody should be criticized for playing any game anytime with an "inadequate bankroll." That's because there's really no such thing as an inadequate bankroll. How much money you want to put at risk is a personal decision, based on how suddenly you seek to succeed and how well you can tolerate the pain of losing.

The greater your bankroll grows, the more you should seek to protect it, because it will be harder to replenish it from real-life assets. Oddly, most players treat their bankrolls just the opposite. They struggle to protect small bankrolls for fear of going broke suddenly, and they're reckless with large bankrolls, because they feel momentarily comfortable. But here's the truth: Since hold 'em is your business, the more successful you become and the larger your bankroll grows over the months and years, the less you should risk losing it. When you eventually build an extremely large bankroll, you should choose stakes that give you almost no chance whatsoever of going broke.

So, here it is, finally, a reasonable answer to your question about how much of a bankroll you need. If you stick to my recommended bankroll requirements and don't con yourself into jumping up to levels without an adequate bankroll, you can probably use this single chart throughout your entire poker-playing career.

The most important concept assumed in the following chart is that the larger your bankroll grows, the more you should seek to protect it. These are the best guidelines I can provide for the broadest number of poker players.

The "Highest Limit You Can Play" column defines the early round and late round betting for either a fixed-limit hold 'em game or for a no-limit hold 'em game with that size of small and big blinds. Multiply each sum in the first "Bankroll Size" column by four for no-limit games. To keep the second number from falling short of the smallest number in the next row, add a few dollars to cover the gap. That means for $1/$2, your no-limit bankroll would be $40 to $1,199 (instead of $1,196). And it could be less than $40, if you can find a $1/$2 no-limit game that allows a smaller buy-in.

I'm not saying that the no-limit games are exactly four times as big at those stakes; I'm only saying that multiplying the bankroll size by four very approximately keeps your risk in balance between the two forms of hold 'em. The "Number of Buy-Ins" column assumes that you can buy-in for a minimum of ten times the smallest bet ($10 in the $1/$2 game). That third column applies only to limit games.

In no-limit, I'm assuming that you will buy-in for moderate

amounts—for no more than three times the standard minimum allowed. For the table to make sense, you must not risk your entire accumulated bankroll at once (except possibly when you're just starting with an insufficient bankroll). The actual comparative risk between limit and no-limit games is difficult to estimate, and it depends largely on your style of play as well as the volatility of opponents.

Anyway, here's the table…

RECOMMENDED BANKROLL REQUIREMENTS
(For Typical Winning Hold 'em Players)

Bankroll Size (Multiply by 4 for no-limit games)	Highest Limit You Can Play*	Number of Buy-Ins**
$10 to $299	$1/$2	1
$300 to $528	$2/$4	15
$529 to $1,081	$3/$6	17.64
$1,082 to $2,854	$5/$10	21.64
$2,855 to $5,036	$10/$20	28.55
$5,037 to $7,535	$15/$30	33.58
$7,536 to $13,293	$20/$40	37.68
$13,294 to $19,886	$30/$60	44.31
$19,887 to $27,178	$40/$80	49.72
$27,179 to $47,946	$50/$100	54.36
$47,947 to $71,725	$75/$150	63.93
$71,726 to $126,533	$100/$200	71.73
$126,534 to $189,286	$150/$300	84.36
$189,287 to $333,924	$200/$400	94.64
$333,925 to $499,531	$300/$600	111.31
$499,532 to $682,711	$400/$800	124.88
$682,712 to $881,233	$500/$1,000	136.54
$881,234 to $1,318,272	$600/$1,200	146.87
$1,318,273 to $1,801,686	$800/$1,600	164.78
$1,801,687 to ?	$1,000/$2,000	180.17

*Fixed-limit early and late betting round amounts or no-limit blind sizes.
**Number of fixed-limit minimum buy-ins you need (applies to limit games only).

CHART EXPLAINED

Here's how to read the chart above. First, determine the size of your available bankroll. This does not need to be cash actually in your pocket, but constitutes money that is readily available to you for the purpose of playing poker. Remember to multiply by four if your target game is no-limit. Find the row where your bankroll fits in the left-hand column.

Follow across to the middle column and find the maximum limit or no-limit hold 'em game you are allowed to play. The amounts listed represent the betting levels for limit games, and the small and big blinds for no-limit games. Never play higher than this limit. If you have backers taking a percentage of your action, adjust the game accordingly. If someone else is covering 50 percent of your action in a $400/$800 game, then you're effectively playing half as large, so make sure you have the bankroll required for $200/$400. If you play in fixed-limit games where the wager sizes stay the same throughout all betting rounds, for simplicity, use the lower number to indicate the limit of game (although these games won't be quite as large, on average). You may, and often should play games lower than this maximum limit allowed, anyway.

The right-hand column applies only to fixed-limit games and shows the number of "buy-ins" that are needed to play the specified level. A buy-in means ten times the size of an early round bet. My bankroll charts all use the methodology of assuming you have enough buy-ins to properly bankroll yourself. I call this Level Two. Here, Level Two is $2/$4, and the number of buy-ins I've selected as appropriate for most people is fifteen. (There is also Level One, which is always playable, assuming you have one legal buy-in, but this, of course, is not for serious players.) Level Two requires an appropriate number of buy-ins (not necessarily a "safe" number of buy-ins) to have a decent chance of getting most potential winning players jumpstarted. If you fail, you will probably be able to come up with another starting bankroll in the real world outside of poker.

If you're playing no-limit or pot-limit games, you'll need to try to pick a level on the chart where the game would be most nearly equal in size and risk. (I'm suggesting a no-limit bankroll four times as large for the stated sizes, so—inversely—that means you might try choosing games where the no-limit big blind is about one-fourth the size of the fixed-limit final round bets, assuming the same-size bankroll.

Also, the chart doesn't factor in your skill, the skill of others, the specific rules, or other factors that might be used to adjust the recommended betting limits. It assumes that you are a winning player who, if you play your best game all the time, will have typical advantages and win typical amounts. If you're better than that description, you can move up levels with slightly smaller bankrolls; if you're not quite that good yet, you will need a larger bankroll to advance. Still, the chart is a good one for most players, and I think you should use it just the way it is.

TECHNICAL EXPLANATION

This part is technical and the non-mathematically minded readers should ignore this paragraph in protecting their own sanity. The requirements for subsequent levels are calculated by dividing the minimum bet for that level by the minimum bet for Level Two, taking that result to the power of the Fluid Acceleration Factor (FAF = 0.4 in the previous chart) plus 1 (1.4) and multiplying by the minimum bankroll for the second level.

A Diminishing Acceleration Factor (DAF) is sometimes used in my charts to temper the exponential amount of increase in number of buy-ins required at larger limits. DAF was not used in the previous chart (or, more correctly, was computed at

0.0, effectively turning it off). By turning DAF off, I am allowing the requirements for the larger limits to become greater than many players would expect. I have done this deliberately, because I believe there are many unexpected obstacles awaiting players at these larger limits, and I wanted to pad the protection in this chart.

GOING UP OR DOWN IN LIMITS

Many players think that as their bankrolls grow, they have a relatively equal chance of reaching the next level as they previously had while climbing the ladder. This might not be true. You can run into larger games that are much tougher to beat. If this happens, you should play smaller limits than the maximum that the chart allows. Remember, the maximum limit listed is just that, a *maximum* limit. If you are allowed to play $100/$200, but the $40/$80 game provides better profit at lower risk, then that's the one you should be playing.

Notice that the number of buy-ins required grows disproportionately as the limits rise. This is in keeping with my concept that when your bankroll is small, there is less reason to spend time and effort defending it. You can simply gamble more recklessly and hope to get off to a good start. But the more your bankroll grows, the harder it is to replace. (That's why the FAF is used in my formula—see the Technical Explanation sidebar. It makes sure that the bigger your bankroll becomes, the more secure it is.)

BANKROLL PITFALLS
DON'T BUY THE NECKLACE

Every once in a while I get the urge to advise new players to poker about how to approach the game more profitably. Nobody I know has ever managed his bankroll correctly from the beginning. Here is an anecdote for those who are just starting their poker careers to consider.

BENNY, THE GIRLFRIEND, THE BANKROLL

His name was Benny. He was 24 or thereabout. I was impressed with Benny. He could have been one of us—one of us who survived the poker wars, made mistakes and grew, and made more mistakes and grew some more. His mind was quick, he was keenly analytical, and he wanted to win at poker. And he did win. But he left us one day, broke, battered, and heartbroken. And here's how it happened.

Benny met Betty. Betty was a people-user, an insensitive manipulator but Benny didn't see it. She was cute and cuddly and 22. She didn't play poker, but she liked the fact that Benny did. She liked the fact that he drove a Corvette—albeit one with body damage and a bad transmission—and the fact that he had a sizeable bankroll stuffed in his right front pocket which he frequently flashed.

Betty also liked jewelry. One day when we were in the restaurant at the Rainbow Club in Gardena, Betty complained, "Did you see that necklace Smithy bought Georgia? Why don't you ever buy me anything like that?" As I sipped my coffee, I could read the conflict on Benny's face. All was not well.

Benny was proud of the fact that he had built his bankroll. Hour by hour and win by win, he had finally

---

achieved a level of comfort in poker. He played for
sensible limits, and knew that even if the next month
brought him poor luck, he would still have an ample
bankroll to survive until the cards romanced him once
again. He was frugal, seldom spending unnecessarily.
He planned for his future.

Then Betty began to fondle and flirt with other guys
in front of Benny, guys more mature, guys with much
more money. And she did this, I think, deliberately to
belittle Benny. I already told you she was insensitive
and manipulating, right? Anyway, Benny's heart began
to break. You could see it happening. And so he took
his $18,000 bankroll, which was significant for playing
poker in those days for those limits, and bought a
necklace that cost $11,400. Betty thanked him with a
kiss and clung to him all that night.

About a week later, Betty announced that she had
found a matching bracelet. "You won't believe this,
Mike," she gushed, addressing me even though her
comments were really intended for Benny nearby, "but
it matches perfectly. You could think it was a set."

So, yeah, you're right, Benny goes down to the
jewelry place and gets her the bracelet. Another $5,000
hit on his bankroll. Now, he has little more than $1,000
to play on and his poker game turns to shambles. Fear
on every call. Missed bets because he's worried about
going broke. Every hand an agony. On the night that
Benny goes broke, he gets ahead about $200, then
hardly wins another pot.

And Betty tells him, walking together off the poker
floor, "You don't know how to manage your money. I
would have quit when I was $200 ahead." I told you
what she was about, right?

THE LESSON

I saw Benny a few times after that, and then I didn't anymore. He came, he played. He had lost his spirit, and he had lost Betty, too.

What can we learn from this? Something very important, my friend. If you want to play poker for a living, then your bankroll is not money that you can spend. Your bankroll needs to be kept separately. Your bankroll isn't designed to buy necklaces, or to buy vacations, or even to pay the rent. Your bankroll is a machine that makes money. Once that bankroll is whole, once it is so large that that you can count on it to do its job and even to survive a very long losing streak, then you can siphon off the profit. And this extra profit, and only this extra profit, you can spend, because this is the benefit of your bankroll.

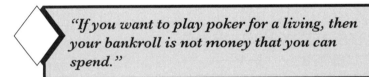

"If you want to play poker for a living, then your bankroll is not money that you can spend."

Think about it. I already told you what would happen if you were a mechanic and sold your tools. If you didn't get the point, try this: If you bought a restaurant and that was how you expected to earn your living, would you sell the stove to pay the rent or to buy a necklace? Of course not, because then you'd be out of business. Well, it's the same with a bankroll. Your bankroll is the stove you need to stay in business. If you spend most of it on an $80,000 car, and then can't stay in action, you'll be losing money everyday you sit home and sulk. Every day.

And the $80,000 might cost you, in the worst case, your whole career at poker if you never recover. In this reality, cars and necklaces can cost millions of dollars and your dreams. That's why I stress this so very strongly to beginners who want to play poker for a living. You should not, you must not, and you cannot spend your bankroll. You won't get good value for your dollar. Betty ain't worth it.

MANAGING LOSSES

Here is a key concept: You'll never be a successful poker player unless you can handle your losses. Most poker players lose a whole lot more money than they should when things go bad. They complain about misfortune, but a lot of it is self-inflicted. You've got to expect things to go bad from time to time in poker. If you learn how to cope with these inevitable losses, you'll have a lot more money to spend overall.

The sad thing is that hardly anyone handles poker losses correctly. But if you play it smart when you're losing, you'll have the makings of being a winning player.

10 STRATEGIES TO USE WHEN YOU'RE LOSING
1. Your Game Plan

It's easy to keep your integrity when you have money. People who can afford to keep their word about paying back debts usually do. But the real test is when you can't easily afford to repay a debt. That's where character and integrity come into play.

Well, a similar concept applies to whether you're winning or losing. It's much easier to stick to your game plan when the cards are running your way. The true test of a player is how you handle losing. This is precisely where many otherwise skillful players fail the test and damage their bankrolls, or even go broke. Repeating: The main reason skillful players go broke is they don't know what to do when they're losing.

2. Don't Forget Poker's Most Important Secret

The secret is simply, "Play your best game all the time." It's a secret that's easy to acknowledge, but hard for players to follow, especially when they're losing.

I believe that playing your best game all the time is so important that years ago I created and sold a recorded audio lecture to drive that single point home. Of course, it seems almost silly to make a big deal out of playing your best game.

What kind of a secret is that? Everybody understands it already. Sure, but not everybody does it. In fact, almost nobody does it. That's what makes it important.

3. Two Types of Dangerous Losses

There are two types of losses that put otherwise skillful poker players seriously off course: Losing sessions and losing streaks.

Losing sessions make some players lose their will to play their best game hand after hand. Frustration takes over. Before long, they're playing as poorly as the opponents they came to conquer. Sometimes more poorly. It's sad, and it happens all the time. But, from now on, I want you to play as perfectly as you can, every hand, every decision. It's those decisions that matter. As I've taught for over 35 years, your lifetime profit will be the sum of your good decisions minus the sum of your bad decisions. And that truth doesn't change whether those decisions are made while you're in the middle of a winning session or the middle of a losing session.

Perhaps more damaging than losing sessions are losing streaks. Every poker player experiences them. Loss after loss, day after day. I know the feeling. It's like you expect things to go bad. One of the most destructive things players do during a losing streak is panic. They play worse because they need to win. But that's the wrong remedy. You don't need to think about winning. You only need to think about making good decisions, hand after hand, session after session. The wins will come when they're ready to come. Winning isn't your job. Making good decisions is your job. Winning is the eventual result of making good decisions consistently.

> *"Your lifetime profit will be the sum of your good decisions minus the sum of your bad decisions."*

4. Don't Think of a Loss as a Session

You can let a losing session destroy you if you think about it as a session to be won or lost. Whether you win or lose during this session, though, really has no bearing on your lifetime profit. A session is just something with an artificial beginning and ending. If you didn't know what they were, you'd simply weigh your bankroll once in awhile to see how you were doing.

Sessions don't really enter into the equation, so why even think about them as wins or losses? And remember during any session to be careful when you pass "Caro's Threshold of Misery." That's when you've lost so much money that any additional damage doesn't feel any worse. But you can only encounter this dangerous condition if you focus on sessions and what's happening right now, tonight. So, don't.

> *"Be careful when you pass "Caro's Threshold of Misery." That's when you've lost so much money that any additional damage doesn't feel any worse."*

The best psychological way to handle losses is to begin every hand fresh. You're neither ahead or behind. You are where you are when the next deal begins. Your good decisions will give you the best chance of rising from that point. But if you lose that hand, forget it. It's on to the next one. Again, you're neither winning or losing. You're starting fresh. You're even when the hand begins. You are where you are. Remind yourself of that again and again.

5. Don't Think of a Win or Loss as a Streak

Streaks, winning or losing, are always something seen in the rear-view mirror. There is never anything in the cards that will dictate that the streak either will or won't continue. So, you're always starting fresh. Just like every hand is a new start, every session is a new start. Never give a streak unwarranted importance that negatively influences your future.

6. Strategic Adjustments When You're Losing

Here are things you should do when you're losing, not because there's any force causing the cards to be bad, but because your image is damaged and your opponents tend to play better.

a. Be more selective about your starting hands.

b. Don't bluff, at least not very often.

c. Don't raise as often.

d. Don't bet for value with the hands you normally would.

7. Psychological Tricks When Losing

a. Remind yourself that you are exactly even right now.

b. Remember that even though what you do now doesn't seem to matter, there will come a time when it will matter.

8. Take a Small Win and Go Home

If you're influenced by the fact that you're on a "losing streak" despite your best efforts to ignore it, build up your confidence by taking a win home with you. This psychological trick works wonders.

9. Play in a Smaller Game

Gong down in limits is a good way to cheaply get yourself back on your feet.

10. Look for Reasons Why You're Losing

If you find reasons, adjust. But if you don't find any, stick to your game plan and keep the faith. Eventually, you'll be rewarded.

PROTECTING YOUR POKER BANKROLL— AND MORE

I'm not a strong advocate of bankroll science. In fact, I think that most things said about bankrolls are not science at all. They are mostly just homespun wisdom.

We've previously explored the concept that the more risk you take, the more likely you are to capture sudden wealth, and the more likely you are to be damaged in the pursuit. The risk is up to you. That's important, and I'll repeat it. The more risk you accept, the more likely you are to suddenly prosper and the more likely you are to suddenly go broke.

So, you see, it's your choice. What's an unacceptable risk for you may be tolerable for someone else. It's a personal decision. It's up to you. And it's up to them.

Also, you should be aware that there are mathematically derived methods that can be used to maximize your chance of success once you've defined your goals.

Most of the concepts in this section have been stated previously, but they are so important, I am stressing them again below.

1. How Big Does Your Bankroll Need to Be?

It is folly to criticize a player for having an insufficient starting bankroll. Taking 100 shots with $50 each time gives you about the same chance of eventual success as taking a single shot with $5,000—provided you play your best game at all times.

Of course, this isn't precisely true. Other factors may influence your fate substantially. What factors? Well, if you play with a single buy-in, you're more likely to go all-in. These all-in situations change your prospects. Actually, being all-in can often work to your advantage. That's because other players may then eliminate themselves from the showdown by not calling bets made by remaining opponents. While this is happening, you are guaranteed to make the showdown. This means you will win all pots where you can stumble into the best hand, while your opponents will not.

On the down side, you may play differently on short money and your opponents may play differently against you. You sometimes will not have the opportunity to stay in a good game long with $50, although you might have stayed and made profit if you had a big bankroll behind you. There are many other factors to consider, but in general, taking 100 shots with just $50 each time can be considered the same as gathering $5,000 before you play the first time. If you play the same type of poker, your prospects will be similar. And when you try to get jumpstarted by taking bigger risks with smaller amounts of money, you might get lucky early and not need to ever invest that whole $5,000.

So, the common notion that short money is at a big disadvantage is a myth. You are much more likely to go broke with only a small buy-in, but the force of all those short buy-ins combined should give you about the same opportunity overall as one big bankroll.

2. Not Everyone Needs a Bankroll

If you only expect to play occasionally, or are playing recreationally, you can just bring whatever you can afford whenever you can afford it. Bankrolls are things you build and are designed for people without infinite assets who want to play regularly.

3. You Really Must Try to Play Your Best Game All the Time

The policy of playing your best game *most* of the time is the greatest destroyer of bankrolls there is. At higher-limit games, players actually seem to take turns going on **tilt**—a poker term that means you've lost critical control of your game and temporarily are playing poorly. If you pass your turn quite often without your opponents realizing it, you'll win the most money. This is known as "Caro's Law of Least Tilt."

I first wrote about this more than thirty years ago and it remains one of the most fundamentally important things you can learn if you want to succeed at poker. You are not likely to succeed if you decide to blatantly take advantage of knowledgeable opponents' super-loose play. If they're taking turns going on tilt, and you come into the game and play perfectly stable, you won't fit in. They will resent you and often they will stop providing you with profit.

The trick is to play along and show some fast action, too. Simulate tilt. Make them aware of it. But pass your turn when they don't notice. Among equally skilled players, the one who spends the least time on tilt (or simulating tilt) wins the most money.

4. Don't Promote Yourself to Higher Limits Just Because You're Winning

You might eventually find a level you can't beat. When this happens, most players refuse to step back down, and they lose or spin their wheels for the rest of their poker careers. This is actually an application of the Peter Principle (about how people get promoted until they reach their level of incompetence) to poker.

5. Be Selective About Your Games

Don't routinely join the first game you see. Most of your profit will come from good games. Even most winning players lose money in tougher games.

Those are fighting words, but they're true. If I could select the worst 50 percent of games that professionals played in throughout their careers, most would be losers for those sessions, especially when the cost of raked pots and other expenses are considered. It is the other 50 percent of their games—and sometimes an even much smaller portion of their games—that supply the profit for most pros. Game selection is much more important than most players suppose. Think about it.

6. You Should Be Less Protective of a Small Bankroll

Do you understand this yet? I want you to win, and I'm going to pound it home until it becomes part of your psyche. The larger your bankroll grows, the more worthy it is of protection and the less chances you should take. That's because a large bankroll would be much harder to replace from sources in the world beyond poker. You can usually get a small starting bankroll from the "real" world, but it's unlikely that you will be able to replace an established bankroll in the same way.

7. Don't Treat Your Bankroll Like a Tournament Buy-In

You can have a "tournament" almost any day you want. Just keep jumping into higher and higher limits until you reach a long-shot goal or go broke. But in a tournament, only one player ends up with the chips. Everyone else goes broke. Don't treat your bankroll that way.

WHEN TO STAY, WHEN TO QUIT

Players are always confused about the best times to quit or how long they should stay in a game to maximize the profits from their poker session. Even worse, they seldom give it any serious consideration. But if you're treating poker as a business—and you should be—that's a mistake.

Here are five concepts to guide you:

1. Go With the Poker Tide

Good games eventually get worse, and bad games eventually get better. In good games, the weak players eventually leave or go broke. They are replaced by tough players trying to capitalize on the game that was better earlier. Strong players eventually leave solid games out of frustration and go searching for easier opponents, and these games become easier. So, it's predictable like the tide. Expect loose games to eventually get tighter; expect tight games to eventually get looser.

When you sit in a loose, easy-to-beat game, be prepared to leave when the tide goes out.

> *"Expect loose games to eventually get tighter; expect tight games to eventually get looser."*

2. Where You Stand

You should never stay in a game hoping to get even, because you already *are* even. Your bankroll is always as large as it is when the cards are shuffled. This attitude will save you the fate of many poker players who destroy their bankrolls chasing an elusive and meaningless goal. You don't need to book a win tonight. You just need to make your best decisions time after time. That's where the money is. Whether you win or lose for a particular session should not be important to you. In the long run, you will earn or lose money in accordance with the quality of your decisions. Nothing more, nothing less. And you are always *exactly* even when then next hand begins.

> *"In the long run, you will earn or lose money in accordance with the quality of your decisions. Nothing more, nothing less."*

3. It's Okay to Lose Back What You Won

There's no disgrace in turning a big win into a loss. It's no worse than quitting now and then coming back tomorrow to meet bad luck. If you're in a good game where you believe you should earn money, then the main consequence of quitting is the same as it would be with any other job with an hourly wage: You'll work fewer hours. And that means you'll make less money.

Poker's all-time stupidest question is, "Why didn't you quit when you were $600 ahead?" Does anyone ever ask that after you stay and win $3,000? Think about it. If you lose $300 for the night, your friends are likely to say, "You should have quit when you were winning $600." Has any friend, in the entire history of the world, ever chided you after you won $3,000 with the words, "You should have quit when you were winning $600"?

Repeating: When you hear, "Why didn't you quit when you were winning?" you're listening to the most illogical question in all of poker. The fact is, you have no idea whether the next hour will bring you a win or a loss, so there's no way to know—based on dollars won so far—when to quit.

4. Beware of Manufactured Streaks

Don't manufacture a win streak by quitting with small wins when the game is good and staying to recover when the game is bad. Lots of players brag about their win streaks. They're just playing mental games that cause them to put in fewer hours and earn less money.

It's easy to put yourself on a win streak. Just quit every time you're a little ahead. And when you're behind, keep playing as long as you can, because there's always a chance that you'll book a win. As soon as you recover and get a little ahead, *then* quit. Yep. That works. You'll have longer winning streaks and a better win-loss record than I will. But you'll have many small wins and notable big losses. And you'll just cost yourself profit.

Worse, you'll tend to invest most of your hours in the worst games, when you're losing and struggling to get your money back. And you'll take hours off from the best games, whenever you quit will small wins that extend your streak, instead of staying for a big payday.

5. Moving Up to a Bigger Game

When you're successful and ready to promote yourself to a bigger game, you don't need to play that game all the time. Stick with your previous limit and make occasional forays into the larger limit. Always watch both games, and be ready to jump from one to the other as conditions dictate. The larger limit must be much better than the regular limit to justify playing it, because there's more risk to your bankroll. This advice is particularly valid if your bankroll is limited.

REASONS TO STAY IN A GAME
1. The game is good.
2. Your image is good.
3. Your spirits are good.
4. There is laughter.
5. You are alert.

That laughter part is important. I always tend to stay in a game where people are having a good time. This generally indicates that they are playing poker for fun and not for profit, and I encourage this attitude in my opponents. Silence is a bad sign. It means your opponents may be serious about the game and are making carefully considered decisions. There's usually less profit in such games, and that's why "silence" makes the list below.

REASONS TO LEAVE A GAME
1. The game is bad.
2. Your image is bad.
3. You've been losing, inspiring opponents.
4. Silence.
5. Your opponents play selectively, but aggressively.
6. The game is too loose for your bankroll—loose games are generally more profitable, but require larger bankrolls, due to increased fluctuations of outcomes.
7. You can't actually spot mistakes opponents are making.
8. You're worried about cheating—this will eat up mental energy, even if your suspicion is ill-founded.
9. You feel "glued to your seat."

Notice that I said you can quit because you're losing. This is not superstition. When opponents see you lose, they play better against you, believing that you're vulnerable. When you're winning and your image is dominating, you're a force to be reckoned with and opponents are often intimidated, predictable, and easy to beat. They'll call more with weak hands because they are numb, frustrated, or amazed. And they'll raise less when they have an advantage because they are less confident. So, you should be less willing to quit early when you're winning.

Also notice that I warned against opponents who are selective about the hands they play but aggressive when they do enter a pot. These, as a group, are your least profitable opponents. They're mostly playing quality hands and getting maximum value from them.

You need to be able to identify mistakes opponents make. If you can't spot opponents making choices that you know are unprofitable and that you wouldn't make yourself, there is probably little profit to be made in the game. So, consider quitting.

> **CARO'S THRESHOLD OF MISERY REVISITED**
> The main rule of quitting: Never cross "Caro's Threshold of Misery." I have defined a point that your losses are so large that your agony is already maximized. Beyond that, additional losses don't register, and they feel no worse. Then you will have a hard time making meaningful decisions. Quit before you get anywhere near this threshold.

Q & A: BANKROLLING
QUESTION

You are building your bankroll. It is growing but not yet large enough to offer you security. You're in a no-limit hold 'em game against weak opponents. You're the favorite here. Your opponents are unsophisticated, and you know you can handle them in the long run. But your bankroll isn't quite adequate for the game? Which is the best advice?

a. Play many weak hands for the first few hours, conditioning your opponents to gamble with you.

b. Always move all-in with medium-strong hands, preventing opponents from drawing out.

c. Throw away a lot of hands when you have only a small advantage.

d. Press your small advantages, because this is where most of your profit will come from.

ANSWER

Actually, the very best advice is to either not play or only buy-in for a small portion of your bankroll. But, for this question, given those choices, the answer is…

C. Playing no-limit hold 'em while building a bankroll can be a frightening experience. Doom can be delivered on the next deal. An opponent's sudden surge of good fortune can shovel you under. You can go broke in less time than it takes to run a horserace.

Limit poker gives you protection. You try to choose the sizes of limit games you are likely to survive. If you have an advantage and a reasonable bankroll, you can usually make it grow. How big is a no-limit game? Well, there's no answer to that, really. It's like asking, "How big is a limit game?" It depends on the limit. The word "no-limit" doesn't determine the size of a game any more than the word "limit" does. This next section further examines the reason why C is the best answer.

NO-LIMIT AND YOUR BANKROLL

What theoretically determines the size of a no-limit game is how much money is in the pot before the cards are dealt. In hold 'em, this money usually takes the form of blind bets. On very rare occasions, there are antes or both blinds and antes. Players gauge the size of their wagers by the amount of money they can gain. Bigger blinds, bigger game. In practice, no-limit games with small blinds are traditionally misplayed. The bets tend to be much larger than what can be justified by the initial size of the pot. That's something to keep in mind, but it has nothing whatsoever to do with what we're discussing. I got sidetracked. Sorry.

So, here you are in this no-limit game. You would like to take advantage of every little edge that comes along, but you can't afford that. You need to survive. Besides, weak players are such that you often can forego high risks in the pursuit of small profit and concentrate on hands with the large edges. If you do this, you're often quite certain of winning their chips.

If you're on a limited bankroll, or even a fairly substantial but not infinite bankroll, you should not commit yourself to pot-limit or no-limit pots with marginally strong hands against pathetically weak opponents. Reckless opponents will likely give you their money sooner or later in no-limit (and pot-limit) games. By playing marginally strong hands you are making two mistakes:

1. You're limiting the certainty of getting the money and adding to your bankroll fluctuations
2. You're accepting a lesser percentage return on your cumulative investments in the pots. This may be all right under some circumstances (it's the total money won that's usually important), but not all right when you're going after a limited amount of money. It's specifically not all right when your opponents only have a finite amount to lose, and you're more likely to win it by being more patient and taking smaller risks.

Usually in no-limit, there's only so much to win (whatever is on the table, plus reserves in opponents' pockets) and you can only get it once. So, why take unnecessary chances? There is an argument in response to that, though. One reason you might want to negate this advice is if several strong opponents are also going after the same money, and you want to keep them from getting it first.

In general, though, the answer is C—just throw away a lot of hands when you have only a small advantage. Wait for better opportunities.

RISKS OF REVERSE MANUFACTURING

Most players, even serious ones, suffer much greater poker losses than they should. One reason is that their losses are "reversed manufactured." In other words, those losses are the necessary byproduct of trying to manufacture a winning streak. You might have manufactured some yourself and not realized it. You're probably manufacturing a winning streak (and, in fact, manufacturing wins) if you like to brag about the number of times you've won in a row. If you go around telling anyone who will listen, "I'm on an 18 day win streak," more likely than not, you're manufacturing wins.

How can you manufacture a win? It's amazingly easy. All you have to do is refuse to settle for a loss and accept small wins whenever you need to. The only requirement is that you fight back when you're behind, hoping to break into the plus column, then quit happy if you succeed, rejoicing in the notion that you overcame adversity, struggled to restack your chips, and are now going home to rest victorious. It will feel like a proud accomplishment to you—but it shouldn't.

HOW YOU MANUFACTURE A WIN

Let's look at how it might have just happened. You're a medium-limit hold 'em player, not competing quite large enough to make a good living, but large enough to supplement your income or to barely get by without a job when required. In this way, you're like the majority of winning poker players, somewhere between just eking out a profit and professional wage-earner status.

Anyway, you sit down in a $10/$20 hold 'em game, hoping to make a profit by showing off your Sunday-best poker skills. Sad stuff happens right away, though. Down goes a king-high heart flush, which you flopped, when a player holding the ace of hearts and deuce of diamonds sees a fourth heart come on the river. Next you flop three jacks, but finish third when two opponents hit straights. Then there's that devastating hand where you get bluffed out of your birdcage by Bruno, who never, ever did that before. And it gets worse. The little medium hands that can go either North or South, all go South. Losses pile up.

You fight back. Hours pass. You grow weary. Hours pass. You fight to stay alert and wait for your luck to change. Hours pass.

It's now 3:40 in the morning and you need to be up at 8:30. Suddenly several pots are pushed to you. Then a small setback. Then you win more pots. After a string of pots go your way, you win a really big one. Is your recovery complete? You don't know, because you haven't had time to count your chips.

"Deal me out one hand," you tell the table. You need to stack these newly won chips, count them, find out where you stand. Down $135, put ten of these $5 chips here, down $85 now, put these two $25 chips off to the side, down $35, oops, three more $5 chips under a $20 bill, exactly even, and that leaves these three $1 chips, change from the rake, so up $3! You did it! Your winning streak continues!

"Deal me out!" you announce. "It's getting later than I thought."

"Don't you wanna play till your blind?" someone asks. "You've got another hand coming."

You're tempted, after all, you can just fold everything except aces, even aces if you really want to. But you just wave away the suggestion. "Nah, deal around me." And within minutes you're cashed out and on your way home. As you're leaving, a friend asks you how you did tonight. Your chest puffs out proudly and you say, "I won a tiny bit. Nothing that matters, but that's nineteen winning days in a row."

Signs of trouble, my friends. Bad signs of trouble. You're manufacturing that win streak just so you can make yourself feel good about it. But you're not manufacturing profit. Sure, you think you're making profit, but really you're putting your bankroll at risk. You have tallied a lot of wins—a couple when you got off to a fast start and kept on winning, a few short ones when you started fast, but faltered and quit before you found yourself in the negative column, some where you'd come from behind and quit when you got ahead. And, of course, tonight when you'd stuck it out and turned a major loss into a tiny win.

Speaking of tiny wins, that's exactly the kind you're likely to have when you strive to extend a winning streak. That's simply because you're willing to settle for them. You'll quit with small wins when you've been winning more to keep from dropping below break even. And you'll gladly cash out with a small win if you've been losing and get ahead. However, there is no such thing as a small loss. You won't accept one. It's either a win or a big loss. You need to keep that winning streak alive if you can, right?

The Danger of Manufacturing Wins

But, all together, this strategy means you're playing more hours than you should when you were losing, because you're trying to catch up. And it means you're playing fewer hours when you're winning, because you're eager to cash out and add to your win streak. By manufacturing a win streak, by forcing small wins, you're also putting yourself in grave danger of manufacturing huge losses. You simply won't experience them as long as your luck holds and your winning streak is extended.

You see, when you try hard as you can to dig yourself out, you risk digging yourself deeper. It's like that popular advice, "When you find yourself in a hole, stop digging." I think those words were tailored for poker. Beware! On the few occasions that you won't be able to experience the glory of cashing out with that $3 profit and puffing up proudly, you're likely to suffer painful losses and depart pitifully from the poker table, all chance of recovery now hopeless. You will have lost way more than you should have. And I'm not talking about a magic stop-loss or predetermined limit on how much you should risk in a game.

I'm saying you lost much more than you should because you played poker in the worst of circumstances. When you're winning, opponents are usually intimidated by you. They're less likely to play their best games, and less likely to make daring bets and raises with winning hands and extract every penny of profit from you. This means you can make value bets that can push your profits to the limit. Opponents who are intimidated usually keep calling in frustration, but seldom raise with anything but obviously strong hands. In doing so, they neglect to take advantage of all their edges, so you rule the table, and your profit soars.

Conversely, when you're losing, opponents are inspired. They play better against *you* specifically. They think, "Hey, there's someone I can beat. There's someone who's unluckier than I am." And they single you out for money extraction.

So, I don't like to hear about long manufactured winning streaks, because I know that those invite huge manufactured losses, too. And, in the long run, long winning streaks usually mean that you've played most of your time under bad circumstances and limited the time you've played under good circumstances. And that isn't a smooth path to poker profit.

There's one more thing you need to know. Players who try to manufacture winning streaks have a statistical signature in their results that identifies them. Remember, I told you to keep records. Well, when you look back over these records, add up the total money won on your winning days. Now divide that by the number of wins. Next add up the total money lost on your losing days. Now divide that by the number of losses.

Here's the secret: If your average loss is larger than your average win over months of play, there's a good chance you're manufacturing your wins. You need to stop doing that.

9 SAGE POKER ADVICE

Sometimes I like to make lists. I'm about to make three of them. One is about some things I've never done at poker; another is about some things I've sometimes done at poker; the third is about some things I've always done at poker. I think you'll find them instructive.

SOME THINGS I'VE NEVER DONE AT POKER

1. I've Never Encouraged Anyone to Gamble With Me Who Couldn't Afford It.

This has been an important part of my creed ever since I started gambling. Yes, I have won money from people who suffered because of the loss. But I have never tried to hustle anyone into gambling beyond his capacity to absorb the losses. If they were bound and determined to do it on their own, I confess that I usually did not try to talk them out of it. But I did not encourage them.

2. I've Never Gone On Tilt.

But, with the game style I have adopted, who would know the difference? My natural instinct is to tighten up after losses and go into a protective and somewhat conservative shell.

3. I've Never Cheated.

I'm proud of that.

4. I've Never Wished I Had Quit Earlier After Losing Money Back.

I'm always philosophical about such turnarounds. I realize that by continuing to play I was more likely to add to the win than to subtract from it. You should look at it the same way if you're a winning player in a profitable game.

5. I've Never Gotten Angry with a Dealer Because of Bad Beats.

I honestly don't associate these misfortunes with the dealer. Neither should you.

6. I've Never Gotten Angry with a Dealer Because of Mistakes that Cost Me a Pot.

I treat dealing mistakes like the weather. Sometimes it makes you happy, sometimes it makes you sad. If I were going to become irritated by dealing mistakes, I'd be wasting a lot of energy that could be better used for more productive purposes.

7. I've Never Refused to Tip a Dealer When I Would Have Otherwise Because an Earlier Mistake Had Cost Me a Pot.

I feel good about that, too.

8. I've Never Borrowed Money from Loan Sharks.

Not a dime, ever. They tell me that's unusual in a casino environment where loan sharks are often nearby and young players sometimes are desperate to get in action—or stay in action.

SOME THINGS I'VE SOMETIMES DONE AT POKER

1. I've Sometimes Gone Broke.

When I was younger, I was willing to risk my whole bankroll at any time, at the mere hint of a challenge. My early poker career was one of building bankrolls, spending too much, going broke, and rebuilding. I never knew from one day to the next whether I was going to have lots of money to flash around or whether I was going to have to return to a smaller game and start all over. Strangely, my memories about those days and the extravagant ways I spent money when I had it—while never holding a job and fighting sometimes fiercely to stay solvent— still thrill me.

But if I had it to do over, I would have sacrificed adventure in pursuit of profit.

2. I've Sometimes Played Silently.

Yep. I did not always put on that wild and crazy act I've written about. I had my moods.

3. I've Sometimes Consumed Liquor While Playing Poker.

Not often. I don't think this is an especially bad transgression at a sociable table. Sometimes this has encouraged opponents to drink also, occasionally even more than I did, which gave me an additional unexpected edge.

4. I've Sometimes Called a Pot When I Couldn't Possibly Win.

Best advertising play there is. And, of course, I've always shown the hand.

5. I've Sometimes Conveyed a Smart, Alert, and Professional Image at the Table.

But not anymore. That image really sucks. All you're doing is alerting your opponents to the fact that they're being scrutinized, and this sometimes makes them more careful about not appearing weak in your eyes.

6. I've Sometimes Made Short Buy-Ins.

Why not? Usually it's legal to make a short buy-in after each full buy-in. There are advantages to being nearly all-in, because opponents can't chase you out of pots and you often win with hands you would have had to throw away had you had more money on the table. Of course, usually I buy plenty of chips, but there's something to say for short buy-ins, too.

7. I've Sometimes Made Proposition Bets While Playing Poker.

I've said I won't take the worst of it, but there's nothing wrong with taking even-money bets if it will loosen up my opponents or distract them more than it distracts me. So, if they want to bet on low spade versus low heart on the flop, I sometimes accommodate them.

8. I've Sometimes Used Game Selection to Make Sure I Was in the Most Profitable Game.

But, unfortunately, not always. Sometimes I opt for the tougher game that is more of a challenge. But I do this much less today than I did when I was younger and still had something to prove. You should be vigilant about finding the most profitable games, even if I don't always do this myself. Choosing the right game is a much more profitable decision than most choices you will make at the table about how to play hands.

9. I've Sometimes Gambled at Things Where I Thought I Probably Had the Worst of It.

But that's only to find out if I really do. There are many things that are worth exploring, not just poker games. You can invest a little money to find out if it's good or bad. If it's good, you often can make a large score. If it's bad, you can take a small loss and move on.

SOME THINGS I'VE ALWAYS DONE AT POKER

1. I've Always Counted My Chips While I Was Sitting at the Table.

That old advice about never counting your chips at the table is nonsense. As I said previously, it's like telling a football coach not to look at the scoreboard.

2. I've Always Stood Ready to Use Optional Rebuys in a Tournament When it Wasn't Mathematically Justified By Profit.

That's because I only enter rebuy tournaments if I'm interested in a trophy. So, I want to give myself every edge toward achieving my goal, even if I sacrifice some potential profit.

3. I've Always Ignored the Stop-Loss Philosophy While Playing Poker.

Stop-loss is a bankroll managing tactic that dictates that you will absolutely quit if you lose a given amount of money. This is intended to protect you from ever suffering super-size losses.

The stop-loss is really a stop-win. If you're a winning player in a good game and you feel like playing, the more hours you put in, the more you'll win. There's no magic number that you should use to stop playing, provided you can afford to continue.

The exceptions may be if your image is damaged because of the losses or psychologically you can't cope with a bigger downturn. Also, you might be in a game that isn't as favorable as you think. Other than that, I say if the game is good, you want to play, and you're in good condition to continue, quitting in accordance with a predetermined stop-loss will just cost you money.

4. I've Always Avoided Gambling at Anything Where I Knew For Sure I Had the Worst of it.

You're looking at a gambling authority who has statistically analyzed craps and roulette, but has never played in his lifetime.

MORE THINGS I'VE NEVER DONE AT POKER

1. I've Never Been Barred from a Game or a Casino.

Well, come to think of it, I was sort of barred once. It was at the old Rainbow Club in Gardena, California. It was actually owned by many of the same people who owned the adjoining Monterey Club. Both clubs have long since vanished. There was a short covered walkway linking the clubs and a mutually accessible tavern right in the middle. Foot traffic back and forth was encouraged, so that it was practically a single cardroom—seventy tables, thirty-five in each club.

A lot of us helped start the biggest game allowed every day at the Rainbow and left our money in player's banks there. One day an inexperienced floorman decided he shouldn't start our game, because it might interfere with smaller-limit games in progress, by taking players from those tables and leaving those games short-handed. We politely understood this, but none of us played the lower limits. So, impatient, we went next door and started our game there. This apparently enraged and embarrassed the floorman and the back-up management that was temporarily in charge.

Suddenly, we were barred from the Rainbow Club premises. We managed to talk our way back in long enough to extract a collective $50,000 (in 1970s money) from our player's banks. When regular management heard about this, hours later, we were immediately called in to receive an elaborate apology. But, I guess, I've technically been barred. But not in the normal sense, for disruptive or unethical reasons.

2. I've Never Berated Weak Opponents for the Way They Played Their Hands.

It's their money and I appreciate their action, whether they draw out on me or not. In fact, that's the primary source of my profit. It seems silly to be mad at that. Yet frequently I see irritated players with winning expectations get angry because opponents played incorrectly and won. Let me tell y'all a secret—you want opponents to play incorrectly. You should encourage it!

3. I've Never Stared Down an Opponent to Try to Get a Tell.

This makes them self-conscious and less likely to display tells in the future. Yes, staring can make them nervous and possibly enhance your likelihood of reading them correctly at the moment, but overall it isn't worth it. Be inconspicuous about watching for tells.

4. I've Never Given Solid Advice at the Poker Table to Players Who Ask.

When asked a serious question about strategy, I usually give a whimsical answer or say you can play it all kinds of ways. Sometimes I giggle and say, "You don't even want to know how *I* play it. You'll just lose money." If I say that, I not only don't have to answer the question, but I have enhanced my image as a confusing player. When asked about odds, I say, "That's why I calculated all those statistics and published them. Now, I don't have to memorize any odds. You're supposed to memorize them so I can just ask you." Actually, there's a bit of truth to that, anyway.

The poker table is not a classroom. And you don't want recreational players to conclude that you're playing seriously. If you do that, they're likely to become self-conscious about their decisions and stop playing as liberally—which will cost you money.

5. I've Never Thrown Cards at a Dealer.

Never even been tempted.

6. I've Never Destroyed Cards in Anger at the Poker Table.

Never even been tempted to do that, either.

7. I've Never Offered a Settlement Deal in a Tournament.

But, I've *accepted* deals that were extremely in my favor, when they only dealt with the distribution of money and didn't determine who would win. All deals should be publicly announced, and I personally believe it would be better if there weren't any deals at all.

MORE THINGS I'VE SOMETIMES DONE AT POKER

1. I've Sometimes Backed Other Players.

I hardly ever do it these days, and only with people I've had long-standing relations with. Backing players just hasn't panned out for me.

2. I've Sometimes Been Staked.

But hardly ever. Over the years, I've almost always played on my own money without even selling pieces of myself. When I first played $400/$800 in the late 1970s, I had a fairly limited bankroll, about $45,000, and I played against top pros on my own money. I later found out that everyone in that game either had pieces of each other , had sold pieces to others outside the game, or had backers. I survived, but I was the only one risking the full $800 on each late-round bet. Go figure.

3. I've Sometimes Gone to Sleep at the Table.

Rarely though. I'm still capable of playing multi-day marathon sessions without drugs or even coffee. I stay awake, usually, but not always. I sometimes try to take micro-naps between hands.

4. I've Sometimes Bet When I Thought it Would Be More Immediately Profitable to Check-Raise.

In fact, I do this very often. This is because I believe check-raising often makes happy losers more aware of strategy. It makes them aware that there's a strategic war happening and that they better be more careful.

They become conscious that the game is serious and not just giggly. Check-raising frequently changes the flavor of a loose game and makes it more hostile. For these reasons, I usually reserve check-raising for special situations, to be used against strong opponents or weak opponents who consider it playful and won't be made uncomfortable by its use.

5. I've Sometimes Raised Blind When it Wasn't Required.

It's great for loose-image building, and if you do it one or two seats before the blinds, you aren't costing yourself much. Heads-up, I do this very frequently and it sometimes doesn't cost anything at all, because many players don't know how to handle a blind raise and I most likely would have raised anyway, even if I'd looked.

6. I've Sometimes Played Very Tight.

I know, it's hard to believe, based on my advocacy of playing a lively game with a wild image. But I started out my poker career as a rock in my first serious games back in high school. If you don't know the term, a rock is a player who hardly ever plays a hand or takes chances without having far the best of it.

Back then, I hadn't done the research and didn't have the sophistication needed to use other tools. But tight play wins against weak opponents, and it won for me. But it didn't win nearly as much as an advanced strategy could have. I quickly learned to maneuver beyond religiously rocky play.

I've also played tight when I was in a new game where I wasn't expecting to stay long, since there was no reason to waste money establishing an image. And I've even played tight as an experiment to see how opponents would react to me in that mode.

7. I've Sometimes Lent Money to Other Players.

But not anymore. In the past, in addition to habitually providing larger loans, I believed that you should give $20 to anyone who was pesky and kept asking. I handed out $20 bills in the 1970s on the hopes the annoying borrowers would never repay it. I figured if these compulsive borrowers owed me a little money, they might avoid me rather than be asked to pay it back. Sometimes this worked, sometimes it didn't. In modern years, I have refined my policy and hardly ever lend money, except to close associates.

8. I've Sometimes Played to Win First Place in a Tournament.

And I sometimes haven't. You need to realize that there's a dramatic difference in strategy between going after the first-place trophy and trying to get the most profit in tournaments. This is because of what conceptually happens in proportional-payout tournaments when the first-place finisher must win all the chips and then surrender most of their value to opponents who came close, but have already been conquered. This first-place penalty makes playing to win the trophy less profitable (and sometimes unprofitable!) than a more conservative approached designed to merely finish high and win the most money in the long run.

9. I've Sometimes Chosen to Check-Call When Almost Everyone Else Advocates Either Betting or Check-Raising.

I often choose to string along consistent bluffers and weak-hand bettors until the final betting round, and then raise.

MORE THINGS I'VE ALWAYS DONE AT POKER
1. I've Always Remained in Games Against Weak Opponents When They Changed From Full-Handed to Short-Handed.

Short-handed is where the money is for me. Most players don't understand how to play short-handed poker, especially hold 'em, and you get to make many more significant decisions, because you play many more hands. In poker, your profit is determined by how well you make decisions. If you're the superior player, the more opportunities you have to excel, the more profit you'll earn. In short-handed poker, you have more opportunities to excel.

2. I've Always Played Hard Against Each Opponent Without Soft-Playing Anyone.

If you feel sorry for a player, you can always give the money back after you've won it. At the poker table, play hard against everyone.

3. I've Always Written Candidly About Poker in a Way That Could Diminish My Profit.

Sure, I recognize that people learn what to expect from me by reading my books and columns or by attending my seminars. Maybe that hurts my profit a little. I'm not really sure, because there are other compensating factors. But my writing doesn't hurt your profit. Most players who read poker books don't master the techniques. They simply feel empowered by having the books on their shelves. Poker becomes more popular; there are more players; and only the most serious ones win. It's just as it always has been.

That doesn't apply to you though. If you're this deeply into the book already, I assume you're taking it seriously.

IF I DID IT AGAIN...11 POKER THINGS I WOULDN'T DO IF I WERE TO LIVE MY LIFE OVER AGAIN
1. I Wouldn't Enter Games That I Worried About.

In old Gardena, California, where I used to play, cheating was rampant. You dealt your own cards, and not everyone dealt fairly. Not every deck remained unmarked. Collusion among players was legendary. However, I was reckless. As an honest player, I didn't believe the cheaters had any right to be in my game. Even when I was quite sure I was being scammed, I would simply stay seated and seethe. I vaguely knew what was going on, but I hated to be run off.

Sometimes I'd spend months building a comfortable bankroll in an honest game only to be lured into a crooked one. If I had to do it over again, I would run away.

2. I Wouldn't Consider Cardroom Management to Be Adversarial.

There's a partnership that exists between a professional poker player and cardroom management. Both make money off the same business, and they need that business to be profitable. In my early years, I thought of management as an outside force, with different interests. I was always cordial, but I didn't think of management as an ally.

If I had to do it over again, I would make lasting relations with casino management from the very beginning, and I'd go out of my way to help make the cardroom successful.

3. I Wouldn't Give Women Money to Gamble in Order to Skip the Preliminaries.

Decades ago, it was unbelievably easy to pick up women. One-night stands were common. I wasn't looking for lasting relationships. Weird time. Different planet. You had to be there. One of the quickest ways I knew to skip even the basic preliminaries of getting acquainted was to tell women I had faith in them as players and give them money to play poker. I would usually agree to keep half of what they won.

Problem was, they almost never won, and I came to believe I wasn't always getting an honest count. Also, all these short-term relationships began with a lie—that I believed they could win at poker. Usually, I didn't. If I had to do it over again, I'd spend a little extra time, save a little money, and go to the damn dinner and movie like everyone else.

4. I Wouldn't Write Books.

Believe it or not, I never wanted to write poker books. I did lots of research, and it was time consuming. It made winning easy. I didn't want to share this information. But in 1977, twice-world poker champion Doyle "Texas Dolly" Brunson talked me into contributing to his soon-to-be bible of poker: *Super System-A Course In Power Poker.* After that, my vow of silence was broken, and I decided to continue to help players who didn't have the opportunity to do research.

It's been rewarding, and I enjoy teaching, writing, and lecturing about poker. But, if I had to do it over again as a poker player, I think I'd just stay off stage and not let opponents know what strategies I use. Of course, that's assuming I would want to remain a relatively obscure poker player for the rest of my life. There are, I admit, financial advantages to the path I've taken. Still, poker was simpler for me personally before I shared secrets.

On the other hand, the psychological benefits of the life I've chosen have been so gratifying that I can't think of anything I'd rather have done. In fact, forget this one. I take it back.

5. I Wouldn't Have Gone Through My FPS Phase.

I teach players to avoid FPS, which stands for *Fancy Play Syndrome.* This is where you often choose the fanciest play, rather than the most profitable, in order to impress your opponents. I suffered from this myself for many years.

If I had to do it over again, I wouldn't try to impress poker opponents. I'd just be satisfied with winning their money.

6. I Wouldn't Gamble Above My Bankroll.

When you gamble too big for your bankroll, you frequently lose and must rebuild. The net effect is that you win less money than you would if you were more cautious.

If I had to do it over again, I would seldom risk more than 10 percent of my bankroll on any single poker session. Usually, the amount would be much smaller.

7. I Wouldn't Spend Too Much of My Bankroll.

Poker players tend to underestimate the amount of money they need to cover a bad run of cards. As yet another example of the same concept we've already visited: They build to $40,000, spend $25,000, lose $15,000 and find themselves broke, even though they won.

If I had to do it over again, I would be much more miserly, from my earliest years on, in keeping my bankroll ridiculously padded. I believe extra profit comes from that extra comfort.

8. I Wouldn't Flash Money and Get Robbed.

One of the big thrills for me was carrying around $40,000 in my pocket while doctors and lawyers might not be able to produce a single $100 bill. This made me feel rich and I loved to flash money. Of course, many of my opponents had much more money than I did when I was young. They just didn't carry all their assets in their pants pockets.

This youthful exhibition of false wealth caused me to be tied up and robbed at gunpoint twice. And I don't think it impressed many people. If I had to do it over again, I wouldn't flash money. And maybe I wouldn't even let anyone know I had money to spare.

9. I Wouldn't Be Embarrassed to Jump Down in Limits.

One of the worst things players can do is to test a larger limit, because that limit looks profitable right now, then refuse to return to their previous limit when the conditions worsen. Ego causes us to think of ourselves as a \$5/\$10 player or a \$20/\$40 player or a \$200/\$400 player. Once you've established yourself at that limit, it can be psychologically damaging or embarrassing to jump down. That's how it often was for me when I was younger.

If I had to do it over again, I would just find the most profitable game at any limit my bankroll could justify and, if it turned out to be a smaller limit than I could afford, I wouldn't care what anyone thought. Often, there can be more profit in a \$40/\$80 game than a \$200/\$400 game or in a \$2/\$4 game than a \$10/\$20 game. It depends on who's playing.

10. I Wouldn't Burn Money.

I'm known for taking a match and burning \$100 bills at the poker table. I've done this to convince opponents that I don't care about money and, thereby, to gain psychological dominance.

If I had to do it over again, I'd only burn \$20 bills. It's more cost effective and accomplishes almost the same thing.

11. I Wouldn't Have Been the Harlem Globetrotters of Poker.

Many times I've played poker just to put on a show. Sometimes I even do that today. I like to prove my superiority by doing magical things nobody else ever envisioned. I call this "putting on poker exhibitions." While I'm usually able to win despite the sacrifice, I wish my nature were a little more conservative.

If I had to do it over again, I'd almost always play purely for profit, not to show how good I am.

But, on the other hand, if I hadn't done all those things, I wouldn't be me.

10 INCREASING PROFITS

Somewhere along the poker path between knowing nothing, where we all begin, and total mastery, is a point where you are now. Hopefully, you will become an even better player. But this won't happen for everyone. Some people stop along the poker path and get no better. They are even apt to regress, revisiting places where their game was much weaker.

I'm going to start with two selected concepts that are essential for you to learn if you are to become a winning player. They are perhaps ahead of you on the path, but I'm going to fast track you directly to those places now. If you are capable of winning a small amount of money now, but often lose or break about even for long stretches of time—even for years—I've got the cure.

Pay attention because this is the most important poker advice I can give you in your quest to increase your profits at the poker table.

MY MOST IMPORTANT POKER ADVICE
1. You Don't Have to Play in That Game

The main reason most break-even players don't earn a lot of money isn't that they lack the skills to win. The reason is that they aren't applying the skills they have in the *right* games. You just can't imagine how important game selection is.

It doesn't make much sense for you to play in a game where you expect to average $5 an hour if there's a game where you can expect to average $50 an hour.

If you're no longer a novice, but not a professional player either, game selection may be the key to winning money. Without using any selection, you'll probably lose dramatically. By using selection moderately, you'll probably lose a little or break even. But by using game selection prudently and consistently, you probably will be a winner from now on.

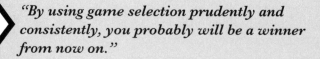

> *"By using game selection prudently and consistently, you probably will be a winner from now on."*

Suppose you were in business and wanted to set up shop. If you don't remember the examples I gave earlier, let me quickly bring you back to speed. It's been said of businesses that cater to the public that the three main advantages you can have are location, location, and location. Fine. So, what does this have to do with poker? Plenty. If you're trying to earn money at poker, then you *are* a business. But you don't have a location, right?

Sure you do. In poker, your business location is wherever the game is. So, unlike opening a storefront and carefully choosing a location that will be profitable over the years, in poker you have the advantage of being able to select your location again and again every time you choose to play. You remember us talking about that, right?

A good poker location is simply one with weak players who are enjoying the game. Good signs are a lot of friendly talk and some laughter. Silence is generally a sign of a serious game among serious opponents who are not planning to giggle and give you their money gladly. Avoid silence.

When you have a choice of games, choose the one that has the weaker and looser players. You want lots of callers in the pots and not too many raisers. This part is important, so listen up: It's much easier to win from players who call too often, but don't raise when they have the advantage. These loose, but timid players are the ones you should seek.

But the main part of this secret is: *You don't have to play at all.* If you're a top professional player, you can sit in the toughest games without losing significantly. If you're an average player, though, and you take my advice to be more selective, then there's something you must know. You are going to lose money in most tough games. You're just not good enough yet to handle these. There may come a day when you will be good enough, but that day is not now. Now is when you need to accumulate a bankroll, and you can only do this by avoiding the games where you will lose.

So, simply, always remember that location is important in your poker business and, also, that you don't have to play today. Unlike that shop owner who must open his door day after day no matter what, you won't harm your future profit if you take off and go fishing.

2. Don't Let Losing Bother You

I have often said that the main key to poker success is to simply play your best game all the time. The difference between playing your best game all the time and most of the time is so monumental that it can make the difference between success and failure in your poker career. In other words, I can't stress this point enough.

Let me just say that most players who lose a little money overall at poker would be significant life-long winners if they simply played their best game all the time. But they don't. Losing can be frustrating, and players tend to become desperate in an attempt to get even or return to their highest level of profit. Players who lose hands that they expected to win often become mentally unstable. Temporarily, I mean. They play too many hands. They call bets unwisely. They bluff too often and at the wrong times.

This tends to turn moderate losses into huge losses. Players need to believe that the money they're readily adding to their loss is as important as any other money. It doesn't feel the same. Most smaller-limit players who lose $387 do not feel any more damaged than they would have had they lost $327. That extra $60 seems to disappear and have no significance, and as a consequence, they don't play the same critical game of poker they would if they'd been losing $5. At that point, cashing out $5 loser or cashing out $55 winner does make a measurable difference to them. It's the same $60; just as real and just as spendable.

Players who have advanced down the poker path, but are not yet winners, need to realize that their main enemy is likely to be themselves. How can I talk in such general terms about a whole group of break-even and small-losing players? Easy. What I'm saying is true for almost every single member of that enormous group of players. That's why I said it, and I'm glad I did.

> *"Players who have advanced down the poker path, but are not yet winners, need to realize that their main enemy is likely to be themselves."*

I've talked a lot about the *Threshold of Misery*. This is what you cross when you've lost more than what you envisioned was likely in a poker session. Beyond the Threshold of Misery lies a land of danger. Here you can add to your disaster without feeling any more agony. That's because your capacity for agony has been maximized. Anything added is unfelt.

People will argue that trimming $60 off that $387 loss I talked about isn't as good as winning $60. They'll tell you that if you win $60, you can spend it. But you can spend the other $60, too. In fact, it's really the same thing. Exactly the same thing. That's right, it's not almost the same thing, or the same thing in some theoretical sense, but exactly the same thing. It's just as real and just as spendable.

Spendable? How can you spend money you don't have? But, my friend, you do have it. You don't believe it? Let's pretend you lost that $387, instead of the $327 you might have lost had you continued to play your best game. Now you're heading for home feeling battered, but I walk up to you and say, "Here. I think you could have done a little better tonight, so here's $60." I hand you three $20 bills and disappear beyond the door before you can react.

"I can't believe this," you mumble aloud. "The Mad Genius just handed me $60 for free. I think I'll go buy me one of those instant cameras." But then it dawns on you that you could have done the same thing yourself. You could have lost $327, instead, and then you could have spent your own $60 on the instant camera. Hey, I guess money won and money not lost are really the same, you realize.

Okay, so it's not going to happen. I'm not going to give you $60, and you don't have any guarantee that you would have saved exactly $60 if you'd played properly. It's just an estimate. But you get the point, right?

Another thing: If you want to start winning today, then stop letting your losses bother you. If you play your best game, losses won't bother you, because you won't have yourself to blame. It's easy to shrug off a loss if you've done everything you're supposed to do. It's not so easy to shrug off if you caused it or added to it.

MAKE WINNING A NEW POKER LIFESTYLE

I want you to win, and there are only two things I'm asking you to do for me:

1. Make game selection your top priority, starting now—and remember, you don't have to play today.

2. Don't let losing bother you—and it probably won't, unless you neglectfully add to your own losses.

If you're anywhere along the main part of the poker path—not a novice and not a pro—these two things can bring you profit quite suddenly. You'll see.

PLAY YOUR BEST GAME

I'll continue with one of my most profitable tips: You must play your best game all the time. But, I can hear you ask, "All of us know that and don't need to be told, right? And besides, haven't you already told us this early?"

Fine. I hear you. But this is how I teach. When you're done with this book, you won't just have mastered these concepts along with the tactics we'll explore, but you'll actually use these concepts and profit from them. That's because I simply won't leave you alone until I know you're psychologically conditioned to win.

You would think everyone would know you've got to play

your best game always. But the sad truth is that few of us play our best game all the time. We need to be told to do it.

What takes place is this. You get caught up in the course of the game. Now and then bad things take place. Let's say you lose a huge pot. Okay. You're a big boy. You can take it. But now there comes one more bad beat, and perhaps one more still. Now, your whole plan to play your best game is apt to break in two parts. One part will beg you to stay on track. The other part will plead for you to take a chance here and there that you had not planned to take. Part two will get its way.

To put it in plain words; you are now on tilt. Or, if you like this term more—you start to steam. I don't care which you choose to call it—tilt or steam—this thing now eats at your stack of chips. "My God!" you think, "I've lost my mind! I mean it. This time I've lost it for sure!" Yes, you know you're on tilt, but your arm seems to reach for those chips, first one bet and then the next, and you have not told your own arm to act that way. It's clear you're not in charge now. Your arm is in charge, and it won't need you to mess with its task of choice, which is to bet, call, raise, and fling chips at the pot when you're holding cards that don't seem to justify it. The word "fold" is unknown to your arm, which you watch as it bets for you.

The war you must win now is the same mind war that all your opponents wage, too. They, too, must learn to play their best game all the time. They will wage that war and lose it. It's their destiny. You will learn to wage it and win. How much is this tip worth? I just can't stress its worth as much as I would like. The fact is that, for most of us who know how to play hold 'em sensibly, this one thing is what will make us win or make us lose in the long run.

So, search deep, deep in your hearts and minds and ask if you can play your best game from now on. If you say *yes*, play. If you say *no*, quit. Tough words, but that's what you need to do. It's up to you.

If you add up all that you lose when you're on tilt, you'll probably find that it is more than what you would need to turn a long term win into a long term loss.

If you play your best game all the time and your opponents don't, you'll soon find that the main source of the chips that you've won comes from the times that they are on tilt and you aren't. You see, they all go on tilt from time to time, but if you just don't join in—if you don't take your turn to go on tilt, if you pass it right back to them—your stacks will soon soar. Trust me on this.

EXPLOITING WEAKER OPPONENTS

I used to drive many miles to play against the toughest players in the world. I'd leave easy games to seek challenging ones. I enjoyed the combat, and I told myself that I was improving my skills by challenging the best opponents.

I survived this long erratic period in my career. In fact, before I began to write, lecture, and research about poker, I had no other job. Poker was all there was for fourteen years. And during those years, I spent a great deal of time bumping heads with some of the most skillful players the world has ever known.

I teased my mind into thinking I was honing my skills by making it hard on myself. But, in reality, I was doing too much honing and too little capitalizing on the skills I had mastered already. I was able to survive these world-class tough opponents and make money. I should make that read, "make some money," if you compare the money I actually won with the money I *should* have won. But I've learned and you should too. My thinking, now that I've become a smarter player, is this: Whenever the money you should have won is greater than the money you actually won, you lost money.

> *"Whenever the money you should have won is greater than the money you actually won, you lost money."*

Clearly, I would have won even more money if I'd spent a greater share of my time facing weaker opponents. Lesson learned. This is the lesson I'm going to bestow on you.

Here are eight points to help hammer that home:

1. Weak Opponents Supply All of Your Profit

Just keeping this concept in your mind at all times will do wonders toward putting you on the path to poker profit. It's easy to forget this, because so much of your poker activity consists of making tough decisions against tough opponents. But that's not where the profit is. In the long run, the profit *always* comes from players who are weaker than you. Nothing else is possible. And the weaker your opponents are, the more money you can expect to earn.

> *"In the long run, the profit always comes from players who are weaker than you. Nothing else is possible."*

Don't confuse this concept with the reality that you also earn profit by making quality decisions against your strongest opponents. This is irrefutable. Also, you may be able to outplay a few opponents who are winners overall. For purposes of your personal profit, you should seek them out. Their special weakness relative to you supplies money.

To make the most money, you need to play as correctly as

possible against both weak and strong opponents. But, overall, weak opponents are the ones who bring the profit to the poker table. If you're not playing against opponents weaker than you, you cannot expect to win money. Period.

2. What's So Great About Beating Strong Opponents?

Beating strong opponents wins a lot of respect and a little money. Beating weak opponents wins a little respect and a lot of money.

So, unless you're honing your skills on select occasions, you should seek out the weakest possible opponents. There is no excuse to do otherwise. The most successful poker players in the world are not the ones who show a profit against the strongest opponents.

> *"Beating strong opponents wins a lot of respect and a little money. Beating weak opponents wins a little respect and a lot of money."*

The most successful players are those capable of extracting the most money from their weakest opponents. These players tend to play fewer hours against strong opposition than they do against weak opposition. Conversely, the strongest opponents often don't know how to extract maximum profit from weak opponents. They are doomed to live pitiful lives of poker mediocrity simply because they know how to play well against rational opponents, but they never learned how to extract the most money from the providers of profit.

And it's actually worse than that! There are many great players who win marginally or even lose over long periods of time because they're pitted against opponents who are too strong. And there are many much less sophisticated players who earn big money because they make sure they sit down at tables against weaker players. In hold 'em, as in all forms of poker, the biggest winners are not necessarily the best players.

If you are the ninth best player in the universe, you will have a losing expectation if you sit down against the eight best players. And you could be the ninth worst player in the universe and have a winning expectation if you sit down against the eight worst players.

> *"If you are the ninth best player in the universe, you will have a losing expectation if you sit down against the eight best players."*

3. Don't Encourage Weak Opponents to Play Better

Never compliment weak opponents on good plays or discuss serious strategy with them. When you compliment weak opponents on correct play, you make them proud. Thereafter, they may struggle to play better in an effort to please you.

Also, it's a very bad idea to discuss serious strategy with weak opponents—at the table or away from it. Doing so makes them self-conscious, and helps them recognize that there are levels of poker they don't understand. They are apt to play more cautiously as a result, and, worse, they may even learn to play well!

4. Make Weak Opponents into "Legends"

When you boast about the pots won by weak players with horrible hands, you feed their ego. They may try to live up to their "legend" statures, especially since you have praised them, rather than criticized them, for their weak play.

For example, "I wish I could play like Harvey! That guy can take 10-9 and win the biggest pots! He knows exactly when to do it. It's not what you play, it's how you play." Then look Harvey directly in the eyes, and say sincerely, "I really mean it. I've seen you do it so many times. It's a joy to watch."

Say stuff like that and learn to mean it and your rewards will be much greater than if you make Harvey feel uncomfortable about occasionally winning with weak hands. You want to encourage his poor play, not discourage it.

5. Say and Do Things to Make Opponents Feel Comfortable Playing Poorly

Tell them you sometimes get lucky with those same hands. Show them an occasionally played hand that is as weak as, or weaker than, those they play.

6. Weak Opponents Don't Play Equally Weak Against Everyone

Try to get more "gifts" than your opponents. You will if:

a. Weak players like you.
b. You're fun to play with.
c. You don't seem to hustle opponents.

It's important to be liked. If you seem to be cheering for your weak opponents more than for yourself, you will be liked by them. You need to make your weakest opponents enjoy having you at the table, and you must never say anything that makes opponents think they're either being taken advantage of or scrutinized.

Some players think their weakest opponents give money away equally to everyone. That's incorrect. Everyone has borderline decisions to make, even weak poker players. Each player, no matter how loose or unskilled, must make decisions to play or not play, to call or not call, with hands that are right on the borderline from his perspective. These will be decided almost at whim. You will profit from more than your fair share of these weak hands and bad calls if your opponent enjoys playing against you and doesn't fear being criticized for poor choices.

Those who believe that encouraging these extra calls ruins a player's chances of being able to bluff miss the point. You aren't going to be able to bluff these weak players very often anyway. They call too much, so bluffing is almost always a poor choice against them. It's calling too often that is their greatest mistake, and that's what you should encourage.

7. Don't Try to Trap Weak Opponents

Check-raising and tricky plays make weak opponents feel targeted and less willing to give you their chips later. Usually, just play your best hands aggressively and use a straightforward strategy. You can be playful without seeming mean. When you make a sophisticated trapping maneuver, you may very well make more money on that specific hand, but you've make your weak opponent uncomfortable and less likely to bestow "gifts" on you in the future.

8. Use Diplomacy to Stop Others from Belittling Weak Opponents

You should do this away from the table. Take the offenders aside and politely advise them that their actions are hurting both of you. Unfortunately, this belittling behavior is standard for even some pros. It makes weak players reluctant to continue their extra-bad play for fear of criticism. And that costs you money.

PLUGGING POKER LEAKS
THE WATER TANK ANALOGY

For years, I have asked students to think about their hold 'em bankroll in a way I'm going to show you now. Once you get this analogy into your head, it's very hard to get it out. It's probably one of the most useful motivational techniques I know. Here's how it works…

> Think of your bankroll as precious water in a world of drought. The more you have, the richer you'll be. All the water you will ever acquire is kept in an aboveground water storage tank, like those used by some cities. Imagine that you acquire water, climb up a ladder and add it, one bucket at a time, to a huge holding tank. When you first start playing poker, your tank is empty. You need to spill a little water into the tank to get the process started. As you continue to play poker seriously, you hope your tank will get fuller and fuller.
>
> But what if there are holes in your tank? Then you have leaks, right? It becomes just plain silly to compensate for these leaks by working harder and harder—playing more hours and learning more sophisticated strategy— because as you put water in, water spills out through the holes. These leaks can be enough to cause you to go broke or, at least, to limit your wins. In either case, fixing these leaks should be done before you spend any more effort learning more poker strategy (or struggling harder to fill the leaking water tank).

Imagine learning everything you can about poker. You play well in most aspects of the game. Working harder should add extra income, not compensate for income lost. But that's not what's happening. So, the first thing to do is plug the holes.

But it's not just leaks you need to worry about. These are problems you can fix. There are other things that can damage your bankroll. Remember, your bankroll is like your water supply, and it can be threatened in these ways:

1. **Through evaporation**—living expenses.
2. **Dry spells**—your luck is temporarily bad.
3. **Extravagant use**—spending your bankroll on things you don't need.
4. **Leaks**—problems with your game that wholly or partially defeat all your hard work.

TWELVE LEAKS YOU CAN FIX

You can't do much about evaporation and dry spells, but you can cut extravagant use (of water or of your bankroll) and you *can* plug leaks. Here are twelve major leaks that you should correct, if they apply to you:

1. Trying to Impress Weaker Opponents

It's very frustrating to know you're better than your opponents but not able to prove it to them or the other players in the short term. That's the way poker is, though. Profit is long-term. For hours, days, even weeks or months, you can suffer bad luck. Remember, this is a dry spell, during which water evaporates from the tank holding your profit. At these times, your weaker opponents seem stronger, and you can get frustrated. It's human nature to want to choose tricky plays designed to impress weaker opponents. Unfortunately, poker isn't a game where it's easy to impress opponents in the short term—especially when the cards aren't cooperating. There's just too much short-term luck in poker. Instead, you should strive to impress yourself with long-term profit. One of the biggest leaks that experienced players have is soothing their own egos by trying to impress weak opponents with fancy plays.

2. Playing More Aggressively When You're Losing

When opponents see you lose, they're often inspired and they play better. All the marginal bets that you normally make for value suddenly become unprofitable. You need to tighten up your game, simply because your opponents aren't as timid or predictable. Failing to do this is a major leak.

3. Raising Too Aggressively When You Have to Act First Next Round

Always be aware of your position. If you must act first on the next betting round, you don't have a positional advantage, and you need to be very careful about raising or reraising. Overaggressive raising from bad position is a leak you should plug.

4. Folding Too Frequently on Late Rounds

Strangely, some players who are disciplined and otherwise play credible hold 'em actually fold too often on later betting rounds. The bigger the pot grows in proportion to the size of the bet, particularly in a fixed-limit game, the more you should call. Thinking yourself out of calling on a he-probably-has-it-this-time basis is a leak.

5. Reluctance to Settle for a Small Loss

Many players treat poker like each session is a separate ballgame. They want to win for that session. This makes no sense at all. Remember, I've shown you that you are always exactly even when the next hand is dealt. Your objective is to make the best decisions *right now*, resulting in the best chance at profit or the smallest loss. Anything else is a leak. When you refuse to settle for a small loss, you're playing a meaningless mental game of win-loss. You are apt to play poorly in pursuit of a victory—and that's not what smart poker is about. It's about long-range profit, not daily wins.

"Winning at poker is about long-range profit, not daily wins."

6. Playing a Bigger-Limit Game When a Smaller Game is More Profitable

Egos can cause some players to enjoy bigger limits. Unless you've decided that occasionally honing your skills against tougher opponents is beneficial, don't play in a higher-limit game if there's more money to be made at a lower limit.

7. Making Marginal Raises Against Deceptive Opponents

This is one of the biggest leaks in poker. Save those aggressive, daring raises for opponents who are intimidated and easy to predict. Doing otherwise will cost you money. Deceptive opponents are terrible targets for aggressive raises.

8. Bluffing With Hands that Can Only Chase Away Weaker Hands

Be careful about trying to bluff opponents who will only call if they have you beat and will always fold if you have them beat. These attempted bluffs have no value (unless they are psychological and planned). For instance, anytime you hold a weak ace in hold 'em on the river against a very loose caller, you should not bluff. You will almost always get called if you're beat (often by a better ace!) and almost never get called if you have the better hand. This is a terrible bet, but not an uncommon one. It's a leak.

9. Complaining About Bad Luck While at the Table

Opponents don't sympathize with you; they just become inspired by your revelations of bad fortune. They think, "Hey, there's someone unluckier than I am! I can beat him!" And they play better.

10. Making Others Self-Conscious About Bad Plays

This is an ugly leak that we need to revisit. When you make opponents feel bad about the way they play, you're making it painful for them to supply you with profit. You're also taking their fun out of poker. Encourage bad plays. Let your weak opponents have fun. If it's in your nature, you can even giggle when you get beat. Chastising opponents for playing bad is stupid. In fact, in every case ever recorded in the history of poker, it's a whole lot more stupid than the play being chastised.

11. Bringing a Serious Winning Image to the Poker Table

The last thing you want to do is look like you've come to take your opponents' money. This can be your secret attitude, but you shouldn't convey it to anyone else. Look like you're there to have fun and you'll make the money for which you came.

12. Betting Marginal Hands after Bluffers Check

Big, big leak here. Habitual bluffers tend to check when they don't have hands worthy of a bluff. A disproportionately large percentage of what remains are calling hands. Players who bluff with hands that would have won in a showdown anyway—in garbage versus garbage situations—are actually not as successful as they think they are.

These players tend to give themselves credit for each bluff, even though many times they would have won the hand without betting. That doesn't mean the bluff wouldn't be valuable against some opponents. If you can chase a garbage hand out by bluffing with a hand that is probably just as weak, you win the whole pot, rather than winning about half the time in a showdown. But, again, this tactic isn't a good play after a consistent bluffer checks.

Repeating: Often, by bluffing against typical opponents, you've taken a situation where you would have won about half the time in a showdown and made it into a certain win. In fact, one of my biggest secrets is that occasional correct bluffing can mean turning fifty-fifty showdown chances into pure profit. But when a habitual bluffer checks, you probably don't have this opportunity and you are seldom getting correct pot odds for the bluff.

Summary

All these leaks, and hundreds more keep you from filling your tank and growing your bankroll. Plugging leaks should be priority one!

PROFITABLE OBSERVATIONS

I believe that many potential winners are inattentive at poker games simply because they don't know what's important. They want to win. But they try to do too much at once. They try to look at everything. They become frustrated. They fail. They begin to lose confidence; and they look at nothing.

This is not an absolute, set-in-stone list of things to look for or how to observe. Everything we're going to talk about is collectively only one example of how you might go about observing things at a poker table. You can incorporate these tips into your own game plan, add some, subtract others. Or you can just take advantage of these specific tips, exactly as presented.

1. Is The Game Worth Your Time?

That's the first thing that demands your attention. If the game is so tough that there's no profit in it or if there is a better hold 'em game available, you shouldn't be in that seat. You can get a good idea about whether a game is worthwhile even before you take a seat, by observing beforehand. Once you sit down, in the first hour of play, keep asking yourself what things are happening that you clearly know you wouldn't (or shouldn't) do. If you don't spot any of these mistakes, the game is probably not very profitable.

And that's one of the key lessons I've learned over my years of playing poker. I need to see mistakes made by others that I wouldn't make myself. If I can't spot these, I'm probably in a bad game. The only regular exception I make is against players who are not making many tactical errors but exhibit powerful tells. Then I'll play because I won't be able to take advantage of such blatant tells in another game, even though opponents seem otherwise to be playing more poorly.

2. What Is Your Fantasy Seat?

Apply this profitable criteria: Sit to the left of loose players so they act before you and to the left of knowledgeable, aggressive players; and sit to the right of tight non-entity players. On that basis, decide what seat you would most like to have. If an opportunity arises allowing you to take that seat, take it.

If you don't focus from time to time on what seat you would ideally like to have, you'll likely be too late to make a switch if that seat becomes available.

3. Focus and Observation

The vast majority of players simply give up on trying to observe seriously, because the task is too overwhelming.

Trying to take poker seriously, but still not being able to discover basic traits or tells in opponents is a classic case of "not being able to see the forest for the trees." There is so much going on at a poker table that—if you try to watch it all—you will almost certainly be overwhelmed and you might as well observe nothing. You will seldom observe the most profitable things in poker if you try to look for everything. The trick is to focus on one thing at a time.

Players who are not yet masters of hold 'em are often amazed by the results they get when they focus on just one thing. When you look for something specific, miracles can happen. Sometimes you see what you're looking for and sometimes you don't. But when you try to focus on everything, you are overwhelmed and important things can go unobserved. You almost never see what you're looking for, because you're looking for too much.

The more experienced you become, the more things you can focus on and still get results. But when you're still learning and having little success spotting poker tells or understanding your opponents, use my "Rule of One."

5. Try to Reconstruct Hands

Nothing else gives you as much insight into the way opponents *really* play as when you try to reconstruct a hand after a deal is over. The trick is to focus on just one opponent. After seeing the showdown, and while the next deal is being prepared, go back mentally and try to equate that player's hand with how he played at each stage of the action.

You will discover wondrous new things about an opponent's habits when you try to put the picture together after the fact and figure out how he arrived at the showdown. Most world-class players do this instinctively.

6. When Looking For Tells, Focus on Just One Player

Other tells from other players involved in the hand might become apparent, anyway. The main reason players can't spot tells is that they don't focus on just one player at a time. Remember, too many trees and you can't see the forest.

7. When You're Not in a Pot and Don't Feel Like Observing—Don't

I believe that one of the main reasons players don't learn observational skills, and thereby sacrifice profit, is that observing constantly is agony. It's better to let your mind rest when it wants to rest. Always observe when you're in a hand. Otherwise, when it's comfortable to observe do; when it's not, don't.

Yes, you can force yourself to concentrate more and play a little better for short periods. But most people will find that they burn out quickly and are unable to play longer sessions in profitable games if they force concentration when their minds rebel. I believe that in those long, profitable games, you should let your brain relax between hands whenever it wants to.

8. A Simple and Accurate Way to Rate Your Table

For twenty-five hold 'em hands that you're not involved in:

a. Add one point for each call.
b. Subtract one point for each raise.
c. Subtract one *extra* point for each check-raise (minus two points total).

First bets in any betting round are ignored in the count. Reraises count as a single raise (minus one point). All players' actions count, even when they act more than once on a single betting round. The higher the score, the better.

You'll have to compare your results to other games of the same size, type, and number of players. But soon you'll know with surprising accuracy how profitable today's game is compared to yesterday's. Twenty-five hands may seem like too small a statistical sample, and sometimes it is. But usually it's enough to tell how profitable your game is relative to others you've played or will play. Try it.

GAINING PROFIT FROM SMALL ADVANTAGES

I'm going to introduce the concept of gaining profit with small advantages with a story whose real-life business application translates directly to your hold 'em game.

THE $15,000 SALE

On the northeast corner of Main and Broadway, is a store named Pete's Poker Trinkets. Prices range from $1 to $10. Since most customers buy more than one trinket, the average sale is $17.42, and the average profit above cost and expenses for each sale is $3.03.

For years, there was one poker item for sale at Pete's that had a higher price. It was a set of solid gold poker chips the owner Paul (who had named the store after Pete, his parrot) once purchased from a homeless sailor for $10,000. Paul was asking $15,000 for the poker chips. A year went by, then two, then five. Nobody bought the gold chips.

Finally one day the richest man on the planet walked into the store. He didn't buy the gold chips either. So, more years passed. Then a frail little boy came to shop after school, hand in hand with his mother.

"Mommy, buy me those chips, please," said the frail little boy.

"But, honey," consoled his matronly mother, "you know I don't have $15,000. Remember, we talked about how we would have to budget more sensibly since your wonderful father passed on."

"Can't you just look in your purse and see? Maybe you've got more money than you think."

"Don't be silly, darling. You know Mommy doesn't carry $15,000 around in her purse." But just to humor her son, she dumped the entire contents of her purse on the countertop, separated the money from her hairbrush and chewing gum, and began counting.

Finally, she shook her head and said, "See, honey. I told you we don't have enough money. I only have $14,992."

Watching this, the owner Paul, being a shrewd businessman and not wanting to see all this money leave his store, steps up and says, "Ma'am, let me make a suggestion. You obviously are $8 short of the $15,000 you need for the poker chips, but we have some really nice decks of cards for $1 each."

The mother examines the decks and offers to buy three for 90¢ each, which the owner quickly accepts, wisely knowing that he could net a profit of 18¢.

So, one more day passes and then, by golly, the owner finally sells his gold chips for $15,000 to the homeless sailor who had originally owned them. On that night, his wife says, "Let's celebrate! You made a big profit today."

And then Paul says something to his wife I will never forget—which is all the more remarkable when you consider that I wasn't even there to hear it—"It isn't one big sale that keeps us in business. It's all the little sales. When you add them all together, they have made us rich. There are so many small sales and so few big ones that the small sales are much more profitable." Of course, arguably Paul should have sold the gold chips the day before for $14,992. But that isn't the point.

His wife smiles faintly and nods in agreement. Suddenly, she understands the value of the small sales.

And, if you want to maximize your poker profit, you need to understand the value of small gains, too.

Now, let's look at seven small edges that lead to profit.

SEVEN SMALL EDGES THAT LEAD TO PROFIT
1. Opportunities for Big Edges During the Play of a Hand Are Relatively Rare

The chance to earn a full extra bet through expert play only happens once or twice an hour—or even less! The opportunity to snare a whole pot through expert play may only happen once in a session. Those are big edges. Moderate edges are also not as common as many players suppose. But small edges are very common, and these small "expert decisions" are often more profitable on a per-hour basis than the major ones. After all, thirty small $1 edges are worth more than two large $10 ones.

2. Not-So-Weak Raises

A major advantage I exploit in a poker game is opening or raising the blinds with hands that seem too weak for my position. Remember, the fewer players that remain to act behind you, the less strict your opening standards need to be. For instance, in a particular easy-to-beat hold 'em game, I might estimate that I need at least a K-J of mixed suits to raise from three seats before the dealer position. But if I'm four seats before the dealer position, this same hand is not quite profitable. Then what?

Well, then I'll need to fold. But, wait! What if I can eliminate a player as a possible contestant? Now, I'm more or less in the position I need to be to raise. That's a small edge.

Sometimes I am able to eliminate two or three (and rarely more) players by watching them before they act. This allows me to earn a profit by raising the blinds or opening the betting with hands I could not otherwise have played. Sometimes the tells are not strong, but I reason that two half tells are worth one whole player missing. Here are a few things to look out for:

PLAYERS ARE LIKELY TO FOLD IF THEY'RE...
a. Staring at chips;
b. Subtly reaching toward their chips;
c. Staring at cards (either their own or the board);
d. Conspicuously watching you.

PLAYERS ARE LIKELY TO PLAY IF THEY'RE...
a. Ignoring chips;
b. Ignoring cards;
c. Staring away;
d. Especially quiet or still.

Note that this small extra edge works two ways: Not only will I profitably enter pots with hands from an earlier position than seems sensible to play when I can eliminate players as threats, I will also fold hands that seem sensible to play when I notice players who are threats.

3. Wait to Rebuy

Don't buy more chips if you have just enough to take the blinds or even a little extra. You'll maximize profit by playing short money and seeing the showdown without being eliminated through betting.

Yes, there can be power in having enough chips to cover all bets. The stronger a player you are relative to your competition, the more you should tend to keep a lot of chips on the table. However, there is also power in having short stacks and in being able to go all-in. Often, this can save you a pot you would have otherwise lost. When you fold a hand, you will never win the pot. But if you're all-in with a hand you would have folded, you will sometimes win the pot. That's the power of short money, and one time this advantage really comes into play is when you're about to take the blinds. Therefore, it's often better to wait until after your blinds before rebuying.

4. Earning That Call

An exaggerated betting motion and chips splashed or spread chaotically will increase your chances of being called. Using this method, you can even bet some hands for value that would otherwise be slightly unprofitable. It's another small edge!

Never forget that most opponents come with a bias toward calling. Anything you do that makes them suspicious increases your chance of being called. Therefore, against most opponents, when you know you have the better hand, a flashy or noisy wager is more likely to earn a call than a calm and quiet one.

5. Did the Hand Begin Short-Handed?

If a hand starts shorted handed, you don't need as much strength to raise in the same position as you do if the hand starts full and becomes short-handed. That's because players who voluntarily pass can be assumed more likely to have folded weak cards than strong ones. On average, this leaves strength among the remaining players. I call this the *bunching factor*. When the deal begins short-handed, this factor is diminished.

6. A Better Seat

If you're in a good game, but opponents have seen you lose and are inspired, you can sometimes "correct" your image simply by changing seats and announcing that you feel confident in your new chair. This has nothing to do with superstition on your part, but it may be on theirs.

7. Hesitation

"He who hesitates is lost" applies to poker. Don't hesitate when you call and are worried about an overcall. And generally don't hesitate when you bluff. Opponents tend to interpret hesitation as uncertainty, and they are more likely to call or to make an overcall that hurts your chances.

PROFESSIONAL TRICKS
1. A Basic Game Plan is Your Lifeline for Survival

A simplified basic strategy demands fewer decisions. Well, this isn't controversial, but it is important. Suppose you're just playing simple, good hold 'em. Nothing fancy. Imagine it. There you are, sitting at a hold 'em table day after day, playing just about as solid and simple a game as any human ever played in history. And you're winning. Got the picture?

Fine. Now, you start to alter your pace a little. You try to adjust to your opponents. You raise a little more whenever the urge comes. And these adjustments help to humble your opponents and bolster your bankroll. So, as you begin to make more and more exceptions in order to obtain ever greater profit, you find yourself straying farther and farther from your original game plan. You're drifting away from where you started.

But you're drifting deliberately, and you hope that doing so will improve your profit. But what if you drift in the wrong direction? What if the adjustments you've made have put you off course? What if you're no longer making a profit?

Well, if you don't remember your original strategy, you can't return to it. You can't grab that basic-game-plan lifeline, and you might drown in the ocean. Therefore, you need to define a basic strategy for survival, a lifeline, so you can always return to it. It's always best to be conscious of when you're making an exception and why. That's why your goal needs to be about making money, not showing off, which is how, unfortunately, many would-be pros misuse additional knowledge.

A basic hold 'em strategy that's in harmony with the tactics in this book is like a buoy in the ocean. You're safe as long as you cling to it. If desirable objects float by, you can swim away from the buoy in pursuit of them. You can always return to the buoy. But what if you swim too far from the buoy and can't find it anymore? Then you're just swimming around in a great ocean with no place to return to for safety. Your basic strategy in hold 'em is your buoy. When you swim away from it and fail to find anything floating by of value, you can always return to it. You know where safety is.

2. Your Advertisements Will Lose Most of Their Value if the Play Seems Reasonable to Loose Opponents

Therefore, reducing your starting-hand requirements a little to advertise is often a poor idea. Make most advertisements sparingly—and make them noteworthy.

It's simply a bad idea to try to make loose opponents think you're not tight by playing hands that appear a little worse than average. That seldom gets noticed and won't make an impression even if it does. Loose players don't see your slightly weaker hands as substandard. They see them as stronger than what they play, and they won't be impressed. They'll just yawn. If you're going to advertise, advertise!

3. It's All Right to Check and Just Call With Extremely Strong Hands

This is half of a sandbag, and what I call a "Slippery Sandbag." Instead of checking and raising, you check and call. It is especially useful if your opponent might be bluffing. Wait until a later round, or even until the final betting round, to raise. (In limit hold 'em games, wait until the betting size doubles on the turn or river.)

A key advantage of the slippery sandbag is that if your opponent is bluffing, you won't lose future-round profit by raising too early and chasing him out of the pot.

4. Tend to Cap from the Final Position

In limit poker, often the house rule stipulates a four-bet maximum number of allowable bets (a bet and three raises) in multiway pots. The final raise is called the "cap." On all but the final betting round, there is much more incentive to cap if you're in the last position than in an early position. That's because, even if you don't think you're a big favorite to have the best hand, you can still make that final raise without fearing a raise in return. This leaves you with the prospect of having everyone check to you on the next betting round. After all, it was *you* who made the final raise. If that happens, you can either take a free card or bet. It will be your option as you exercise the power of position. You earned this luxury by capping from last position.

5. Fold Borderline Hands When You're Last to Act Unless Your Call Closes the Betting

Otherwise, you're often in too much jeopardy. With borderline hands, there is no obvious best decision. When the borderline choice is between calling and folding, I often look to a single consideration to help me decide. What is it? If my call will close the action, I'll call. Otherwise, I'll fold. What do I mean by "close the action"?

Well, if I bet and there's a raise and then a call, my call will close the action. Nobody can raise again after my call. But if I bet and there's a call and then a raise, I have to be very careful. If I call, the original caller can still reraise. The raiser may even then raise again before the action returns to me. This close-the-action factor is especially valid when you're doubtful about whether to call in the big blind. Before calling with that borderline hand, ask yourself if that call will close the action. If the answer is yes, go ahead and call. If the answer is no, fold.

6. Early Round Advice

On the second round of betting from the last position, tend to be very liberal about betting marginal hands back into players who seldom sandbag (check-raise). You can take tactical control of the pot by betting. In fact, you can often save money by being last to act on subsequent betting rounds, because opponents will frequently check to you. Then you get to decide whether to take the next card for free or to wager.

FIVE WAYS TO INCREASE PROFITS
1. How to Handle a Bully

It's not uncommon to find players who, through their demeanor and actions, try to bully the game. Your best strategy isn't to retaliate. It's simply to call more often, to decline to make aggressive bets, and to otherwise play rationally. There is no meaningful defense for this tactic.

Hold 'em bullies try to dominate. But in doing so, they must bet too many questionable hands, they must bluff more often than is mathematically proper, and they must get maximum value from their quality hands. Put it all together and you can see that the first two traits are mistakes and the third means that you should be careful about betting marginal hands when you might get punished.

You can destroy any bully's attempt to terrorize the table and make a profit from you simply by taking advantage of his mistakes. Call more often. Bet and raise less often with marginal hands.

2. Strange, But True—One Pro Can Play Twice as Many Hands as Another and Both Can Earn the Same Money!

Earlier in this book, I told you something that perplexes students and leaves casual players shaking their heads in disbelief. One winning player can play twice as many hands as another winning player—and they can both earn about the same profit over twenty years of hold 'em action! That's because the bulk of "playable" hands are marginal. Tight players can avoid these hands almost entirely and loose players can play a few too many of them. These two types of not-quite-perfect pros may make identical profit with vastly different styles.

Of course, the player who errs on the liberal side—without psychological skills to take advantage of the effect loose play has on opponents—will usually suffer much bigger up-and-down bankroll swings than the player who errs on the conservative side. That means more risk for the same money. But if you know how to use a loose image to manipulate opponents, you can make opponents give you extra money with their sub-marginal hands. Still, the concept that one winning player can enter twice as many pots as another winning player is an important one. One might seem to be playing too loose, and the other might seem to be playing too tight. But they can both earn the same in the long run.

3. The Less Often an Opponent Calls...

The more you should bluff and the less you should bet medium hands. I see many otherwise skillful players damage their bankrolls day after day by betting marginal hands aggressively into tight opponents. These are the people you should bluff, not the ones you should value bet.

4. The Looser Your Image

The more easily you can fold strong hands! Most opponents bluff you less often when you're loose or wild.

5. Against Deceptive Opponents

Seldom raise with marginally strong hands. Violation of this rule is also among the main reasons strong players damage their bankrolls. Value bets *and* value raises work best against opponents who call too often but don't maximize their profit by raising with medium-strong hands. If you just choose loose-

and-timid opponents as targets of your value bets and raises, you'll do fine. Make it your policy.

SEVEN ERRORS TO AVOID

In hold 'em, there are lots of ways to damage your bankroll. You can run short of discipline and do things you know you shouldn't. Playing hands you know you shouldn't play and making calls you know you shouldn't make are two common poker faults, even among experienced players. Playing games you shouldn't play is another fault, because you can feel lazy and fail to shop for a better place to invest your money. Playing too big for your bankroll can take you out of the game quickly and put you on the rail watching the action. And playing when you're tired is often unprofitable.

Here, I want to deal with a whole category of mistakes that relate solely to good judgment. I hope to talk you out of some bad habits you may have and help you increase your profit potential. Can I really do that in just this one section? Don't know. I'll try, though.

So, if you're ready, let's examine these seven errors in poker judgment.

1. Error: Raising Players Out on Early Rounds (especially in a rake game)

Oh, I know this is controversial. There's a whole group of people who strongly believe—deep, deep, in their hearts—that it's better to raise in an effort to limit the field of competition.

Well, let me assure you, those people's hearts are in the right place. It's their thinking that's faulty. Even in those instances when you have a significantly strong hand and you can prove that it would be better to play against fewer opponents, raising may not be the answer. Why? Because if players remain to act after you, you often succeed in chasing away the weak hands you hoped would call, but not chasing away the strong hands you hoped to scare away.

> **"Raising may not be the answer if you often succeed in chasing away the weak hands you hoped would call, but not chasing away the strong hands you hoped to scare away."**

Many years ago, my research showed that limit-the-field tactics were often less profitable than the-more-the-merrier tactics. Later I was able to pinpoint the main factor contributing to this, and I've just told you what it is. In raising to limit the field of opponents to the right size, you're often eliminating the wrong hands. So, the limit-the-field strategy, in itself, is often an error in judgment. Not always, though—and that's another story.

In rake games, you should usually raise only to build pots, not to eliminate opponents. This advice takes into consideration both the loose nature of typical opponents in these games and the effect of the rake. As we just examined, even in non-rake games (e.g., seat rental and button pays), the thin-the-field strategy is often wrong. But in a rake game it tends to be wrong more frequently, because the burden of the rake is split among fewer opponents if the field is reduced. This means that, when the pot is raked, you often need a bigger edge than you might expect to justify betting. This is especially true before the rake is capped. (A "capped" rake is one that has already reached the maximum stated amount that the house will extract during the hand, so future betting isn't raked.)

Just to make this concept clear, let's suppose you have a sure winning hand and only one opponent. The rake is 10 percent with no cap. You bet $10 and your opponent calls $10. That's a total of $20 wagered, and the house takes 10 percent (much higher than typical at most casinos, by the way). So, that's $2 in rake. This means you have wagered $10 in an effort to gain $8. So, the "tax" on your winnings is 20 percent against a single opponent. But suppose there are three of you. You bet $10, Player A calls $10, and Player B calls $10. The house takes $3 of the $30 total wager (still 10 percent), but the tax is now only 15 percent on your winnings ($3 out of $20 you can win, instead of $2 out of $10).

So the percentage of rake is reduced with every extra opponent you face. Even if the rake is capped, this concept is very important on the first round of betting and often means that you should *not* raise in an effort to eliminate opponents. Violation of this concept is an error in judgment.

2. Error: Showing too Much Caution When the Board Pairs Big in Hold 'em

Let's say you're holding K-K and the board pairs aces on the turn. In this situation, you're often better off, not worse off. The new ace diminishes the chances that your opponent has you beat (although you might be badly beat) and thus, improves your chances of winning. If your opponent had an ace, you're trailing, anyway. Don't be afraid to call, bet, or even raise in this situation. Remember, when you hold a pair and see an ace overcard on the board, there are three aces that could be in opposing hands. But when there's a pair of aces on the board, there are only two aces that could be in opposing hands.

Folding when higher-ranking cards pair on the turn or river, when you were willing to call on the flop, is often an error in judgment.

3. Error: Letting Tight Players Bluff You

Many tight players restrict the number of reasonable hands they play but don't restrict the number of bluffing hands.

The result is that they're bluffing more often than you might expect.

You'd be surprised how many conservative players bluff too much and don't know it. (Some do know it, but realize they can get away with it.) Although they only bluff occasionally, they bet far fewer medium-strong hands than well-rounded quality players do. As a result, the hand you're thinking about calling is either very strong or very weak, and the percentage of bluffs is large. It is, therefore a mistake in judgment to routinely lay down your hand on the last betting round when a solid-as-a-rock opponent wagers. You don't want to be rolled over by a rock!

4. Error: Backing a Skillful Player for 50% of the Win on a Single Night

This very common type of "sponsorship"—where the backer takes half the win and absorbs all the loss—is silly and is almost always skewed in favor of the player. If you give or get half or more of the winnings, the contract should be long term. Otherwise, the player should take less and the backer should take more.

Let's suppose you backed a player basis that had these results for seven sessions:

COSTS OF BACKING A PLAYER

Session	Result	Player's Overall P/L	Backer's Overall P/L	50% Per Session Player's P/L	Backer's P/L
1	Win $4,580 (Winning $4,580 overall)	+$2,290	+$2,290	+2,290	+2,290
2	Lose $3,100 (Winning $1,480 overall)	+$2,290	-$810	+$740	+$740
3	Lose $2,510 (Losing $1,030 overall)	+$2,290	-$3,320	$0	-$1,030
4	Win $6,400 (Winning $5,370 overall)	+$5,490	-$120	$2,685	$2,685
5	Win $230 (Winning $5,600 overall)	+$5,605	-$5	$2,800	$2,800
6	Lose $8,490 (Losing $2,890 overall)	+$5,605	-$8,495	$0	$2,890
7	Win $3,480 (Winning $590 overall)	+$7,345	-$6,755	$295	$295

P/L – Profit or Loss

Although the 50 percent per session method of backing has become fairly common, it isn't fair. As you can see, splitting profits fifty-fifty over the long-term, with the backer absorbing the overall loss, if any, makes more sense. Mathematically, the more sessions played and the stronger the player, the smaller the backer's take should be. For a single session, an 80/20 split in favor of the backer may be fair. Over a year's play, it might be 80/20 in favor of the player. But an even split on a given night, with the backer taking all the risk, is almost never fair.

5. Error: Using Tricky Plays Against Weak Opponents

If opponents are already giving you their money, don't make them uncomfortable or inspire them to play better.

6. Error: Calling With 7-7 Against a Player Who Three-Bets Before the A-6-2 Flop

This type of mistake is very common. That opponent is very likely to have either an ace or a bigger pair. Although you, indeed, hold a pair higher than any rank on the board except the ace, it isn't enough to warrant a call, even in a limit game. However, if you hold a pair of kings or queens, your call makes more sense. Then you're hoping your opponent three-bet with a strong pocket pair that you can beat.

7. Error: Never Taking a Chance on a Game When You Might Have the Worst of It

This applies to many situations in gambling and in life—not just to poker. The best gamblers know that it's often worth risking a little to find out! If it's a bad situation, get ready to back off early. If it's a positive situation, you can sometimes make a big score. You should have the discipline to quit if things go badly. Most of the people you bet against won't have that discipline.

PROFITABLE ADJUSTMENTS
1. You Don't Need to Adjust

If you're playing perfectly and your opponents aren't, then you profit from the value of their mistakes. This means if both you and your opponents begin by playing perfectly and they stray—by playing too loose or too tight—you have the advantage. You don't need to adjust to fare better than you would have. That's a very important theoretical concept and

I'll repeat it. You don't need to adjust at all to make a profit from opponents' mistakes.

Now, sometimes the interaction among three or more players complicates this concept. Mistakes by opponents, while costly to them, may not always benefit you specifically. But when opponents stray from their best strategy, the money they lose goes somewhere. And normally, you'll earn your share, even if you don't adjust.

However, even though you don't need to adjust, you usually will make much more profit if you do. That's what we're talking about right now.

2. If You Don't Adjust Correctly, You'll Lose Money

Because you will almost certainly profit from mistakes your opponents make, you are better off stubbornly refusing to adjust your strategy than adjusting incorrectly. "Adjust" implies that you are varying from your normal best strategy. You need a solid reason to justify the cost.

When you adjust, you're sacrificing something. We talk a lot about shifting gears and modifying the intensity of your attack. But the main reason you do this is because your opponents are human and will be influenced by this. If they simply ignore you and play perfectly, randomizing some decisions in accordance with game theory, then there's no reason for you to adjust. If under those circumstances you do adjust, you're making a mistake and your opponents will profit.

Fortunately, your opponents are influenced by what you say and do. So you can adjust to manipulate them. Also, because they're human, they don't know how to play perfectly. So, you can adjust to take extra advantage of that.

3. Shifting Gears

Changing back and forth between high and low gears can make it very difficult for opponents to correctly respond. Yet, if your opponents stick to their game plan, they may actually gain by your random shifting. This is why it is important to shift gears at the right times for the right reasons. But let's get specific…

4. When an Opponent Folds Too Often on the River, How Should You Adjust?

Theoretically, you should not just bluff more often with your hopeless hands, you should bluff always. Of course, if you do that there is a chance that your opponent will see the error he's making and start calling more often. For that reason, you should bluff as much as possible without causing your opponent to correct his mistake. Similarly, if an opponent calls too often on the river, you should theoretically never bluff.

5. Adjusting to Early Raises

If a tight player raises in early position, adjust by folding the worst of the strong hands that you would have raised with in his position. In other words, if the worst hands you would have raised with in his position were A♥ J♠ or K♣ Q♦, you should fold, rather than call. If a loose player raises in early position, adjust by often *reraising* with the worst of the strong hands that you would have raised with in his position. In other words, if nobody else has called, you might reraise with that same K-Q offsuit. You're making an aggressive reraise in an attempt to drive stronger opponents out and compete heads-up against this weak opponent. You're also reraising with a hand that has a good chance of winning, because that opponent likes to enter pots with weaker-than-average hands. Consider the minimum hands you would need to bet or raise, as an opponent just did, in his position. If that's a tight opponent, usually fold if *you* hold those minimum hands; if that's a loose player, often raise.

6. What if an Opponent Has Been Losing and Complaining?

Adjust by betting almost all marginally strong hands for value. This opponent is:

a. Unlikely to bluff because he'd rather just let his misery continue in a quest for sympathy—so checking and calling has little value.

b. Likely to call—because he doesn't care.

c. Unlikely to raise when he has small advantages—because he believes he's defeated and doesn't expect to win.

7. Value Betting

Value bet when you're winning and in command, and seldom do it when you're losing and not in command. Value bets—pushing marginal hands for extra profit—work best against opponents who are intimidated and are not pressing for value in return. When you're a target, often because you're losing and opponents are inspired, value bets don't work. In fact, when you're losing, you should often return to your tightest strategy and wait for the cards to bring you out of your shell again.

8. Major Tip—and One of the Hardest Adjustments

Seldom do anything fancy against deceptive, lively players to your left. These players hold a positional advantage over you to begin with and they increase it through deception and aggression. You can't get into a long-term creative war with them, because they get to act last most of the time. You might occasionally reraise as a warning, hoping they'll become more timid in the future. But that's not the main adjustment you must make.

The main adjustment against deceptive, lively players to

your left is simple—just check and call more than usual. If you're a regular player handling this any other way, you're probably costing yourself thousands of dollars every year, even in middle limit games.

BIG POKER SECRETS THAT HARDLY ANYONE KNOWS

We're going to discuss things that very few players know. But after I tell you about them, they'll become part of your poker wisdom. And then you might feel smug because others don't know these things. If that happens, think back to the time when you had read up to this point—and no further.

1. Pause Two-and-a-Half Seconds Before You Bluff

This is serious advice. If you bet instantly or wait too long, you might make opponents suspicious. You are likely to trigger their "calling reflexes." As I've stressed, most opponents want to call. They didn't come to the cardroom to be bored and throw hands away. So, they have a bias toward calling, and anything you do that seems even slightly suspicious can trigger their calling reflex.

I have carefully observed opponents in this regard for many years. While I have no conclusive scientific answer, counting mentally, "One thousand one, one thousand two, one thousand—" works best before you bluff. Although you might think a longer pause in no-limit games might be appropriate, this two-and-a-half-second delay seems to work best, whether the hold 'em game is limit or no-limit. Now, be aware that the length of time may be different for various situations and for specific opponents. No two people react precisely the same way to stimulus, but two-and-a-half seconds is the perfect pause against most opponents.

However, if you determine that an opponent already has mentally surrendered on his hand, bluffing instantly may be better. Doing so doesn't give the opponent time to reevaluate. He is prepared to fold, and you take advantage of this with an instant wager. Usually, though, an instant bet just makes opponents suspicious. Also, if you pause too long before you bluff, opponents become suspicious and are likely to call.

Wait the two-and-a-half seconds. Try it. And remember, in limit games your bluff isn't likely to succeed most of the time whether you pause appropriately or not. In limit hold 'em, you only need to win once in a while to justify a bluff. That's because the pots are much bigger than the wagers, making the rewards much bigger than the risks.

2. An Opponent Clearing His Throat After Betting Has a Medium-Strong Hand and Almost Never Anything Else

Often you'll hear a player (always a male) clear his throat after making a bet. This is a little-analyzed, unconscious male trait. It is a way of preparing psychologically for whatever may come. Players tend not to do this when they're bluffing. When they are bluffing, they're typically quiet and unmoving, fearing that any action may trigger a call.

And, if they have especially strong hands, they don't have to prepare themselves for the possibility of being beaten, thus no throat clearing.

3. Two-Handed Bets Are More Likely to Be Called

Sometimes use this technique when you're sure you have the best hand. The two-handed action looks suspicious to most opponents and triggers their calling reflex. I have been using this technique successfully for years, but I guess I'll have to stop after blurting that out. Oh, well.

4. Opponents Who Don't Pause in their Conversation When They First Look at Their Hands are Likely to Fold

If an opponent looks quickly at his starting hand and keeps talking flawlessly, he probably holds an unplayable hand. Observe and use this information to mentally move yourself to a later position (with reduced opening requirements). When you know that opponents waiting to act behind you won't play, you can be much more aggressive in attacking. This wins extra profit and helps your image.

When players first look at their hold 'em hands and see something they like and intend to play, it is natural for them to pause and consider exactly how they will proceed. Raise? Just call? Lure players into the pot? All these questions and many more go through their minds. So, if they're carrying on a conversation, they will pause or stammer when they see potentially playable cards. In the absence of this pause, usually cross them off the list of possible threats and pretend you're in a later position. You can then play slightly weaker hands because not as many opponents have a chance of beating you.

5. One Way to Maximize Your Sandbagging Profit is to Threaten to Call after Checking

If you threaten to call, players may bluff, thinking you're insincere about your verbal remark or gesture. And if they have medium hands, they feel safer about betting them, not thinking they'll face an uncomfortable raise. But that's exactly what they'll face.

By checking and then threatening to call, you've actually forced your opponents into what I call an "either/or" evaluation. Either you'll call or you won't. In addition to making it seem safe for your opponents to bet marginal hands, often they may try to bluff, seeing their chances for success as a virtual coin-flip. The third possibility (and the truth)—that you'll raise—seldom occurs to them.

6. Try to Identify Opponents Who Are Playing Above Their Normal Limit

These players typically are uncomfortable. They are more likely to just call with borderline hands than to raise. They often can be bluffed. The unfamiliar higher limit makes them among your easiest-to-beat, most predictable opponents.

7. If You'll Earn More on Average if Everyone Folds, Often You Should Still Try to Get Called

How come? If you could get everyone to fold, you would. Unless you hold an unusually strong hand, there's usually more money in the pot right now—comprised of blinds, antes, and initial bets—than you can expect to earn on average (considering wins and losses) by playing to a showdown. But usually, players will call, even if you don't want that to happen. So, your biggest profit, in those cases, is usually to encourage extra calls from weak hands.

8. Caro's Great Law of Betting: You Should Only Bet if the Value of Betting is Greater Than the Value of Checking

Some players think checking shows weakness. That's wrong. Checking simply shows that you've decided not to bet right now, but reserve the right subsequently to call or raise. Never forget that checking is a poker weapon. It has the potential threat of deception, and more. Checking and then calling may earn more than betting and hoping to be called. There's actually a lot more to this concept, and the reasoning gets fairly complex. But, for now, just remember the big premise.

Repeating: In order to justify a bet, the value of betting must be greater than the value of checking. If you begin to think about wagering that way, you'll earn a lot more money.

UNKNOWN FACTS ABOUT BAD BEATS

The first thing you need to know is that I'm usually very accommodating when poker players tell me bad-beat stories. In fact, I was almost convinced years ago to establish a 900 number that players could use to phone in their most miserable experiences at poker. A fully trained and sympathetic staff would, for $4.95 a minute, listen attentively.

Our skilled Bad Beat hotline employees would know precisely when to sigh empathetically, and when to use one of the three permitted responses: "Oh, my gosh, no!" "That's just awful!" and "I can't believe you didn't kill yourself after that hand!"

I caution players never to talk about their bad luck at the poker table. The reason is simple: Opponents are inspired by your bad luck. They then think of you as someone they can beat, and they play better against you. It's not a good idea to discuss your personal poker misfortunes, because that tends to reinforce the bad experiences, even in your own mind. At my seminars I explain how complaining about missing twenty-seven flushes in a row might actually make you want to miss the twenty-eighth one so that you can show your cards and say, "See, this is what I mean."

WHO SHOULD YOU ROOT AGAINST?

That's why players sometimes root against themselves after they've complained to others about their bad fortune. I even think it's usually wrong to share your bad beats with others away from the table. It becomes negative reinforcement in a poker lifestyle that works better if you feel lucky.

When they're complaining, I will seem to listen to bad-beat stories, but that this is just an act. I will nod and mutter sympathetic-sounding, but randomly generated, words. I will shake my head sadly. I will feign deep compassion. But I will not be listening. Instead, I'll be using that time constructively to ponder unrelated things.

Despite this fair warning, players still approach me all the time and convey in great detail their losing experiences. And, as promised, I nod. I mutter. I offer occasional sympathetic words that flutter randomly through my mind. I shake my head sadly. I appear deeply compassionate. And, also as promised, I never listen.

This is not rude of me, and it does not matter. The players telling the sad stories get every bit of psychological soothing that they would gain if I actually gave a damn. And this way I don't need to clutter my mind with the details. So, it works well for everyone.

BUT WAIT! THIS HAPPENED TO ME!

Now, having told you that, I'm going to share something that will sound like a sad story. You can do what I do, and only pretend to listen, or you can actually listen in the hopes that listening might be worthwhile. It's up to you. If you feel like gambling, think about this…

TWO BAD BEATS IN A ROW

I once played in a limit hold 'em tournament run by the premier director of tournaments Jack McClelland. It paid nine places. There were ten players remaining. To my left sat an obnoxious drunk, who turns out to be a nice guy sober. He boasted that he was going to, "Knock Mike Caro out of the tournament." Many onlookers gathered. I am dealt a pair of jacks. I raise. He reraises with 7-5 offsuit. The final board, after much more betting, finds me all in with no card over a jack showing. But the drunk makes a straight on the last card.

Well, this victory did not bring glory to the drunk,

> because the onlookers had all seen the play and several showered me with unsolicited sympathy. I simply smiled and wished the drunk well. He was eliminated shortly thereafter. I finished 10th, one place out of the money.
>
> I played another event at the series of tournaments, a no-limit one that paid eighteen places. With fifteen players remaining, I had semi-significant chips, although the accelerated size of the blinds threatened to turn the proceedings into a crapshoot—as usually happens toward the end of ten-hour tournaments. Blinds were $800 and $1,600. A player from the second position to the left of the blinds raised about $7,000. I called all in for $6,000 with my long-awaited miracle pair of aces. The flop was Q-7-Q. The opponent had made his move with Q-J offsuit from an early seat. So, three queens beats a pair of aces, I guess. Well, goodnight. I smile, wish everyone luck, and collect my meager 15th place winnings.

At the first event at the 2006 World Series of Poker, I held 8-8 when the flop was 8-8-6. You're right. I lost to a straight flush. Couple this with a myriad of two- and three-card "miracles" with which opponents recently eliminated me from the rare tournaments I enter and I could get to feeling sorry for myself.

Now, are those sad stories, or what? At least one kibitzer thought so. On my way out the door at a tournament, he commiserated, "I saw that beat you took with the two jacks last time, too. You really get a lot of good hands beat, don't you?"

I said, "I think I get beat, on average, with better hands than almost anyone else."

He seemed surprised that I would say that. "So, you're usually unlucky?"

"No," I corrected, "I'm not unlucky at all."

"But you just said you got beat with big hands."

"That's right," I told him. "But I don't mind."

MORAL OF THE STORY

Getting beat with bigger hands on average than your opponents is not a sign of misfortune. Aspiring professional players need to understand that. If you play skillfully, if you have a winning game plan, if you succeed, then you will absolutely lose, on average, with bigger hands than your opponents. That's because the hands you play are, on average stronger.

Players complain about being drawn out on. Even world-class players complain about it. But, if you're a great player, you should be drawn out on much more often than other players. Why? Because you usually have the stronger hand to begin with. In fact, if you always started with the best hand against an opponent, then every single time you lost, you would take a bad beat. How else could you lose?

So, now you have new goals in poker.

Your New Goals

1. To have as many of your losing hands as possible be bad beats, and

2. To never complain about it.

Q & A: TIGHT GAMES AGAINST CONSERVATIVE PLAYERS
QUESTION

A major ability that separates consistent winners from consistent losers is finding the most profitable poker games. If you stubbornly decide to enter and keep playing in a very tight game against conservative players, what will most likely happen?

a. The game will become looser and more profitable.

b. You will go broke trying to bluff your opponents.

c. The game will become even more unprofitable because weak players will avoid sitting down.

d. You will find it hard to beat the game, because check-raising doesn't work well against conservative opponents.

ANSWER

A. The game will become looser and more profitable. Before I explain, remember that it's very important to find the best games. Previously, I've told you how businesses that enjoy great locations are much more likely to succeed. Well, in poker you *are* a business, and you get to choose your own location every time you play. Choose wisely, and you'll fare better.

I've also pointed out that many lifelong winning players lose money in most of their games. They are saved by the few rare games where very weak players unload huge chunks of money. If you eliminated these rare and wonderful sessions from their careers, all the rest of their play combined would be negative. An overall loss. Wasted time. Failure.

This doesn't apply to all serious players or to many top pros, but it does illustrate how important it is to find the best games. If you're contentedly sitting in a same-size game, earning $40 an hour, but you could be in a game earning $65 an hour, then in my book, you're actually losing $25 an hour.

Anyway, that wasn't the question. The question was: What will happen if you stubbornly decide to sit in a tight game and stay there. An interesting thing about poker is that loose games tend to become tighter over time. That's because the loose players, who are typically losers, will tend to go broke and be replaced by solid and conservative players seeking winning opportunities.

Conversely, tight games tend to become looser over time. The conservative players abandon the game, looking for greener felt. They most often are replaced by looser players and reckless gamblers, since potential tight replacements tend to decline the game. So, if you just sit in a tight game, it will probably get looser and more profitable. That doesn't mean you should sit in a tight game and wait for things to improve, though. There usually are better uses of your time.

If you answered B, that's wrong. Tight players are typically easier to bluff than loose players, so if you go broke trying to bluff them, you're doing something terribly wrong. We already discussed why C would be a wrong answer, and D makes no sense because check-raising (sandbagging) often is a perfect tactic to use selectively against conservative players.

BOTTOM LINE TO MAKING POKER PROFITS

In poker, the only measurement of your eventual success is the difference between your skill and your opponents' skill. If you're a good player dancing around with world-class opponents, get ready to lose. If you're a bad player battling against terrible opponents, expect to win.

What does that tell us? It tells us that mastering the science of poker, both tactical and psychological, is only half the job. The other half is finding the world's weakest wimps and pouncing.

Sure, I've told you before that I enjoy playing against tough opponents. When I was younger, I would drive hundreds of miles to challenge the most skillful players I could find, abandoning soft, soothing games that were minutes away. Yes, I was trying to hone my skills, but ego was also involved.

If you want to make the most profit, you should only occasionally test your skills against the best opponents. Usually, you should take the skills you have and use them against opponents far weaker than you are.

There's a dramatic truth in this statement. The truth is that, as valuable as it is to improve your poker game, it isn't your skill that determines how much you win at poker. And the truth is that, as valuable as it is to play against weak opponents, it isn't your opponents' weaknesses that determine how much you win at poker. Your poker destiny is decided by the *difference* between your skill and your opponents' skill.

Now I'm going to tell you something shocking. Ready? There are players who are in the top one percent in skill who lose for their lifetimes at poker, simply because they don't look for soft opponents. They end up challenging players who are equal to or better than they are, and there's no profit in that.

Wait, there's more! There are players who are worse than average in skill who win for their lifetimes at poker, simply because they choose opponents who are much worse than themselves.

Now here's the point. A player from that elite one-percent group might not qualify as a professional player, but one who is worse than average might. Think about what I've just told you long and hard. When you're done thinking, you'll know what to do and which games to play.

SIX OFTEN-OVERLOOKED STRATEGIES FOR EXTRA PROFIT
1. Often-Overlooked Strategy #1

When to thin the field by reraising and hoping to share what's already in the pot with a reduced number of opponents is a complicated issue. This strategy is often wrong, but sometimes it's right. You need to keep this in mind: Often, reraise with medium-strong hands when weak opponents have already called and strong opponents remain to act. This increases your profit by forcing the weak opponents to call one more bet, often solidifies your last position, and chases away stronger opponents who might otherwise call the raise with hands that might beat yours.

Thinning the field is a righteous ambition, but actually attempting to thin the field often costs money. This is because you too often chase away the opponents with the weak hands you would like to play against and limit yourself to facing the stronger hands who refuse to be thinned.

But one really good opportunity to thin the field happens when you hold a marginally strong hand and can reraise a potentially weak hand. By reraising, you often make it too expensive for sophisticated opponents to enter the pot behind you with semi-strong hands that might beat yours. You should always look for this opportunity. It's profitable to reraise liberally on the first betting round when weak opponents have routinely raised the bring-in bet or blind and more challenging players are waiting to act after you.

Let's suppose it's a $200/$400 limit hold 'em game and I hold A♥ K♦ as the fifth player to act. The first player to act raises to $800 and the third player to act calls.

Scenario 1: The raiser and caller are strong players and many weak players remain behind me. Actually, I'll sometimes fold in this situation, depending on how selective the players are about competing from early positions—but that's a very rare choice. I'll usually just call, hoping to lure weak opponents into the fray. I don't really have much advantage against the players already in the pot, anyway. They're likely to have pocket pairs and unlikely to play an ace with a kicker worse than my king. Occasionally they'll hold A-A or K-K and I'll really be in a tough spot. Put it all together and I'm better off just calling and inviting weak players into the pot—players who'll provide me more advantage. This is a scenario where I *don't* want to thin the field.

2. Often-Overlooked Strategy #2

Scenario 2 (see scenario 1 in tip above): The raiser and caller are weak players and many sophisticated opponents remain behind me. I'll usually raise to $1,200, hoping to discourage sophisticated players from entering the pot. I'll also be taxing the two weak players already committed against my probable best hand. In this scenario, I *do* want to limit the field.

Let me repeat the concept. Often, attempt to limit the field when weak players are already committed to the pot and strong players remain to act. But seldom attempt to limit the field when strong players are already committed to the pot and weak players remain to act.

So, from now on, you'll seldom reraise with medium-strong hands when strong opponents have already called and weak opponents remain to act. This inadvisable reraise pushes your luck against possibly superior hands while chasing away the weaker opponents that you'd often like to see call the pot. This strategy works for exactly the opposite reason as #1.

3. Often-Overlooked Strategy #3

There are five basic reasons why you might choose to reraise:

a. To drive opponents out when you're vulnerable.
b. To win more money with great hands.
c. To bluff.
d. To send a necessary message.
e. To leverage position.

If you're reraising for any other reason, you probably have either "entertainment" or "ego" on your mind.

I believe very strongly that even sophisticated players sometimes lapse into the bad habit of raising "by feel." It can be a very profitable self-discipline to ask yourself why you're reraising and make certain that the reason matches one of those sanctioned above.

4. Often-Overlooked Strategy #4

Usually *don't* reraise when you have a very strong hand and you will force opponents to call a double raise or to fold. Analysis suggests that you'll make more long-range profit by just calling and "inviting" opponents to also call.

Here are two hold 'em situations where I will almost never raise and often choose to just call:

I hold A♥ A♠ in seat #7 in a 10-handed game, which means I'm fifth to act after the blinds and five players must act after me (seats 8, 9, and 10—plus the blinds in seats 1 and 2).

Limit Game Situation: The blinds are $200 and $400. Seat #3 (first to act after the blinds) calls. Seat #4 folds. Seat #5 calls. Seat #6 raises to $800. Instinctively, we're all tempted to make it $1,200 here. But wait! If I do that, I'm likely to scare away the two early callers, as well as the five players waiting to act behind me. It's very likely that I'll succeed in isolating myself against just Seat #6. Is that what I really want? Probably not.

My analysis has proven that a pair of aces in limit hold 'em games makes most money, on average, when played against four or five opponents, not just against one. In accordance with this knowledge, I just call, inviting more players into my pot. Sure, this is risky and I'll lose many more pots than I would otherwise; but I'll average more profit—and that's all I care about. I call.

No-Limit Game Situation: The blinds are $50 and $100. Just as in the limit game above, Seat #3 calls. Seat #4 folds. Seat #5 calls. Seat #6 raises to $225. What should I do here? Move all-in? Triple the raise? What? In no-limit hold 'em, there are a whole lot of things to consider: How many chips I have as opposed to the other players; how aggressive or timid the opponents are who are already in the pot; the traits of the players remaining to act; and a lot more. But, again, if I raise moderately, I'm likely to scare everyone out except Seat #6.

And if I make a large raise or move all-in, I'm likely to just take what's in the pot right now. I want to win more.

I realize that by just calling, I'll probably average more profit (assuming I could replay this situation thousands of times). By not raising, I'll also gain built-in deception that might work in my favor on later betting rounds, having chosen not to provide a clue about the true strength of my hand just yet. Even in no-limit games, you can expect to make more profit with aces against multiple opponents, not just one. But, as before, playing against many opponents implies a greater risk of losing, along with a greater expectation of profit. Sometimes I'll raise, but usually I'll just call.

5. Often-Overlooked Strategy #5

This illustrates one of the governing truths about chasing down hands in hold 'em. It's often correct to call a bet against a lone opponent and keep calling until you see the river with just an overcard and an inside straight draw. Earlier, we've examined why an overcard and an inside-straight draw is usually superior to two overcards. However, you shouldn't do this if two suited cards flop, unless you hold an ace of that suit. Having the suited ace has benefits. Obviously, if both final cards are of that suit (runner-runner), your flush will win (even if your opponent has two of that suit), and it's less likely that an opponent even has a flush draw, because you have the ace and that's the most motivating card for playing suited hands.

Let's say your hand is A♣ 4♦ and the flop is 7♣ 6♦ 3♣. While it depends on your opponent, you should usually call a bet. The main reasons you should call are:

a. Your ace might win against a bluff.

b. The ace and inside straight draw is generally better than just two overcards, which many opponents strangely are more likely to play. There are four matches for the inside straight and only three for a second overcard. And you have a slight bonus chance of winning by pairing your lower rank (though not as good as pairing your lower rank if you hold two overcards).

c. You can get lucky and win with a pair of aces (though they're less likely to win than if you held a larger kicker).

d. A bluffing opportunity might arise for you.

Put these factors and more together and it becomes clear that you can't just routinely fold against a lone opponent with an ace and an inside straight draw. If you do fold routinely every time the board misses your hand and your opponent knows it, he'll run all over you. This advice applies to times when you hold two overcards or sometimes even less glamorous hands, too. Don't fold automatically on failed flops against a single opponent. Often fold, but not every time.

6. Often-Overlooked Strategy #6

On all but the final betting round, when you hold semi-big hands, you should tend to raise when you:

a. Already have last position secured;

b. Can gain last position by chasing players out behind you.

This constant quest for position should become an almost automatic part of your strategy when you have medium-strong hands.

Q & A: WHAT MAKES A WINNER WIN?

Here are two statements about winning at poker:

Statement #1: How much you win at poker is mostly determined by how good you are.

Statement #2: How much you win at poker is mostly determined by how bad your opponents are.

QUESTION

Which one of the following assessments about the two statements above is true?

a. Both statements are false.
b. Both statements are true.
c. Statement #1 is true, but Statement #2 is false.
d. Statement #2 is true, but Statement #1 is false.

ANSWER

The answer is A, clearly and overwhelmingly. Both these statements are false.

Confused? Want to know why they're false? Okay, I'll tell you. Both statements are false because your own skill won't make you the favorite against opponents who are better than you are. And your opponents' weaknesses won't make you the favorite if your weaknesses are more significant than theirs.

So, there you have it. You can practice and practice. You can study all the math, concentrate on all the psychology, condition yourself to exert the greatest discipline, and you'll probably still lose against world-class opponents. You'll need more practice, better math, stronger psychology, and greater discipline than they have to stand a chance.

And if you don't have sufficient skills at poker, playing against weak opponents won't save you. They could be terrible, but you could be worse.

11 SPECIFIC STRATEGIES FOR LOW-LIMIT GAMES

People read books on poker and they study and study. Then they sit down for their first cardroom experience. Then what?

I'll tell you then what. Then these readers most likely have chosen to seat themselves in a $1/$2, $2/$4, or $3/$6 hold 'em game and *nothing* seems the way it was promised. What good does it do to know about check-raising, about reraising aggressively to get extra value, or about tricking your opponents if these strategies don't work?

Opponents in low-limit hold 'em games don't know that they're in danger of being check-raised or what it means when that happens. They don't understand why a medium strong hand is okay to play against a single raise, but often not okay to play against a reraise. And they aren't likely to be tricked, because they don't have a firm understanding of what a non-tricky play should look like.

Instead of going into casino poker games unarmed, as was necessary years ago when no credible books laid out winning strategies for cardroom poker, lots of new players today do something very smart. They decide that they don't want to waste a lot of money learning the game by trial and error. Instead, they take advantage of the already-paid-for, hard-learned lessons of others. Heck, if these experts are willing to make their experiences, their research, and their profit-making advice available for under $100, well, why should novices risk thousands of dollars trying to figure it out themselves?

And that makes sense. You should take advantage of a head start if it's available. But with a few exceptions, everything you're likely to study before attacking your first very-small-limit hold 'em game will be aimed at a different type of player than you're going to encounter. These lower limits are likely to see the majority of hands decided by a showdown, many with three or more players participating to the final card. In low-limit hold 'em games, it's not uncommon to see six and often more players pay to see the flop.

The common complaint is, "How can anyone beat these games?" What good is A-K in hold 'em if everyone stays around to make their hands. Getting drawn out on again and again is bewildering to beginners and frustrating to experienced players.

Nothing seems to hold up. It's hopeless. You start with aces. The flop is A-7-6. The turn is 5, the flop is 9. You feel queasy. You just know in your heart that somebody has an 8 and will beat your three aces with a straight. You learn to expect it.

When serious-minded new players sit in what's become known as a "no-fold-'em" low-limit game for the first time, much of what they've studied makes no sense. All the sophisticated plays they've mastered seem to have no impact on the outcome of the hand. They win only a small portion of the hands they play, despite the fact that their choice of starting hands is superior to that of their opponents.

Well, there's good news. I have profitable answers for you.

REAL LOW-LIMIT SECRETS FOR WINNING

The most important thing I can teach you about playing the lower limits is that you usually should not raise from early positions, no matter what you have, because all of those theories of thinning the field and driving out opponents who might draw out on you don't hold true in these smaller games. In low limit games, you're usually surrounded by players who often call the big blind with nearly hopeless hands. But they're much more selective versus a raise.

Which is better, playing against a few strong and semi-strong players with possibly a small advantage for double stakes, or playing against a whole herd of players, mostly weak, for single stakes?

Clearly, when you're not likely to win the pot outright by chasing everyone out, you want to play against weak opponents, and the more the merrier. So, why raise? There, I've just described one of the costliest mistakes in low-limit poker. The mistake is raising when many potential callers remain behind you, thus chasing away your profit. Don't do that.

Thinning the Field: Five Points to Consider

1. When you raise with a strong hand with the intention of "thinning the field" of opponents, you are usually employing the right strategy for the wrong reason. Why? First, because you'll usually make more money if most players call. Second, if you do succeed in thinning the field, you are most likely going to chase away the players you want most to call you and become isolated against the players you wanted to fold. In other words, thinning the field usually results in you chasing out the profit-providing hands and failing to chase out the stronger ones. That's a problem with the thin-the-field theory.

And it's an even bigger problem in low-limit games where players would call indiscriminately if you don't raise, but will fold their weak hands if you do.

2. The flip side of this coin is: There really are some hands that play better against fewer opponents.

3. If you have the second-best hand possible and people are drawing to beat it, there comes a point when there are too many callers and your profit dwindles.

4. There comes a point beyond that when your hand is not profitable at all.

5. There comes a point beyond that when your hand is almost worthless.

ARE MORE OPPONENTS BETTER?

In a real-life nine-handed hold 'em game, some hands play best against an exact number of opponents. I first announced this peculiar truth at a poker seminar at the Las Vegas Hilton about twenty-five years ago. It turns out that if you encounter more than the ideal number of opponents, these hands fare worse. Fewer opponents and these hands also fare worse. Of course, the exact number of opponents that most hands—in fact, all but the very strongest hands—play best against is zero! This means that you will usually make more instant profit by winning the blinds outright than you will make, on average, if you are pursued by opponents.

People have surmised that you can have too many pathetically loose callers, and it is better if you choose a game where there are only one or two opponents who seem to play every hand and are destined to destroy their bankrolls. However, that is not true. In most ring games consisting of the usual number of opponents, you will make more money if you are surrounded by the weakest opponents you can find—and the more of them, the merrier.

There has been a lot of debate about whether games with too many callers are unprofitable. My answer is no. The more weak callers you get, the better off you'll fare overall. The money weak players lose goes *somewhere*. It doesn't evaporate. However, there are exceptions, as you will see.

Here are some more thoughts about this.

When Do You Want More Callers?

1. Very strong hands fare well against a single caller.

2. Very strong hands usually fare better as you add a second, third, and fourth caller.

3. At some point, if you had a table large enough and a deck deep enough to accommodate millions of players, there can be so many callers that even the second-best possible hand loses money.

4. You really can be better off theoretically if there are sensible players in your game, limiting your field of opponents to the right number of weak callers. (This doesn't often happen in real low-limit poker games with the usual number of players, though.)

5. If there are sensible and unsensible players in a game, you are sometimes better off if the sensible players act first! Why? Because if you're in a situation where too many callers can destroy the value of your hand, then you are less likely to face too many callers if the sensible players fold before the unsensible players act. If the unsensible players act first, the odds may be correct for the sensible players to call by the time the action reaches them. Of course, the sensible players can call in anticipation that the unsensible players will call later, but they may not have the conviction do this.

The previous is all wildly theoretical and not practical in real-life hold 'em games. Even if the too-many-opponents theory did frequently apply in regular poker games, the act of trying to take advantage of it by limiting the field is likely to cost you money. That's because, as we've discussed, you are apt to chase out the weak opponents who could supply profit on future betting rounds and leave yourself against your least desirable opponents. The cure can become worse than the disease.

ADJUSTING FOR LOW-LIMIT RAKE GAMES

You should know that in a rake game, the house fee comes directly from the winner of the pot. In typical rake games, $3 to $4 or so is taken from the winner of each pot. Players wonder, "How can anyone hope to win under such conditions?"

But, you *can* beat these games. Here's how:

1. You Need an Edge

Except for image enhancing reasons (which are usually not valid in smaller rake games), you should only play hands with enough of an edge to overcome the rake.

2. You Need Good Starting Hands

Only the very best starting hands have enough of an edge to overcome the rake.

3. Adjusting from Your Seat-Rental Game

The majority of hands you could play profitably in a seat-rental game (including rare by-the-hand rental games when the button pays the fee) are unprofitable in a rake game. You should simply not play them.

The point here is that if you were either playing in a home game without rakes or in a pay-by-the-hour (or half hour) game, you could press many marginal hands for value. As a group, these hands would each add a little to your overall win rate.

Cumulatively, this extra money won would be significant, even though none of the hands individually would have a large profit expectation. But when you're raked, most of these marginally profitable hands actually lose money! They're good enough to make a little money without the rake. But the amount they win is less than the average cost of the rake when you take the pot. The bottom line is that if there's a rake, there's a whole herd of otherwise-profitable hands you simply can't enter pots with. You need to play tighter.

4. Don't Loosen Up Your Play

The no-fold-'em games, where many players "survive" to see the showdown, tempt you to loosen up your play somewhat. But, as we've just examined, that strategy backfires in a rake game.

5. Play Less Liberally Than Your Opponents

If it were not for the rake, you should play much more liberally in very loose games. You'd just need to play, on average, less liberally than your opponents.

6. Avoid Tricky Plays

Tricky plays fail to maximize profit in these games. That's because loose, weak opponents are not fully conscious of what's normal and what's tricky. In these cases, the most obvious best tactic is usually the most profitable.

7. Don't Worry About Getting Drawn Out On

You will get drawn out on. Since you will normally be entering the pot with the best hand, the proportion of hands you will be drawn out on will be much greater than your opponents. Don't get frustrated about this. It's where your profit comes from. Winning players are drawn out on much more often, among the hands they choose to play, than losing players. And in loose games, your hands tend to hold up even less often.

8. Good Starting Hands Are Important

In theory, great players can enter pots with hands that would be losing prospects for weak players. The great players can overcome this initial disadvantage by outplaying opponents on later betting rounds. But this strategy is almost never true in a rake game. Even great players can't make up enough of the disadvantage to overcome the rake.

9. The Skills in Low-Limit Games are Different than Higher Limit Ones

You will not find lower-limit rake games very useful in developing the majority of tactical and psychological tools that will help you beat larger, non-rake games against rational opponents. But the smaller games can be good training in other respects, as long as you understand this.

10. Better Players Tend to Move Up

There are very few consistent winners in rake games, because most people capable of playing excellent poker find the profits better at the larger levels. And most not-quite-as-good players who could beat these lower-level rake games eventually move to a higher limit where they flounder or lose.

11. Play Tight

The old too-simple adage, "Tight is right" is actually quite powerful advice in loose, lower-limit, rake games.

Yes, you can beat most loose rake games. But, in addition to basic skills, you need to have a whole lot of patience.

12 TELLS

Tells are mannerisms, often body language, that, when correctly interpreted, allow you to determine what type of hand your opponent is holding and whether or not he is bluffing. It's magic. Sometimes your poor opponent might as well turn his cards face-up on the table! Beyond fundamental strategy, tells are the most powerful and profitable weapon available to any poker warrior.

Tells are worth studying, because they, along with related psychology, can account for most of the profit you make at poker once you've mastered the fundamentals. Poker tells are all around you, but you must learn to see them. If you don't, you'll consider them to be like the fairies of lore, magical manifestations of minds that meander—not real, not serious, not valuable, and not verifiable by photograph. But tells are real, serious, and valuable. And you *can* photograph them. In fact, I did exactly that for my *Caro's Book of Poker Tells.*

It is tells and psychology—not statistics and complex tactics—that account for most of my profit. But, if you don't first understand the fundamental concepts of winning poker, you won't win with tells alone. You've got to master the basics first. So, with that in mind, let's move on.

OBSERVATION FLAWS AND STRENGTHS

The majority of typical poker players haven't discovered one single tell in their lifetimes that they can reliably use over and over against more than one opponent. Sure, many have spotted tells now and then. When Jeff is bluffing, he often reaches for his coffee cup, grabs the handle and stops. Stops dead. Doesn't bring the cup to his lips. Doesn't even lift the cup. That's a tell.

But it's a tell in isolation. In order to use it, you have to be playing poker against Jeff. He has to have coffee nearby. He has to make this one move. And this habit must remain from session to session. That's a problem, because most peculiar tells are just short-term habits and will soon fade as repeated mannerisms, to be replaced by others.

So, wouldn't it be better if you knew some reliable tells that apply to Jeff all the time? And why stop there? Wouldn't it be better still if you knew reliable tells that apply to Jeff *and* other opponents, too? Is that asking for too much? Nope.

UNIVERSAL TELLS

Universal tells that are shared by many, many opponents are real. They are the basis of my more than thirty-year investigation into the science of reading body language at poker. All common tells arise from a single fact: Most of your weak and average opponents are forced into an arena where they feel uncomfortable, because they are, in effect, forced to lie about their hands. They can't just tell you the truth or you'd always know what they held and be able to beat them for all their money.

The "lies" are not usually stated mistruths. Instead, they are typically comprised of what your opponents try to imply through body language and tone of voice.

Your opponents will usually try to act as if they have weak hands when they have strong hands and strong hands when they have weak hands. So, when an opponent sighs, shrugs as if bewildered, and says "I bet" in a sad tone of voice, you can be pretty sure he holds a very strong hand. If you don't hold a strong hand also, you should usually fold. Conversely, if an opponent makes a subtle extra movement to bolster his bet and make it seem a little stronger, there's a good chance he's weak.

TELL CATEGORIES

There are two types of tells; **natural tells** (tells exhibited by players who are unaware of them), and **actor tells** (tells from players trying to fool you into believing they have a type of hand they don't). Natural tells include things like neatly stacked chips and slumped posture. Actor tells are the more profitable category. They include tells like deliberate sighs, misdirected bets, and reaching for chips out of turn.

Is Your Opponent an Actor?

In general, your job is to figure out whether an opponent is acting or not. Usually, if he is acting, you should determine what he is trying to get you to do and react opposite. If he is not acting, react directly in accordance with the tell.

In *Caro's Book of Poker Tells—The Body Language of Poker,* and subsequently in my video covering the topic, I examined poker tells that are either voluntary or involuntary. Many of these clues come from players who are not acting. For instance, when you hear and see an opponent breathing fast, loud, or erratically, there's a great chance that he holds a strong hand. This is involuntary. Conversely, a player who is bluffing is often afraid to breathe. You will encounter very shallow breathing from typical bluffers. Sometimes they don't breathe at all. Again, this isn't an act.

When someone who was formerly steady, makes a bet, and seems suddenly to be trembling in the midst of a hand, this is not likely to be an act. Nor is it a bluff. While many people think a shaking hand is suspicious and indicative of nervousness associated with a bluff, this isn't the way life works. Players who are bluffing tend to bolster themselves and become rigid. They show few outward signs of nervousness. They are afraid of being read, and so they steady themselves and do nothing out of the ordinary. This, too, is not an act. It is instinctive reaction.

Your opponents do act, however, when they decide to convince you of something. Usually, this takes the form of acting opposite of the true strength of their hand—weak when they hold strong hands, and strong when they hold weak hands. That's why you'll see those players with unbeatable hands shrug, sigh, and bet sadly. They are trying to convince you that their hands are not worth getting excited about. But it's a deception.

In short, your first mission is to decide whether your opponent is acting. If he is, figure out what he's trying to get you to do and disappoint him.

NATURAL TELLS

Natural tells, involuntary tip-offs of which your opponents are unaware, include things like trembling hands—which are almost never a sign of true nervousness about whether they're going to win a pot. Bluffers do not shake. They bolster themselves so as not to give you clues that they're bluffing. They're afraid to move for fear you will read them. Bluffers are often rigid and sometimes they don't breathe.

Players with real hands are more relaxed and animated. These are powerful clues. Also, players who have strong hands often pretend to not be interested. They'll look away while the action approaches. They don't want you to have any clues that they're going to bet or raise, so they pretend to be focusing on something else. Sometimes they look as if they're watching imaginary butterflies dance to their left as the players to their right decide what to do. Conversely, when their hands are weak, they'll scrutinize the action as if interested. These are easy tells. They're all around you.

But why doesn't everyone see them? Good question. It's not just that everyone doesn't see them. It's that *most opponents* don't see them. And that's even stranger. Worse yet, some players deny that tells exist or profess that they have little value. This is like the blind preaching to the sighted about what isn't there.

Look for these four natural tells:

1. Pay Attention to the Tail End of a Bet

Watch for the tail end of a bet. A little extra emphasis usually means a weak or vulnerable hand. This is one of the most profitable tells in poker, but also one of the hardest to spot. You need to really practice observing. The reason it's hard to see the tail end of the bet is because you're apt to be overwhelmed by the more obvious motion.

After awhile, you're going to get used to watching for a little extra push with the tip of the fingers. The bet finishes with a subtle flare, a little extra force, often a flick of the fingers. It's very subtle, and when you see it you can profitably call with a medium-strong hand. You're facing either a bluff or a daring bet from a less than stellar hand. Psychologically, the bettor reasoned that he needed that subtle extra emphasis to make his hand seem stronger than it is. Tend to call these bets.

2. Watch for Wiggles

On a final-round bet, if you act as if you're about to call and your opponent freezes, this usually means you're facing a weak hand or a bluff. If the wiggling continues, you're usually facing a strong hand and the bettor isn't concerned about a call. This is a powerful category of tells you should pay special attention to if you want to extract the most money from your opponents.

Bluffers and weak bettors become less animated when they're in danger of being called, because they fear that any action will make you suspicious.

3. Motion

Watch to see how much general motion an opponent normally makes. If that opponent is quite jittery, taps his foot, shakes his legs, drums his fingers, shifts around in his chair, or shows other signs of life, you should be concerned if the opponent bets and continues in this mode.

Players who are normally animated and continue to fidget after a bet are generally comfortable with their hands.

Players who suddenly freeze after betting are often bluffing, as we've just learned in point #3. This holds true for humming, whistling, and talking, too. When it stops, that's often a bluff or a weak hand. If it doesn't stop, beware.

4. Breathing

Finally, I'm going to remind you again: Listen to the breathing! This is the main indicator of whether many opponents are bluffing. Watch for heavy breathing. That's almost always a sign of a strong hand. Breath holding, though, means weakness. It's what people do when they're hiding in a corner hoping the murderer won't find them. It's also what bluffers do when they're trying to seem less noticeable so they won't get called.

ACTOR TELLS

Let's talk about tells from actors. Remember, opponents will typically act opposite of the true strength of their hands. This means, trying to seem weak with a strong hand and strong with a weak hand.

Here are two favorites:

1. Shrug Tells

When you see an opponent shrug his shoulders and bet, you need to interpret the shrug. Try to put the gesture into words. It means, "I'm not sure, but I'll take a chance." But since shrugging is an act designed to deceive you, always consider that the opponent is trying to convey indecision and weakness and is therefore very strong. Be reluctant to call a shrugged bet. Note that the shrug does not need to be obvious. Especially among experienced players, you'll seldom see an exaggerated shrug. More often you'll see a movement so slight that is merely the suggestion of a shrug. Learn to interpret this and seldom call.

2. Finger Tells

Be very aware of your opponent's fingers as you make your bet. Often, you'll be thinking about making a borderline bet with a marginal hand. Should you or shouldn't you? Well, players who hold weak hands often act as if they're eager to call by letting their fingers slide slightly toward their chips as you begin to bet. When you see this, your bet is usually safe. Your opponent is trying to subtly discourage you from betting. If, instead, you see the fingers holding the cards start to inch toward the discards, this is dangerous. Your opponent is trying to encourage your bet. What should you do? Want a quick tip that's easy to remember? Do this: Complete that marginal bet when your opponent is discouraging it by inching toward his chips. Abandon that marginal bet when your opponent is encouraging it by inching toward the discards.

TELLS MISSION #1

The first objective is to ignore everything your opponents say or do and concentrate only on the way they play their cards. You'll do this for exactly one-and-a-half hours.

During this 90-minute period, you must not be influenced by any body-language tells or by any verbal tells, even if you're 100% certain of their accuracy! It is very possible that you'll sacrifice some advantage during this period, but it is extremely important that you participate in this observational exercise.

In particular, pay no attention to anything your opponents do to influence you. Often, using your knowledge of tells, you'd figure them for a hand exactly opposite in strength from what their acts convey, but that is not important now. Ignore everything but the way your opponents play their hands.

During this preliminary period, play conservatively and use a straightforward strategy, one that contains no tricky tactics. After each major hand, reconstruct what happened, omitting all behavioral clues such as gestures and comments. Remember who made the early bets and raises and equate that with the final known strength of the hands.

Get as vivid a picture as possible, but do not strain your mind. Don't concentrate too hard. This exercise must be painless. What sinks in, sinks in. What doesn't, doesn't. Your only objective is to observe the card-playing tactics of your opponents and to ignore their words and actions. Pretend these opponents are faceless and formless. Pretend you know only their final decisions and that you observe nothing leading up to those decisions.

In fact, even though you're playing in a real-world hold 'em game where it's possible to observe opponents, ignore this opportunity and, instead, imagine that you're playing online. You can think of your opponents as lifeless robots who merely write their decisions and display their hands on a video screen.

After one and a half hours exactly, get up from the table for a few minutes. Mentally circle the table clockwise beginning to your left. Based on the way they played their cards and not on their actions or comments, rate each opponent: loose, average, tight, or insufficient information.

Now, mentally circling the table once more, rate each player: predictable, average, tricky, or insufficient information.

Finally, make a third mental circle and identify any player who you feel is dangerous enough to cost you money.

Now, return to the poker table...

TELLS MISSION #2

Listen to the voices. For half an hour, try to determine the natural tones of voices of your opponents. Each may have his own manner of speaking, but try to focus on it. Try to speculate how each would sound and what he or she might say under these two situations:

1. Expressing sorrow to a friend over the death of a beloved Saint Bernard.
2. Winning a large bet on the super bowl due to a last second miracle.

Deciding how these opponents might react will not be easy, but give it a try. Keep those two events in mind. Every time a player says anything, decide which category it most fits. Of course, very little will fall into either category, but don't let that discourage you. You're on your first step toward mastering one of the most powerful techniques in poker. You won't be very good at it today and, in fact, you don't even know what I'm talking about yet, but try to place these opponents into the sad category or the happy category by the sounds of their voices alone.

Simply do that for the rest of your mission. Now, before

actually carrying out these experiments, reread the previous instructions. Take notes, if needed. Make sure you know exactly what you must accomplish. Then do it.

Two-Mission Review

Did any of the categories your opponents fit into surprise you? It doesn't matter. What's important is that sometimes the players we fear—or the one's we think are the most liberal—don't play the way we perceive that they play. Remember to tune out and observe from time to time.

What should you have heard in Tells Mission #2? It's a very well established fact that, with few exceptions, the players who bet using voices you correctly put in the sad (Dead Saint Bernard) category are much less likely to be bluffing than those you placed in the happy (Super Bowl Miracle) category. For now, that's all you need to remember.

TALKING TELLS

Some of the most important tells you can't see at all. They're audible. You simply have to listen for them. And if you listen well enough, you can almost beat poker with your eyes closed!

Pay attention to:

a. What the player says.
b. When the player says it.
c. How the player says it.
d. What the player *doesn't* say.

It's important to listen carefully to what your opponents say. Hostile or goading speech generally means a strong hand. Most players fear that their combative words will irritate you into calling, so this verbal behavior is seldom a bluff, though rarely it can be—so know you opponents! Natural, non-poker conversation is an indication of a player at ease. That player is seldom worried about his hand and isn't likely to be bluffing. He is also, at that moment, a poor target for a value bet.

If a player suddenly starts talking as you're betting or calling, that's almost always a last-second desperation effort to make you reconsider. The reason for this powerful truth is that if an opponent wants you to finish your bet, he won't do anything whatsoever to change your mind. Particularly, he won't suddenly start speaking.

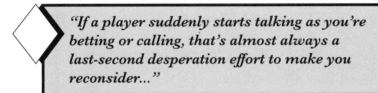

> *"If a player suddenly starts talking as you're betting or calling, that's almost always a last-second desperation effort to make you reconsider..."*

If a player speaks in negative tones about his hand, he is usually strong. If he's excessively cheerful or friendly in his voice, he's usually weak. If a player tries to avoid engaging in conversation after betting, that's a clue that he is more likely than usual to be bluffing.

Here are seven talking tells to be aware of:

SEVEN TALKING TELLS
1. Listen for Talk That Sounds Natural

The more naturally an opponent engages in conversation, the less likely he is to be bluffing. And the more casual an opponent's conversation seems when it's your turn to act, the less willing you should be to bet. This is just another way of acting uninterested, similar to looking away. When a player is looking away, he is trying to make your bet seem safe by giving you nothing to worry about. When a player keeps talking casually, he is also trying to avoid giving you clues that he may be interested in the hand.

I have used this audible tell to great profit. If someone is talking about how to fix his washing machine as you start to bet, and if he continues to talk about his washing machine, you should be careful. Don't make any weak wagers or value bets. True, sometimes this player is so weak that he just doesn't care. He's simply waiting to throw his hand away. But, more often he's not worried. He has a significant hand. It's when a player stops talking or has trouble sounding rational while talking that you should suspect weakness. When that happens, the opponent is worried—and probably weak.

2. Humming and Soft Whistling

This often ceases either:

a. Immediately when an opponent bluffs.
b. Later when you look as if you're beginning to call.

Those rare opponents who whistle under their breath are goldmines. They will almost always stop whistling when they bluff. Same for humming.

3. Believe Them!

Players who tell you they have a big hand are usually telling you the truth! Not always, of course, but usually. They are waiting to take pride in showing down their hands and saying, "I told you so," in words or gestures of their choosing.

4. Listening to the Word "Bet"

Listen carefully for an opponent to say the word "bet." If there is anything sad or reluctant about it, this usually means a strong hand, so seldom call.

5. Breathing

Players that pause to catch their breath quietly, as if they don't want you to know they're struggling to breathe normally, are usually bluffing. Remember, bluffers have trouble breathing naturally and sometimes choose not to breathe at all. Players who hold big hands also often have trouble breathing naturally, but their breathing tends to be quite audible and less restrained, and you should seldom call their bets with medium-strong hands.

6. Forced Conversation

Let's fit a concept we've already visited into a simple rule: Whenever an opponent has bet and his conversation seems unnatural, unfocused, or forced, there's a very great chance that he is bluffing. That's because it's hard to concentrate on casual conversation when you're in immediate danger. You should call much more willingly than you normally would.

7. Major Tip

When considering a borderline bet for value, first look away. Just listen. Even close your eyes if you choose. You can often "hear" the silence and sense the stillness. After an opponent has bluffed, he will usually be silent, too. But the action I'm talking about is *before* your opponent has acted. It's your turn to act and you begin to bet. Ominously silent players who are waiting to act are often trying not to do anything to discourage your bet. That usually means your opponent is ready to pounce. So, don't bet!

Do you see how these two situational silences mean opposite things? Silence after betting usually conveys weakness; silence when waiting for you to complete a bet usually conveys strength.

"Silence after betting usually conveys weakness; silence when waiting for you to complete a bet usually conveys strength."

FOUR TELL FAILURES TO AVOID

There are four major reasons why serious poker players fail to win significant extra profit through mastering tells.

Tell Failure #1: Looking All Around You

You're never going to master tells if you look all around you to spot them. Yes, I've said that tells *are* all around you, but if that's where you look, you probably won't see any. There are so many things happening at the poker table that interpretation becomes monumentally difficult. You've got to focus on just one player while you're learning to spot tells. As you get more proficient, you will automatically spot other tells while still focusing mainly on just a single player. It's magic. You'll see.

But you'll never see by trying to grasp every tell all at once. I can't do it, and neither can you. And don't expect to see what you're looking for immediately. Observe and be patient. Find an opponent who is likely to exhibit tells. Some aren't. Eventually, you'll pick up the opponent's mannerisms. And what's really exciting is that most of them will conform to my broad theory of tells—many opponents are actors pretending to be weak when strong and strong when weak.

Don't expect to see a lot of tells, either. If you can pick up three powerful tells in an hour, be very happy. Some of these will save you a whole pot. There may be many lesser tells, but these minor ones should be weighted and factored into your fold-call-raise and betting decisions, just like other factors—like the opponent's wagering habits and deductions you make from betting sequences.

Minor tells are things to be weighed. They help tip the balance on tough decisions. They don't dictate, in themselves, what decision to make.

Tell Failure #2: Looking for Tells that Make You Call

If you're like most players, you have a bias toward calling. You didn't drive to the poker game hoping to throw hands away. This is where a rudimentary knowledge of tells can be dangerous. You need to fight the urge to only look for tells that indicate that you should call and, at the same time, ignore those that indicate you should throw your hand away.

The truth is, there are more tells that indicate that you should fold than those that indicate that you should call. And those should-fold tells are usually more blatant. These are the ones where opponents act weak—sigh, shrug, use sad voices, look away—and they're the most profitable overall. The problem is, that profit is hard to measure directly. After all, each time you act in accordance with these tells, you've folded and you've won nothing stackable. However, you won something theoretically—the money you didn't lose. And that adds up in a hurry.

"There are more tells that indicate that you should fold than those that indicate that you should call."

Of course, if you only looked for tells that caused you to call, you'd still be ahead of where you'd be if you didn't use any tells at all, right? Probably not. That's because players tend to manufacture let-me-call tells in their minds and, also, put too much emphasis on weak indications. I believe the result of this is that many players end up using tells as a justification for playing bad hands and making weak calls. I don't want you to do that.

Tell Failure #3: Showing Pride in Your Success with Tells

One of the worst things you can do is to convey to your opponents how proud you are about having spotted a tell. This makes your opponents aware that you're scrutinizing them. It also makes the player you just profited from aware of the specific tell you spotted. This means he's probably going to correct the mannerism and not provide the same tell in the future.

I've even seen professional players make a quick winning call and then explain to the opponent, "I knew you were bluffing as soon as you blah, blah, blahed." Well, that's sure to keep the opponent from never blah, blah, blahing again, and it will cost you a ton of money.

If you spot a profitable tell, be quiet about it so that you can use it again and again to make money. Don't use it to show off.

Tell Failure #4: When You See a Tell, Don't React Right Away

Sometimes pride tempts players to react immediately to a tell. Instead, when you spot a tell, try not to appear that you're reacting to it. Hesitate and pretend to ponder first. Finally, make your move as if still indecisive. If you hesitate briefly before you fold or call in reaction to the tell and act as if you're uncertain, you'll probably be able to profit from that same tell again in the future.

This is one of the things that is hardest to teach, because players naturally have pride in their poker skills. But it's a profitable poker skill in itself to not make others aware about what you know about them.

The more quickly you react to a tell, the more likely you are to tip off your opponent that you are reading him, and the more likely he is to correct the behavior. I go to the trouble of hesitating when I'm 100 percent certain that I've spotted a tell. I then pretend to act indecisively. That way, my opponent is less likely to realize that he's broadcast a tell, and I'm more likely to profit from it many more times.

CREATING TELLS

I don't recommend making it apparent to opponents that you're carefully watching them. Doing that often can lead them to believe you're playing seriously and they'll often respond by being more cautious in their hand selection, costing you money.

Despite this, sometimes if you scrutinize opponents in key betting situations, they may put on "acts," making them easier to read. If your opponents don't think you're paying attention, they're much less likely to go to the trouble of acting in a way designed to deceive you and, unintentionally, in a way that makes them easier to read.

The more your opponents believe they are being watched, the more likely they are to act deceptively in an effort to deceive you. So, just making opponents aware that you are watching them closely can sometimes help generate tells.

Conversely, there are some non-acting tells that you are more likely to spot if opponents don't think you're watching— quick, secretive glances at their chips in preparation for a bet, for instance.

When I can't pick up a tell on a player in a key situation, often one will suddenly appear when I make it obvious to that opponent that I'm pondering what to do while I study him. The more I scrutinize, the more likely my opponent is to exhibit a tell in a failed effort to hide the truth. But use this tactic sparingly, when it really matters.

IF THERE'S NO TELL, PONDER

So, let's put it all together. As a general rule, don't scrutinize opponents conspicuously. But, if you have a close decision about calling or folding, hesitate for a few seconds and watch. Pretend to be pondering the situation. Often, you won't get a tell from your opponent until you drive home the fact that it's necessary for him to sway your decision. Your hesitation will often shift your opponent into acting mode, where the same "weak means strong" and "strong means weak" clues apply as usual.

When in doubt, conspicuously ponder for a few seconds, and observe how your hesitation affects your opponent.

USING TELLS WISELY

Repeating: You should not think of most tells as absolute clues to an opponent's hand. The vast majority of tells are only indications that push a decision in one direction or another.

You can think of most tells the same way you'd think of someone trying to make a heart flush in hold 'em when there are three hearts on the board. He may have the flush and he may not. Tells, except for the rarer ones that are almost 100 percent positive indicators, should be used as additional information. They should be weighed along with many other factors in coming to a conclusion.

---

13 ADVANCED BETTING CONCEPTS

Sometimes in poker, things aren't as they appear to be. Some of the following concepts might be known to seasoned professionals. Some won't be. Most aren't obvious the first time you sit down to play hold 'em.

I've decided to select items from my list of things that should be a fundamental part of your betting arsenal and others that don't immediately make sense to poker players.

CALLING CONCEPTS

Winning hold 'em is all about aggression. But sometimes, for a variety of reasons, calling is your most profitable option.

For example, you should consider calling, even if the call is not quite profitable, if your opponents know you have a strong hand. That's because, one of the worst things you can do is make your opponents think you make carefully considered laydowns. That's just inviting unexpected bluffs and long-range disaster.

In fact, I try never to let my opponents know that I ever make studious decisions, period. I want my image to be one of impulsiveness, perhaps that of a loose cannon, firing everywhere, at everything, not aiming, not caring. When I stop to ponder or count pots to see if the odds are exactly right, I'm destroying that image. And that image (and it's only an image and not reality, remember) is precisely what fools opponents into providing me with extra profit.

WHEN CALLING IS PROFITABLE

If you are making excessive money-catching bluffs or making calls, you most likely aren't calling enough! You're probably costing yourself money on the somewhat less profitable—but still long-range money-making—calls you didn't make.

Players who take pride in being right when they call are usually losing money in limit poker games and to a lesser degree in no-limit games. If a pot is eleven times as large as the amount it costs you to call, and you expect to win one in ten times, you will make a long-range profit by calling. But you will lose nine times for every one you win. That can get frustrating. But, the point is, if you wait for just the calls you know are extremely profitable, you will need to sacrifice all the other calls that are reasonably profitable, and that sacrifice will cost you a lot of money.

CALL MORE AGAINST TRICKY PLAYERS

When you first started to play poker, you probably were bewildered by a certain style of play. Some opponents would make strange and unpredictable plays, and you couldn't quite figure out how to handle them. Should you respond by making strange and bewildering bets and raises right back at them? Many experienced professionals believe doing that is the answer—but it isn't.

To get to the best answer, you must first identify those who habitually use deception. You'll recognize these players because they often bluff, they consistently check-raise, and they seem to suffer from Fancy Play Syndrome.

Fine, but how do you beat them? Easy. You simply call more when they bet, and you bet less when they are waiting to act.

Can it really be that simple? Yes! That's just another poker fact that may not make sense at first. But it's powerful advice. Try it. Against FPS opponents, simply call more and bet less.

HANDLING A BULLY

It's tempting to get into an ego war with a poker bully, someone who wants to establish dominance by bullying the game. Sometimes, it's a good idea to fire back with a few raises and sandbags (check-raises), especially if it will make the bully behave. This is good strategy if the bully is a winner.

But, most often, the bully is not a winner. In that case, your best strategy is to simply call and let the bully "declare" his dominance. His declaration will not match his results.

Most players do not know how to react when an opponent tries to control the game through super-aggressive play. The solution is simple. If it's a strong opponent, it is in your best interest to neutralize this behavior. Raising back will do this. If it's a weak opponent, your maximum profit comes from letting him "rule."

By letting your weak, overly aggressive opponents rule, you are allowing them to increase their most common mistakes—betting too much, raising too much, bluffing too much. You should tend to simply call. If you raise or use other counter-strategy to make their poker lives miserable, you are likely to bring them back in line. They may stop their poor and unprofitable bets and raises—and your bankroll will suffer.

There are some words of caution here. Letting someone else rule the game runs contrary to my general philosophy of establishing an image that makes you the one force to be reckoned with at the table. For this reason, I will only let weak opponents rule with bad bets and raises. I will tend to counter-attack both strong opponents and break-even opponents who try this tactic. Also, position comes into play here. If you're sitting one or two seats to the right of the opponent, you are not in a good position to declare war. You should be much more willing to launch counter attacks if you are on the left of that opponent, giving you a positional advantage.

RIVER PLAYS
Calling from Middle Position on the River

Let's never forget this powerful poker concept during the heat of hold 'em combat. The middle position is frequently misplayed on final betting rounds, even by seasoned professionals. If you have a strong hand that is not a cinch, you will usually make more money by just calling than by raising. Why? There are several reasons:

1. Your hand might not be best.
2. You might lose a call from a weaker hand behind you.
3. The original bettor might be bluffing, making a raise futile.

There are other reasons as well. If the player behind you has a hand that is better than yours, you probably won't chase him out with a raise, anyway. Save this middle-position raise for weaker hands when you think the bettor is bluffing and wish to chase away opponents waiting to act—and use it sparingly.

Analysis of many key situations shows that, when you have a fairly strong but vulnerable hand, just calling is usually better in the middle position on the last betting round.

Overcalling on the River

A common mistake made by some advanced players is to overcall on the river with the same kinds of medium-strong hands they would need to make a single call. Your hand needs to be much stronger to overcall.

A very simple way to explain this is to show that the pot odds change dramatically when someone else calls. Let's say the pot is $100 after an opponent bets and it costs you $10 to call. This means the pot is laying you $100 to $10 or 10 to 1. In such a situation, you would only need to have one chance in 11 of winning to break even. If you have a better chance than that, you should make the call. If you have a worse chance than that, you shouldn't. Still confused?

Okay, suppose you played the same situation just 10 times. You called $10 each time, hoping to win that $100 pot. You figure you were a 9 to 1 underdog, and you were right. As fate would have it, by golly, you won exactly as many times as you projected for those 10 calls—namely, just once. So, nine times, you lost $10, for a negative total of $90. Once you won the $100 you were pursuing. Overall you came out ahead $10 after 10 calls and each call was theoretically worth $1. We now see that if you're a 9 to 1 underdog when the pot is laying you 10 to 1, you can call and make money. Now what?

Here's what. If someone else calls that same pot before you do and you think you have just as good a chance of beating the opener as the caller does, you might be tempted to overcall. After all, the pot is now bigger than before. It is now $110 ($100 after the first wager, plus $10 after the other player called). So, an overcall is tempting.

But, wait! That caller only added $10 to the pot, but your odds of winning were disproportionately lowered. We already said that the caller has just as much a chance of beating the bettor as you do. That means, even if you are right and you beat the bettor one in 10 times, you still need to beat the caller.

Since you only have a 50 percent chance of doing this, your odds of success are twice as bad. You now only have one chance in 20, not one chance in 10, of winning the pot. That's 19 to 1 against.

Is the pot laying you 19 to 1? Heck, no! Only $110 to $10, or 11 to 1. If you call you will be losing forty cents on the dollar. It works out this way. Nineteen $10 losses, or $190 negative total. One $110 gain. Total for 20 calls is an $80 loss, which averages a $4 loss for each $10 call—or 40 percent of your investment. That's 40 cents on each dollar down the drain.

And, my friends, this is exactly why so many overcalls don't compute. Most players, even seasoned professionals, don't realize that in hold 'em, as in any other form of poker, their hands need to be significantly better to overcall than to call, not just marginally better. And, yes, although the example used limit hold 'em, this concept is quite valid for no-limit games, too.

BETTING CONCEPTS

Sometimes, playing good, winning poker means pushing chips into the pot and forcing opponents to make tough decisions. Often, you want your bet to win the pot right there. Other times, when you have a big hand, or your opponent has a weaker hand than you, you'd like to get a call.

In limit hold 'em, most of the time that you bet, you would rather not be called. You can't believe I said that, right? If that's true, why bet? It's because most of the time that you're betting with quality hands, your opponents are correct in calling. The pot is laying them money odds that justify them continuing to play, despite the odds against them winning.

We've just stumbled upon a flaw in limit poker. The size of all bets is mandated, and as the pot grows, since the bets don't tend to be large enough, the caller usually gets a bargain.

In no-limit, you get to size your bets according to your own desires. In theory, your no-limit bet should be just large enough so that it doesn't matter whether your opponent calls or not—he's getting a neutral deal. Of course, we go beyond that by taking an opponent's traits into consideration when pricing a bet. But in limit games, that kind of bet tailoring isn't possible, and you're usually under-betting your hands. That's why there are so many more calls in limit hold 'em than in no-limit. It's also why bluffs fail so often in limit games.

Of course, we could partially alleviate this limit-poker flaw by doubling the bets on every betting round. That still wouldn't completely solve the problem, but it would help.

Just keep in mind that in limit hold 'em games played under the typical betting structure in use today, you'll usually be happy if everyone passes. You need an exceptionally powerful hand not to be happy when opponents desert the pot, leaving their money behind. Most of your betting is done with the hope of marginally improving your profit. In almost all of those cases, you're somewhat better off betting, but you're much better off if you don't get called. Sound strange? It's because the amount of money already in the pot is a bigger prize if you win it right now then the average profit you'd make if your opponents called in a million similar situations.

The simple governing concept here is this: If the call is bad for your opponent, you want him to call; but if it's good for your opponent, you want him to pass. Usually, when you bet correctly for value in limit hold 'em games, the bet is good for you and the call is good for your opponent. Therefore, you want him to pass. Only when the bet is good for you and the call is bad for your opponent do you want him to call.

Here are some more betting concepts to keep in mind.

1. When to Bet Weak Hands

Betting weak hands into other weak hands is one of the most fundamental talents you can master in poker. If you check them, you are likely to be outplayed and will have to surrender the pot.

It's especially important to bet out on the final round when there's a reasonable chance that your opponent is also weak. If you check, you may be bluffed into, and be unwilling to call. That costs you a whole pot! Checking and hoping to win in weak showdown situations is usually the wrong choice. When you're reasonably sure your lone opponent is weak, but it's near fifty-fifty whether you can win in a showdown, then the best choice is usually to not risk a showdown. Just bet, instead.

2. Betting on the Come

In hold 'em, you often start with two suited cards and catch two more of that suit on the flop. If everyone checks to you, the decision to take a free card qualifies as a tricky situation. Sometimes, you simply should check and take the free card.

In this situation, you should usually bet unless your opponents are deceptive and likely to check-raise. By betting, you will often get a free card on the next round. And if it's limit hold 'em, where the limits double on the next round, this advice is especially valuable. If you connect, you can just keep betting your flush, which has gained deceptive value. The same holds true for two cards higher than the board, for one card higher and an inside straight draw, and for an open-end straight draw. With those hands, often bet when everyone checks to you on the flop. Then, if you pair one of your overcards on the turn or make a straight or flush, keep betting. Otherwise, usually check on the turn and take the free river card. Ideally, when everyone checks to you on the flop, if you bet and miss, the last *two* cards are free.

3. Betting Second Pair

Players make key mistakes in hold 'em when it comes to betting a pair of the second-highest rank on the board. You should not be afraid to make that bet into one or two opponents when you're first to act. If you only bet top pair, you are being too conservative.

However, you should routinely check second pair, even with a good kicker, if players behind you bluff too frequently or are especially deceptive. The bigger your kicker, the more likely you should be to bet. You need to mix it up, though. Sometimes check; sometimes bet. You should be more willing to bet second pair if the top board card is small, such as 9-8-4, than if it's large, such as K-8-4. That's because an opponent is more likely to hold a king than a 9 to beat your pair of eights.

It's easy to go overboard once you give yourself permission to bet second pair, so you need to strike a happy balance. Against typical opponents, betting about half the time or a little less will adequately mix up your strategy, add to your aura of deceptiveness, and enhance your overall profit.

DID YOU KNOW THAT YOU CAN LOSE A POT BY BETTING?

When you journey beyond the basics of hold 'em, you start to think about strategy more intricately. You realize that by not betting hands in key situations, you can not only cost yourself extra money, you can sometimes cost yourself the whole pot.

Sometimes, on an early betting round, you check and the player behind you checks. On the very next card that player connects for an inside straight. It's a tragedy for you, but one you often could have avoided had you bet. That opponent likely would not have called a bet in an attempt to make an inside straight. He wouldn't have been around to receive the card that brought you misery. So, in that case, betting could have saved the pot. And even if you were called, you could take pride in knowing that you got good value for your bet against an inside-straight attempt.

The most obvious event in which betting wins an entire pot is a bluff. That's what a bluff is all about, right? You're probably going to lose in a showdown, so you bet and hope your opponent doesn't call. If that happens, you win. Again, an entire pot has been won by betting.

What if you have a medium-strength hand and you figure your opponent does also? So, there you sit on the last betting round, holding a hand that seemingly is not quite strong enough to bet or maybe even to call with if you check and your opponent bets. You might win in a showdown, but you might not. Now what? Now, you should often consider betting. Notice that I said *consider* betting. It isn't automatic that you should bet, and, in fact, you probably don't want to bet most of the time. But sometimes you should make a daring bet in this situation.

You sometimes should bet because, although you don't have an advantage in strength, which is the most common reason to wager, you have your opponent trapped in a situation where he may not call. It takes the right kind of opponent to justify this bet. And it takes the right kind of action leading up to the bet. Often, the bet is a good idea if your opponent is in an analytical mode, off tilt, and has reason to suspect your hand may be strong.

If he perceives the situation the same way that you do— that you're both holding about the same strength hand—the bet will be futile because he will just call and hope to win. And if it's a limit game, the pot will overwhelm the size of your bet and, therefore, your opponent will be gaining much more if he calls and wins than what it will cost if he calls and loses. In limit hold 'em, these pot odds dictate that you should usually call with any reasonable hope of winning.

But, if this opponent has reason to believe that you probably have the best hand, he may fold a hand that would have won in the showdown. That sometimes makes your bet worthwhile. It can be much better to risk, say, a $20 bet into a $100 pot, if it means your opponent will sometimes fold, than to just see the showdown and hope. Even when your opponent calls, you still have an excellent chance of winning.

Your chance of winning in this bet-call showdown isn't quite as good as it would be in a check-check showdown, however. That's because, presumably, your opponent will tend to fold the hands at the lower end of the spectrum of possibilities and call with the hands at the higher end.

Let's say that by betting and being called you win only 40 percent of your showdowns, but by checking you win 50 percent. That sacrifice still might be worthwhile if your bet occasionally causes your opponent to throw away the superior hand. Another thing that's good about betting is that you can sometimes make extra money. If you do have the best hand and your opponent does call, that's an extra bet you would not have earned had you checked. Of course, this advantage is largely offset by the times you bet, are called, and lose.

Betting or Checking

The analysis gets even more involved than this, and there are other powerful reasons why betting is sometimes the best choice on the final round when you think you have about a fifty-fifty chance of holding the better hand. You should even consider betting hands that have *less* than a fifty-fifty chance of winning in a showdown. And I'm not talking about bluffing. The fact is, you don't know if you're bluffing, so you're betting for a different reason—or a combination of reasons.

There is another risk of not betting. If you check, your opponent might bet and you might not call. Theoretically, this should not usually happen in limit games, because if you have a borderline betting hand, you should almost always be willing to call. The size of the pot so dictates. But, in the real world of hold 'em, many players check the weaker portion of their medium-range hands and then fail to call. That could be a disaster and another reason—if you're inclined to make the mistake—to simply bet, rather than check.

In spite of all this, I believe that many experienced players bet too often in some key situations. There are many advantages to checking.

Overview

I think you're convinced by now that betting in some marginal situations can be profitable. But that wasn't the key question. Remember, that question was: "Did you know that you can lose a pot by betting?"

How? I'll tell you how. When you make the kind of daring bets that I've just described, you better make sure you're against a predictable player. That sort of aggressive betting with fifty-fifty or worse hands only tends to work in the long run against players who are not especially deceptive.

BETTING INTO A DECEPTIVE OPPONENT

If you bet a somewhat worse-than-average hand into a deceptive opponent, you may be met with an unexpected raise, one that you might not call. Again and again this aggressive bet backfires against deceptive opponents. If you check and they check, you might win the showdown. In fact, let's say you have substantially worse than an average hand for the situation. You check. Your opponent holds a truly miserable hand and decides not to bet. You win the showdown.

But what if it's a deceptive opponent. You think both of your hands are weak. You bet that same substantially-worse-than-average hand, hoping to drive out a hand that might be better than yours. But, instead, the deceptive player raises. You fold. If your opponent is bluffing, you've lost the entire pot by betting. And this happens quite regularly where certain types of opponents collide. It's in the chemistry. Yes, you might decide to call the raise, reasoning that the deceptive player often bluffs. In that case, your decision to bet paid off. But the truth is, that player usually has the advantage by acting last. And when you bet first into a deceptive opponent with a marginal hand, it allows him to maximize his position. Mix it all together—the positive outcomes and the negative ones—and it's clear that you lose money by betting marginal hands into deceptive foes.

To take this concept further, there's a danger in bluffing when both you and your opponent are very weak. You won't be able to justify a call if raised, and you might win the showdown if you check and your opponent doesn't bet. But, you're saying, if the opponent is apt to raise, isn't he also likely to bluff if I check to him? Probably, but not always.

I know what you're thinking. You're wondering if this advice contradicts what we've already learned—that sometimes you should bet on the final round when you think both you and your opponent are weak. By doing so, you hope to avoid showdowns which might only win half the time. You win all the time, instead. The answer is *no*, that isn't a contradiction. In hold 'em, each tactic has a time and a place. In this case, we're not talking about the "weak-versus-weak last-betting-round" scenario generically. We're talking about it in specific terms of the opponent being deceptive. And, as always, you must use much more caution against that type of player.

The more deceptive your opponent, the more likely he is to raise with nothing when you wager your weak hand. But that doesn't mean he will bluff just as often. There are some situations in which deceptive opponents fear that you'll call in an obvious bluffing situation, for example, after they've been checked into. Still, if you bet, they think that you might be bluffing or weak. They figure their raise might secure the pot, and they'll try it.

This happens more often than you might suspect in the

bigger-limit games against sophisticated opponents. In no-limit hold 'em, you can be raised right out of your seat by making small- and medium-sized bets into lively opponents. Unless you're prepared to call in advance, make it a policy to bet less frequently into volatile opponents.

I'm not saying that in general you will lose more pots by betting than by checking. I'm just saying it's something you need to consider. Betting can win you an entire pot sometimes. And sometimes it can lose you an entire pot. Think about it.

VALUE BETTING

Among the most obvious traits that separate poker superstars from the players they pulverize is an understanding of value betting. Great players value bet at the right times and for the right reasons. Lesser players often understand that value betting is a good idea, but they don't quite know when to do it or what the true purpose is.

I'm going to tell you what value betting is and how I employ it in the heat of poker combat. This is a very important topic, but if you're like most players, you'll often forget these guidelines and value bet by whim or emotion at the poker table. Don't make that mistake.

Some players think value betting means a bet that can profit in many different ways, and therefore has "value." For example, your bet with a medium-weak hand might cause an opponent to lay down a slightly stronger hand—or you might get called by an even weaker hand. Or, your bet with a flush draw may confuse an opponent and cause him to check to you on the next betting round; or that same bet might cause your opponent to fold, leaving you with the pot and immediate profit. A bet that can profit in many different ways is one of the common definitions of a value bet, but it's not mine. Those are multi-purpose wagers, which I call **utility bets**.

A **value bet** is simply a daring wager that correctly goes after every extra penny in profit. Sometimes a value bet actually is a utility bet, too, but usually it's just a very perceptive bet when your profit expectation is slightly greater if you get called than if you don't. The value is in the money that's made from these aggressive wagers—wagers made when lesser players probably would have just checked along had you not bet.

NINE CONCEPTS IN VALUE BETTING
1. Psychological Control

There is even more "value" in value betting than earning a little extra on the play itself. You help establish an image that gives you psychological control over your opponents.

2. Value Bets Are Usually Wrong on a Limited Bankroll

Although value bets theoretically add to your profit, they also add to your risk and bankroll fluctuations. If you are in the process of building a bankroll, think twice before you value bet. Also, in proportional-payoff tournaments, value betting is usually a bad idea. Survival is generally more important than extracting slight extra profit.

3. Direct and Indirect Value of Value Betting

The direct value comes from earning extra money you would not have earned by checking. The indirect value comes from enhancing your image.

Players who frequently value bet cause most opponents to feel insecure and to call more often. These opponents also, strangely, raise less often, because they are intimidated. A sensible counter strategy would be to raise *more* often, but typical opponents just plain don't. Your fast-action and unpredictable image makes opponents behave. It gets even weirder, because this image, which is enhanced by value bets, allows you to make even more value bets than you would be able to make otherwise.

4. Players Who Are Good Targets

The most profitable targets of value bets are opponents who like to call and are not deceptive. Think "loose and timid" before you value bet. This doesn't mean that you can't sometimes pick other opponents as targets, too, but you need to value bet with stronger hands against them. And, of course, the livelier, luckier, more confusing, more deceptive, and more controlling your image, the more likely your opponents are to call and the less likely they are to act deceptively.

5. When You Should Not Value Bet

You seldom should value bet when you're losing. That's when players are least intimidated by you and are unlikely to be as meek and predictable as you need for a value bet to have value.

You should also be reluctant to value bet against opponents who bluff too much. Let them bluff and make your profit calling. And, remember, if these consistent bluffers have already checked, they often have strong calling or check-raising hands, usually making value bets wrong. It's true that they also have a lot of semi-weak calling hands, but after deceptive check-raisers check, it is not usually a good value bet opportunity, because there is too much danger. Also, opponents who both value bet and bluff frequently should not be your value bet targets after they check. Usually, your best strategy is to just check along. You can be in a world of trouble here if you bet, especially in no-limit. Deceptive players are much more likely than most opponents to be plotting a check-raise.

Tricky opponents, who might raise unexpectedly for value, are also poor value bet targets. Tight opponents are poor targets, too, because they will only call with quality hands. So, while you should often bluff against tight players, don't stretch medium-strong hands by betting for value.

6. Being Slightly Better on the River Isn't Enough

When you value bet, you need to be a favorite if called. However, an exception might occur when your opponent will randomly throw away some hands that are better than yours and, at the same time, call often enough with hands that are worse than yours. You might lose most of the showdowns, but the value bet is made profitable by those instances when your opponent decides (often by whim) to fold hands that would have beat you. Surprisingly, this happens quite often on the river, and it makes betting for value occasionally correct with medium-strong hands that will be an underdog if called. Always consider your opponent before value betting. If you're not sure the chemistry is there to give your value bet a profit expectation, you should probably check.

7. Value Betting After Someone Checks to You

Do this often against players who never check-raise and almost never against players who often check-raise.

8. Preventing Others from Value Betting for Profit Against You

If your opponents are predictable value bettors, raise more liberally with hands that average slightly more strength than the typical hand they bet. Specifically, raise with the top half of the hands you would have value bet. If that value bettor tends to check-raise predictably with strong hands, that makes your raise even better. You're more likely to be facing a hand weaker than the one you're raising with, because the possibility of big opposing hands is diminished. After all, this opponent most likely would have checked a huge hand, hoping you'd bet and he'd raise.

Essentially, you're responding to an opponent who value bets too frequently with a "value raise." However, some players bluff quite frequent, bet large hands whenever they can, and value bet extensively. Even though these fit the "value bettor" category, you shouldn't liberally raise them. You'll make more money just calling these unpredictable bullies.

Follow that advice when you're trying to decide whether to call or raise against a value bettor. If you do, it will ruin their strategy.

9. A Tight Image and Value Betting Don't Mix

Players with tight images can't bet medium-strong hands for value and make a profit. Opponents don't call as frivolously with moderately weak hands against tight players. This absence of many calling hands that would lose often makes a typical value bet unprofitable for tight players.

RAISING CONCEPTS

Raising is the heart of any profitable approach to hold 'em. It's the ultimate form of aggression. Raises take pots away from opponents and puts chips into your stack. But there is risk involved when you throw chips at the pot—you may get action from a better hand, or even get reraised. So, for your raises to be effective money-making tools, you need to make them for the right reasons.

There are two equally valid approaches to raising. You can meet every single opportunity with an attitude that silently asks, "Why should I raise?" You then try to see if there are any reasons why a raise, rather than a call or a fold, would be appropriate. Or you can ask, "Why shouldn't I raise?" You then try to see if there are any reasons why a call or a fold, rather than a raise, would be appropriate in the situation.

One way, you're assuming that you won't raise and try to argue yourself into it. The other way, you're assuming you will raise and you try to argue yourself out of it. Conceptually, either of these approaches should lead to the same conclusion provided all factors are weighed correctly. But whichever route you take toward making your decision, raising at the wrong times can be very costly. We're about to talk about that.

NINE RAISING CONCEPTS
1. Ask Yourself the Reason Before You Take Assertive Action

If you're betting, make sure you know why. Just a vague notion is not good enough. Justify your choices. Once you get in this habit, you're apt to discover that you have been taking actions for the wrong reasons—or for no reasons at all.

You should do the same exercise before you call and especially before you raise. There are more experienced players than you who might raise for faulty reasons or without a clue as to the reason. From today on, unless you have a reason to raise, don't. That means never. Quite simply, you need to adopt the approach to raising where you first assume that you won't raise and then argue yourself into a raise if it makes sense. I know we've talked about doing it from the opposite perspective: Always assuming you *will* raise and then exploring reasons not to do it. Theoretically, that will lead you to the same decision, if you carefully consider everything. But, for now, I want you to stick to the no-reason-no-raise method of evaluation.

2. Two Reasons to Raise

Excluding the psychological aspect of poker, there are really only two basic reasons to raise:

a. To build a bigger pot.
b. To increase your chance of winning.

Sometimes you need to evaluate both these factors to decide on a tactic. Building a bigger pot means more money if you win, and is often the best choice for a strong hand. But it sometimes actually decreases your chances of winning a pot. This can happen, for instance, if you would build a bigger pot by not raising with an exceptionally strong hand, inviting many players in. You are then more likely to lose, because there are more opponents remaining who might get lucky and beat you. But you're hoping that the increased risk will be overwhelmed by increased chance of profit from a bigger pot if you do win. Conversely, if you raise from an early position, you may be making the pot smaller by chasing opponents out, but you will tend to win more often.

In addition to these two key strategic reasons to raise, you might sometimes raise to enhance your image—and profit later. When you make an image raise, you are working toward being the one force at your table to be reckoned with. It is not necessary that the raise will add an expectation of extra profit on that pot itself. The extra profit can come from subsequent pots, because your raise has helped to build a commanding image that lets you manipulate your opponents. So, when you begin with the premise that you will not raise, image can sometimes be a factor in changing your mind. But be careful.

Don't let yourself be argued into a raise frivolously. If you don't really need to enhance your image right now, or if the raise would be too costly for the benefits, just call or even fold.

3. Be Careful Whom You Drive Out

You should usually not raise if you expect to drive out the weak hands and remain against the strong ones. As we've discussed, this is a common result of the "thin-the-field" strategy. Often, you would prefer to play against fewer opponents. Some hands simply make more profit that way. But what if your raise will thin the field in the wrong way? What if the most likely callers are those you least want to play against and the most likely folders are those you most want to play against? In that case, a raise can be wrong, even though you did want to thin the field and play against fewer opponents. That's because you didn't want to thin the field if it meant playing against only opponents with the stronger hands. And that's often the case. This is why, in general, I'm not an advocate of thin-the-field raising for many common situations for which it is advised.

4. Raising Preflop

Before the flop in hold 'em, most players raise too often. This is not just guesswork, but a viewpoint I've formed after studying hold 'em opponents for many years and comparing what they do to the ideal strategies I've devised through computer research and other analysis.

I believe that you should often just call and see what develops. Since most of a hold 'em hand blossoms on the flop, you aren't usually raising with the advantage you assume. This doesn't mean you shouldn't be very aggressive in short-handed games and when attacking the blinds from late positions when no one else has entered the pot. But it does mean in full and nearly full games that there are many times when you should opt to just call before the flop, rather than raise. Yes, you *should* often raise, but not nearly as often as some players assume. When in doubt, I believe you're usually better to just call.

5. When Opponents Are Deceptive

One of the biggest mistakes made in hold 'em is routinely raising with marginal hands against deceptive opponents. Since a raise with a marginal hand is a borderline decision that won't earn much extra profit, on average, even in ideal situations, it will often lose money against deceptive opponents. How come? It's because those opponents won't behave. You can't count on them to just call with stronger-than-average hands. Instead, they are likely to get full value by raising with their marginally strong hands, and they may occasionally even be bluffing. These possibilities can often remove all the value and more out of that value raise.

Also, don't raise in middle position on the river with anything except a super strong hand, a bluff, or a weak hand designed to drive out a bluffer. You'll make more by just calling and giving the next player a chance to overcall. This advice isn't obvious, but it's the right answer. Research proves that middle-position raises, in most common situations on the final betting rounds, should seldom be made with hands of secondary strength.

> *"Don't raise in middle position on the river with anything except a super strong hand, a bluff, or a weak hand designed to drive out a bluffer."*

6. When to Steal Blinds

If the blind players are aggressive and unpredictable, abandon most blind stealing. The best types of opponents to steal against are tight and timid. Always remind yourself of that before you barge into the pot with your precious chips.

7. Handling a Bluffer

Don't raise with strong hands on an early betting round against a frequent bluffer. Let him continue to bluff. This strategy can sometimes work against you, but overall you'll make more money if you allow your opponent to exercise his most glaring weakness—in this case, bluffing too much.

8. Wrong People to Raise

By now we've discussed simpler concepts from other angles, so this tip shouldn't surprise you: Don't chase away your profit by making daring raises against solid players when weak players remain to act after you. When you do this, you are just chasing out the wrong people. One concept of poker that is seldom talked about is that you should be *much* more willing to raise when a loose player has bet and tight players remain to act behind you than when a tight player has bet and loose players remain to act behind you. The reason is that often you'd like to be able to chase others out and face only the loose bettor. But you seldom want to chase the loose players out and face only the tight player.

9. What if You're Losing?

One of the most important lessons is to stop value raising when you're losing. These daring bets for extra profit only work when your opponents are intimidated. When opponents see that you're losing, they're inspired and they become more daring and deceptive. And as we discussed in point #5, you definitely do not want to be making marginal raises against deceptive opponents.

There is a lot more to the science of raising. But you'll be on the path to mastering it if you always make sure you have a reason before you raise.

SIX MORE RAISING CONCEPTS

I can tell you in one word the main motive for most raises. Whim. That's right, most of the raises you're ever going to encounter in your poker lifetime are made at whim. They're not carefully analyzed raises. They're not goal-oriented raises. They're just made at whim.

The spirit strikes and opponents raise. A telltale shiver tickles their spine and they raise. They raise for the thrill of it, out of aggravation, to impress, because calling doesn't feel quite right, or to send a hazy message. Who knows why? They don't. Ask them and you'll see what I mean. They raise for reasons vague to their conscience minds. And it is whim that rules. And it is whim that makes their decisions for them.

Of course, there are some hands so powerful that players

raise on that basis alone—often correctly. But most raise decisions aren't obvious. These borderline choices should be decided rationally. But they aren't. Repeating, they are decided by whim, and that's a very expensive method.

You can add significantly to your profit if you consider key factors when deciding whether or not to raise. Here we'll look at some of them.

1. Don't Raise to Get Even With an Opponent

In poker, it doesn't matter whom you get even with, just so you get ahead. Taking bad beats personally is a common mental mistake. If Jerry beats you out of $100 and you beat Norman out of $500 ($400 total profit), that's better than if you beat Jerry out of $150 and Norman out of $150 ($300 total profit). It's the overall profit that you're after. So, there's no reason to adjust your strategy in order to get even with Jerry.

One of the instinctive ways people try to get even with opponents is to raise more liberally than usual as an act of retaliation. You should never do this. I don't mean that you should never raise them. I mean that you should never raise them for that reason.

It's okay to send a message by raising, but you should do so against someone who will be influenced by the message and might back down on future warfare, thus leaving you in control. Many opponents won't react that way. Players who have been beating you are motivated. They are not timid or predictable. But it is precisely against timid and predictable players that borderline raises work best. If instead, you choose borderline raises against deceptive and aggressive opponents, you will simply lose money in the long run. This is not just theory. I have simulated these situations by computer. It turns out that borderline raises against volatile opponents simply don't work. You need to win control over these opponents, and you can't do it by overbetting vulnerable hands.

2. Tend Not To Raise from Early Positions

Hold 'em is largely a struggle for position, and when you don't have it, you're often wise to just call (or fold). In general, you will lose money trying to assert dominance from an early position. Save these early raises for your very best hands, and even then, you can often make more money just calling. When you raise from an early seat, you are apt to chase away opponents you would profit from most if they stayed.

How often have you seen weak hold 'em opponents win with the weirdest hands that players just called with from middle positions? It seems like all the time, right? Let's look at some…

1. The final board is 10♣ 10♦ 4♥ 4♠ K♦. Someone wins with 9♦ 4♦.
2. The final board is J♣ 8♣ 6♥ 4♣ 2♣. Someone wins with Q♥ 5♣.
3. The final board is K♥ J♦ 4♠ 7♥ 7♦. Someone wins with K♣ 7♠.
4. The final board is 6♦ 5♦ A♦ A♣ 3♠. Someone wins with 7♣ 4♣.
5. The final board is K♠ 10♦ 8♣ 2♦ A♣. Someone wins with 8♠ 2♥.

What do these hands have in common? For one thing they all won. But that's not what should amaze you. What's truly amazing is that for every hand like that you see miraculously win a pot, there were many more similar hands played that were *unseen* and did *not* win. Weak players are entering pots with these sorts of hands quite often. Typically, they get inspired and call the big blind with them, or overcall after others have just called the big blind. But most weak players are at least a little discerning about the hands with which they enter pots. If you raise the blind, they're much less likely to play those same hands.

I hear you saying, "But I don't want them to play those hands, because they won." Wrong. You do want them to play those hands. Overall those hands are unprofitable for your opponents. Yes, such questionable hands sometimes win, and that can be frustrating. But usually they don't win. Instead, they are a great unseen source of your profit. When these hands lose, you seldom see them. They just disappear into the discards. But you're winning a lot of money from their original overcalls, when the big blind wasn't raised.

Don't you believe that the only incredibly bad hands opponents play are the ones you see winning pots. That's simply not the case. Most of these hands lose when played. You want them to be played, because they supply you with profit. And when you raise the big blind, you're often chasing away this easy profit.

This doesn't mean you shouldn't frequently raise from an early position. Raising is often the best choice. It just means you need to know why you're raising and to keep in mind that calling may bring bigger profit.

3. Tend to Raise from Late Positions

Hands that would lose moderately from early positions win moderately or heavily from late positions. This means you can easily establish psychological dominance by raising when you act after your opponents. Most serious players know this, but they fail to realize the extent to which this concept can be profitably applied.

"Hands that would lose moderately from early positions win moderately or heavily from late positions."

When it comes to raising, position shouldn't just be a concept that you intellectually acknowledge. It should be a primary factor in deciding whether or not to raise. Think about your strategy. If you can't honestly tell me that position is a main consideration every time you think about raising, then I'm betting that you're making much less money at poker than you should.

4. Often Raise When You Will Chase Away Players Who Would Otherwise Act After You on Future Betting Rounds

This primal struggle for position can be the main factor in deciding whether to raise. It's often worth taking slightly the worst of it by raising with a borderline hand *now* to gain position on *later* betting rounds. Note that this opportunity seldom presents itself when you're in an early-to-act seat. Most of the decisions to raise or reraise in order to establish position happen in late position.

5. Raise Less Liberally When You're on the Button

On the button, you don't need to gamble to get position, because you already have position. However, you should mix up your strategy and sometimes raise hoping to chase the blinds out and isolate (with better position) the original bettor or raiser. Also, you should tend not to reraise as the big blind against a late-position raiser, because it's unlikely that you can ever get position. Very rarely you might be able to isolate against the small blind, immediately or on future betting rounds, by choosing to reraise and act last throughout the hand, but this isn't usually worth the risk of a reraise.

Of course, if your big blind hand is exceptionally strong and there are lots of players already committed to the pot, you can raise to extend your profit. But with anything less than superior strength, I seldom raise in the big blind position other than against the small blind alone. I will often make an exception to this rule, though, if I can reraise and force players who have so far only called a single bet out of the pot. This is where it's important to know which opponents will usually fold if faced with a double raise. When I'm in doubt, usually because I haven't watched opponents play long enough to form an opinion, I seldom reraise as the big blind. That's because the assumption that typical opponents will call a double raise is usually right. And if they do, I'll have invested risky money in a situation where I will have a positional disadvantage throughout the hand. So, I don't do it.

6. The Governing Rule of Borderline Raising Decisions

Tend to make borderline raises mostly against timid opponents. Rarely make a borderline raise against a deceptive opponent—and only when you have, or can acquire, a positional advantage. Repeating: These close-decision hands only show profit by raising with a positional advantage or against timid opponents.

CHECK-RAISING: LIMIT POKER

When you check-raise to get extra money, you prefer the player immediately to your left to be the most likely bettor. That way, the sequence can go. You check, bet, call, you raise, call, call—giving you two bets from each opponent, a total of four. If the most likely bettor is the last of three players, the sequence is apt to be: You check, check, bet, you raise, fold, call—this leaves you only two bets captured. It's better to bet, in that case.

RERAISING CONCEPTS

The reraise is one of the most misunderstood strategies in poker. Hardly anyone reraises correctly, and this includes some top professional players. There are many average players who would make more money if they never reraised. That's because when they choose to reraise, they are often doing it at whim and are simply costing themselves money.

There is an old poker adage that in limit poker your hand needs to be a 2 to 1 favorite to justify a bet, a raise, or a reraise. The thinking is that it will cost you double if your opponent has you beat and raises. But this logic is flawed for many reasons, including the fact that either your opponent might not reraise if he has the better hand (for the same reasons that you wouldn't unless you had a big enough edge), he might raise with a losing hand that he only thinks is the better hand, or he might be bluffing.

In general, I believe a 3 to 2 edge is a good all-around target advantage that could justify a reraise. But just because you could justify that reraise doesn't mean you should always do it. It is a complicated decision whether or not to reraise. We'll look at a few of the elements that help us decide.

SEVEN RERAISING FACTORS
1. Who's Behind You?

When you want players waiting to act behind you to fold, you don't even need a 3 to 2 advantage over the raiser to justify a reraise. Sometimes, you can raise as the underdog! But if you don't want players behind you to fold (usually because you have a very strong hand that will make more money if they call), then you should often just call, even with more than that 2 to 1 likelihood of having a hand better than the raiser.

2. The Big Secret about Reraising - A

If you have a hand big enough to justify a reraise, usually just call if players waiting to act behind you are loose. There is usually not an advantage to chasing them out when you have a big hand.

3. The Big Secret about Reraising - B

But you should usually reraise with big hands if the waiting players are tight, because you aren't as likely to lure them in by calling and if they do come in it may be with hands big enough to cut into your profit expectation. So, in most cases, you should reraise when players acting behind you are tight.

That's so important that I'm going to explain it one more time. If you are considering raising or reraising and there are other players involved, consider the nature of the players who will have to call an extra bet if you raise. When you have a very strong hand and your decision would otherwise be borderline, usually just call with loose players waiting to act, and usually reraise (or raise) with tight players waiting to act. Following that simple advice will add a lot to your bankroll over the years.

4. How Position Affects Reraising

a. Seldom just call in an early seat hoping to reraise. The strategy often fails because you'll have poor position on future betting rounds. Such a sandbag is almost an act of war, and should be used sparingly against weak opponents, because you want them to have fun giving you their money, not feel hostile towards you.

b. Almost all your reraising should come from last or late position or in an effort to gain last position.

c. As a limit-poker exception, before the final betting round, you should often cap the betting in last position, even with hands that are slight underdogs. This helps your image and often manipulates players into checking to you on the next round.

Let's talk a little more about C. The cap is your friend. It's much easier to raise when you're capping, because nobody can reraise. You don't have to think about what we explored earlier—whether your edge should be 2 to 1 or 3 to 2. You just need to swing out there and reraise with any kind of advantage, for speculation, to establish an image, or just on raw courage. Your opponents don't know that your hand wasn't strong enough to keep raising beyond that. They don't know that you wouldn't have reraised if it weren't for the cap. This works especially well if you're in the last position with betting rounds to come. You can often get everyone to check to you on the next round and decide what to do then.

5. When Not to Reraise

a. Against bluffers. You can often make more if you let them continue to bluff.

b. From early seats, because positional advantage often is what makes reraising worthwhile.

c. With extra-strong hands and loose players waiting. You want them in.

6. When to Reraise

a. When establishing an image. This helps make you a force to be reckoned with, and opponents will become more timid and less apt to maximize their advantages in the future.

b. From late seats. Position is then working in your favor.

c. With strong hands and tight players waiting to act, because you have less to gain by inviting them in.

7. Don't Overdo the Reraise

Good players can win at most poker games without ever reraising before the river. But they might not be able to win if they reraise too often.

FOLDING CONCEPTS

Folding is a powerful weapon in poker, a lot more powerful than most players realize. It saves you bets, which means it saves you money. And at the end of the day, that means more profits to you.

If you walked up to almost any average poker player involved in a hand and asked what the goal is, the most likely answer you'd get is, "To win the pot." But among my favorite poker lessons is this: The object of poker isn't to win pots.

I keep saying it and saying it and some people keep not getting it and not getting it. But it's really very simple. If you wanted to win as many pots as possible, all you'd have to do is bet and raise at each opportunity. Then you'd either win the pot because everyone passed or you'd win in the showdown if you had the best hand. Every hand that could possible win would win.

While your money lasted, you'd be the world champion of winning pots, but how long would your money last? Probably not very long, because calling and raising all the time is a sure way to lose. Trying to win every pot is not profitable. In poker, you need to be selective about the hands you play and how you play them. The profit comes from making the right decisions. Each time you make the right decision, you earn money. Folding is often the right decision. So, when you fold correctly you earn money.

> "Each time you make the right decision, you earn money."

That doesn't make sense to some people, because they figure, "How can I earn money if I throw my hand away? Doesn't that mean I lost money?" No, not if you folded correctly. The profit is always the difference between the money you have now by making the right decisions and the money you would have had overall if you'd made the wrong decisions. That difference is real, and you can spend it. Folding is, therefore, potentially profitable.

FOLDING FOR PROFIT
1. It's Not the Absolute Size of Your Hand That Matters; It's the Relative Size

Top two pair is always a big hand in hold 'em if you don't take anything else into consideration. Big hands are presumed to be powerful, unless you know something about the opposing hands.

And that's where even experienced players make beginners' mistakes. If the pot is $120 and it costs $20 to call, some players make a poor call with a straight that only has one chance in ten of winning (instead of one in seven, which is the mathematical break-even point). However, these same players won't call with an ace-high garbage hand that has one chance in ten of winning. So, they play correctly with the garbage hand, but feel obligated to call with the "big" hand.

They are making the common mistake of thinking in absolute values, rather than relative values. The only reason to call with a big hand in an unprofitable situation is if its strength is obvious to your opponent. Then folding might inspire the opponent to bluff more often than you expect in the future and cost you money overall.

Obvious strength happens often in seven-card stud, where you might have three-of-a-kind exposed. I often call in such cases against a very probably flush, just so my opponent won't think I make big laydowns and bluff me in the future. Fortunately, this factor doesn't matter as much in hold 'em. You can always fold a big hold 'em hand without your opponents knowing for certain what your cards were.

Often your biggest hands are the easiest and most profitable to fold, especially if the action doesn't make them seem big and you're sure an opponent would only bet a strong hand. It's not the size of your hands that matters; it's the size of the pot and the likelihood that you'll win.

2. Whenever Calling or Raising is Unprofitable, Folding is Profitable

What else would be possible? In other words, there is profit in losing a pot if it costs you money to pursue it. The profit is the difference between the amount you'd lose in the long run by continuing to play in thousands of similar situations, and zero. You win the difference between nothing, which is what it costs you to fold, and what you would have lost.

Don't think of that fold as costing you whatever you had already invested in the pot. What's out there is out there. It belongs to nobody until the pot is awarded. Once you put money into the pot, it isn't yours anymore and you have no investment to defend. Decisions must be made in conjunction with the size of the pot, independent of where that money came from or the amount it has previously cost you to play.

3. When Folding a Strong Hand That Looks Weak, Make Your Opponent Think That You're Going to Raise (Or at Least Call) If You Make Something

This ploy always works. Squeeze out a card and pass unhappily and suddenly. The fact that you had two pair, rather than a missed flush, will not occur to your opponent. So, he won't think you made a big laydown.

Making it obvious that you are willing to lay down big hands is a sure way to encourage opponents to take shots at you at unexpected times. While you can adjust your strategy accordingly, it's much easier to win if your opponents stay predictable and uninspired.

4. Overcalling or Folding

    a. Never overcall on the river unless your hand is much stronger than what you would need to make the first call.

    b. Never make the second overcall on the river unless you have major strength.

Let's examine this critical concept one more time before I turn you loose on the tables. So many players make the critical error of overcalling in unprofitable situations that the discussion bears repeating.

Overcalling is really a mathematical issue. Let's say there's a final-round bet and you have the same chance of winning as the first caller. In a $50/$100 limit game, if you're last to act and the pot is $900 and it costs $100, you only need one chance in 10 of winning to make this a break-even call. (In a much smaller 50 cent/$1 game with a $10 pot and a $1 call, the reasoning is exactly the same.) If your chances are better than that, you're expecting a profit if you could play this situation out thousands of times. If your chances are less, you're not.

The math is easy: At one win in 10, you snag the $900 already in the pot once and lose $100 nine times. It comes to nothing. So, if you're last to act, you could call if you have one chance in 10 of winning, without losing money.

But what if someone else beats you to the call? The pot now grows $100 to $1,000. Now your pot odds (the amount the pot offers versus the cost of your call) are even more attractive. Now, though, it's time to fold. But wait! We said that your chance of winning is just as good as the first caller's. So, why wouldn't you call?

You wouldn't call because you earn money by folding. If you would have beat the original bettor once in 10 times, then you still will. Nothing changes. But you will only beat the first caller once in two times. This means that you will only win this pot by making that final call once in 20 times (half of the time for each of the one in 10 times you beat the original bettor). And, although your chances of winning fell to half, after that first call, the pot only grew from $900 to $1,000—making your pot odds grow only from 9 to 1 to 10 to 1. That isn't nearly enough to make the call. In fact a call now would cost you $45 on average. So, by folding, you earn $45!

5. When to Fold

You need to fold most hold 'em hands before the flop or on the flop. Seldom commit yourself further with defensive hands.

6. The Art of Folding

The great art of folding profitably is to never let aggressive opponents know you folded a significant hand. If knowledgeable opponents suspect from the action that you have a strong hand, it's often better to call, even if calling is slightly unprofitable at the time. Of course, in no-limit hold 'em games, the cost may be much too great to justify a call in order to help your image. Still, in limit games or in no-limit games against puny bets, this advice holds true. Experienced opponents can take advantage of you if they think you lay down big hands. And, finally…

7. Try Not to Fold if Folding Will Turn an Opponent Who Never Bluffs Into an Opponent Who Seldom Bluffs

This will mean the opponent will steal a pot from you once in a while, but not often enough that you should call. A conspicuous fold with a seemingly strong can cost you whole pots later. So, never act as if you're making a smart laydown with a big hand.

FIVE MORE FOLDING CONCEPTS
1. Calling a River Raise Instead of Folding

One of the most costly mistakes made by experienced players is that they call too frequently on the final betting round against a bet and a raise. If you could tally all calls made by all players in this situation, you would quickly see that an overcall against a river raise loses money.

Why? It's because players don't seem to realize how much extra strength they need to make this call. They get caught up in the moment and are awed by the size of the pot. But, actually, the pot size is much smaller, relative to the size of the call, than it would be if there had been no raise. That's because the call costs double, and the pot is only one bet larger than it would have been without the raise. This means, for a very big pot, your pot odds are only about half as good, but your hand needs to be much stronger than usual to win. The second player is probably figuring the bettor for a big hand, and yet he is still raising. This tells you that your run-of-the-mill strong hand isn't enough in most such situations. You need extra-special strength to call.

Also, remember that most players who are squeezed between you and the first bettor are reluctant to raise without super-strong hands. They'd rather play it safe, and maybe win a call behind. (Beware that some tricky players will try to freeze you out of the pot by raising if they think the bettor might be bluffing, but this is rare.)

The point is this: I have no doubt that most readers understand what I just said and that it isn't news to them. Still, the fact remains that most sophisticated players—and almost all weak players—call far too often on the river against a bet and a raise. If I could take a statistical sample of all such calls ever made in poker games, I'm betting that the result would be a significant loss.

2. Getting Overcarded

In hold 'em, you should almost routinely fold any large pair if the flop contains two different higher ranks.

This is another great mistake made by many players who otherwise pride themselves on correct decisions. When you're dealt J♠ J♦ in the pocket and the board is A♥ Q♣ 4♠, you should not hesitate to make a laydown against a bet. It's simply not a big laydown. Of course, there are certain players and certain situations in which you might make exceptions and call, or even raise. But your basic strategy—the one you should choose in the absence of factors indicating a contrary decision—when you have a high pair and two higher cards of two different ranks flop should be to fold.

This is much different than having a less-significant pair when two or even three higher unpaired ranks flop. In that case, it's not the fact that those ranks are higher than your pair, but how much higher that should dictate your decision. Especially if there has been raising before the flop, high cards are more dangerous and more likely to pair your opponents than medium cards. Therefore, if you hold 6♠ 6♦ and the flop is 9♥ 7♣ 2♠, you should not fold quite so routinely, even though there are two overcards.

3. Image Matters

The looser and more unpredictable your image is, the more successfully you can fold strong hands. Think about it. You are less likely to bluff or bet borderline hands into loose or tricky opponents. Your opponents think the same way. So, when they bet, they typically have stronger than average hands against your loose and treacherous image.

4. Don't Show

We've talked about why you shouldn't make big laydowns in limit games if your opponents think that's what you're doing.

Well, worse still is voluntarily showing the cards when you make a big laydown. You should never show a good laydown. Don't show, even if you're proud of it. Showing good laydowns invites unexpected bluffs later.

5. Best Times to Fold

There are two types of players that are especially profitable to make laydowns against when you hold medium hands with which you might otherwise call. They are:

a. Non-bluffers who bet.
b. Non-bettors who raise.

You should fold against the non-bluffers because typical calls that are barely profitable earn a big share of that profit by catching bluffs. When there are no potential bluffs to catch, you need a much stronger hand to justify a call. And players who are reluctant to bet are typically reluctant to raise with marginally strong hands, also. So if you have a marginal raise-calling hand against them, you should fold. You need something much stronger.

SHIFTING GEARS

Shifting gears is simply the act of changing tactics suddenly between tight and loose, between aggressive and passive, and then back again

There is no world-class player who stays in the same gear all the time. You can't maximize your profit without shifting gears, but shifting gears for the wrong reason can just cost you money. Sure, if your opponents are playing strict game theory without making any adjustments in accordance with how you play, you can only lose money by shifting gears. In that case, there's simply no reason to do it.

Doyle Brunson talks a lot about shifting gears. Of course, now that almost everybody drives a car with an automatic transmission, the concept of shifting gears may not have the impact it once did. So, pretend you're driving a big old truck or a small sports car without automatic, and need to shift to match driving conditions.

In poker, you can shift gears by changing from a very aggressive style of play to a more defensive one, from tight to loose, from bluff mode to non-bluff mode and back again. The object of shifting gears is to keep opponents off guard.

The nice thing about shifting gears in poker is that you always know right away that you've shifted, but your opponents may throw thousands of dollars your way before they figure it out. But, what if your opponents aren't paying any attention to you? Then, shifting gears is silly. You might as well just make your most profitable long-range decision on every play. There's no reason to sacrifice the top choice in an effort to throw your opponents off-guard, because they simply aren't reacting to you.

But that last type of opponent is more theoretical than actual. All opponents react to what you do to some extent, whether they realize it or not. Still, changing gears just for the sake of it doesn't accomplish much. You need to use the right gear at the right time. No sense cruising along the highway, making good time toward your destination, with no traffic, thinking, "Hey, I haven't shifted gears for a while, maybe I'll shift down to first gear and gradually rebuild my speed from there."

So, we'll talk about correctly shifting gears.

1. Shifting Gears for the Right Reasons

Shifting gears should only be done to confuse opponents or to enhance your image. There is no other reason whatsoever to shift. However, this does not mean that you shouldn't randomize your decisions, even against some opponents who may not be paying attention when you change tactics. If you're playing against an excellent opponent who is using game theory to his benefit—whether perfectly or imperfectly, consciously or unconsciously—you need to vary your decisions. Bet sometimes, but not always, with given hands. You need to bluff at random, but at the right frequency.

But shifting gears is different from this kind of sudden randomization. Shifting gears means you've changed your basic mode of aggression or deception and intend to stay in that new mode for many hands, many minutes, or maybe for hours.

2. There Are Only Four Good Reasons to Shift Gears

a. To be less predictable and more confusing.

b. To attack *their* money.

c. To defend *your* money.

d. To let opponents self-destruct.

3. Shifting to Appear Less Predictable Only Matters Against Certain Players

There are players who otherwise (consciously or unconsciously) would understand how you're playing and who would and could take advantage if you stayed in the same gear—thus, you should change gears at the appropriate time.

4. Don't Shift Unless You Need To

Stay in your most profitable gear as much as possible. If you don't need to shift, don't!

5. Which Gears Work Best?

Consider a low gear (conservative and unaggressive) against tight, sensible opponents in rake games, because a fast strategy will eat up your profits in rakes. Also use a low gear when you've been seen losing or otherwise haven't been able to establish a dynamic image—but have tried. This is very important, because borderline bets and raises are unprofitable against opponents who are inspired by your bad luck and may play better and become more deceptive as a result.

Middle gears (sometimes aggressive, sometimes defensive) work best against aggressive and sensible opponents, but you should often shift up or down from middle gears. Middle gears should also be used against opponents who bluff often. In that case, middle gear often can mean calling, but not raising.

High (fast) gears should be used against opponents who are intimidated by you. Also use high gears while you are building your image. When you're winning against weak opponents whose main fault is that they call too much with bad hands and don't raise enough with valuable hands, go into high gear and stay there unless conditions change.

6. The Simple Truth about Shifting Gears

Your primary goal should be to get into medium-high gear and stay there as much as possible. But, except in rare games where opponents call too much, raise too little, and don't adapt, you will lose money if you stay locked in the highest gear.

7. When You Suddenly Shift Gears, You Have the Advantage!

Even the most observant opponent has no way to tell that you shifted right away. The advantage of acting first in shifting your strategy before your opponents shift in response is available to all players. Make sure you use it often and hope that your strongest opponents don't use it as much.

8. Even Unobservant Opponents Can Be Confused by Opponents Shifting Gears

Unconsciously opponents sense volatility and become more timid and play worse against you.

9. When You're Controlling the Game, Don't Shift Gears

Doing so is a huge mistake. You should almost *never* shift down to play a big hand deceptively when you're in control. Just keep betting and raising. As long as it's working, take advantage of your aggressive and deceptive image.

Q & A: DECEPTIVE TACTICS
QUESTION

In poker, a bad time to use deceptive tactics with a strong hand is when…

a. Your opponents hate you.
b. You're breaking about even.
c. Nobody has made a raise on an early betting round in half an hour.
d. The most obvious play has a great chance for success.

ANSWER

D. You need to realize that choosing deception with a strong hand is an alternative strategy. By saying that it's an alternative strategy, I am also saying that you should consider using it only when there is something wrong with using the obvious best strategy.

One bad thing about the obvious best strategy is that if you use it all the time, your opponents may be able to take advantage. You'll be too predictable. For instance, in hold 'em, if you only raise with aces and kings from the early positions before the flop, eventually some of your opponents may realize this. They will no longer wager any inferior hands against you, and your profits on that play will evaporate. So, you might occasionally invoke an alternative strategy. Like what? Like just calling with those aces or kings.

Fine. But what if the obvious strategy works very well? If betting is a clear choice, you should usually bet.

That's the point. The better the chance for success that the obvious play offers, the less reason you have to use deception. This is even true against whole classes of opponents. The more vulnerable they are to the obvious strategy, the less deception you need to use. That's why against a table full of weak opponents who call most of the time, you should rarely choose anything except your obvious best tactic.

Are you a football fan? Well, one of the big mistakes sometimes made by coaches or quarterbacks is passing on first down and goal to go from the one- or two-yard line. Using every down necessary to rush straight into the line toward the goal is so likely to result in a touchdown that using deception by throwing a surprise pass is simply wrong. The obvious strategy has too great a chance of success for deception to be considered. Same in poker. Same in *anything*.

14 TOURNAMENT CONCEPTS

SURVIVAL IS THE MOST IMPORTANT CONCEPT

The most common types of poker tournaments are the proportional payoff variety. That's where, as players are eliminated, tables are consolidated until the survivors meet at a final table and first place wins all the chips. But first place doesn't get to keep all the money, so there is, in effect, a penalty for winning—as I'll explain. This means survival is more important than using many sophisticated tactics that would earn extra profit in non-tournament games. So, you should avoid high-risk, seemingly profitable finesses and play more conservatively in order to survive and win more of the prize pool.

Correct strategy for tournaments requires that you concentrate your attacks on players with fewer chips than you have. This provides two advantages:

1. You can't be eliminated by those players, so you'll survive even if you lose the pot.

2. If you win the pot, you'll eliminate the short-stacked opponent and automatically move up in the money (or, at least, toward the money).

IS IT CORRECT TO ELIMINATE PLAYERS?
The incorrect concept is this: You should almost always seek to eliminate opponents in a percentage-payoff tournament.

The thinking is that the more players you can get rid of, the closer you are to the money. For example, if the prize money will go to only the top eight finishers, then if you can eliminate all but eight players right this second, guess what? You're in the money!

For this reason, most serious players believe that it's worth a sacrifice to eliminate an opponent. And, actually, that's theoretically correct. But what players don't seem to realize is that the sacrifice they might be willing to make should be a very small one. In fact, the adjustments you can correctly make in an attempt to knock a player out of a tournament in the early stages are so insignificant that they should rarely affect your decision. That's important, and I'm going to repeat it: Early in a tournament, you should seldom change your strategy in an attempt to eliminate an opponent.

Let's straighten out the misconception once and for all. I'll do this with a little anecdote (which happens to be true).

> I remember one tournament where, by the second round, one player—I'll call him Tim, because that's what everyone else called him—had experienced such misfortune that he had less than $200 left of his original $1,000 in tournament chips. I had somewhere around $600 remaining. Tim finds himself heads-up at the river. The pot is small. At this point, he has $150 in front of him and decides to make an $80 wager.

> The opponent, an extremely knowledgeable player with a charming disposition—okay, it was me—thinks about it and decides to call (and not raise). On the showdown the bettor has a pair of kings and I have tens-up.
>
> Immediately, the woman to my right starts complaining, "How could you let him survive? Why didn't you raise and put him all in? You have an obligation to knock him out of the tournament. It's not fair to the other players when you play soft."

KNOCKING OUT AN OPPONENT: DO THE MATH

Of course, I hadn't played soft at all. In fact, I had almost not called the bet. If I hadn't, then the player would have won the pot worth hundreds of dollars more in tournament chips, rather than having just the $70 I had left him with. Had I raised in an attempt to knock him out, I would have risked almost an amount equal to his $80 bet ($10 short) in a situation that barely justified a call. Looking back I figured that I would have lost three out of four times had I made a similar call forever.

If I assume that my opponent would have always called and my handicapping is correct, that means that for every four raise attempts, I would lose $70 three times and win $70 (eliminating the opponent) once. That translates to a loss of $140 every four attempts or $35 per attempt. What this means is that I would need to sacrifice $35 on average if I made an attempt to eliminate this opponent. Of course, there are other factors to consider: The raise might cause Tim to fold a better hand and Tim might not call the raise, among others. But let's just assume Tim is always going to call my raise and that I'm a 3 to 1 underdog. That way, we can simplify and accept the $35 projected cost as valid in order for me to make my point.

So, let me ask you a question: Would it have been worth $35 to me to attempt to knock Tim out of the tournament? Remember, that is the cost of the attempt, not the cost of eliminating him. By my prediction (although he would have lost, as it turned out) I would have won only a quarter of the time.

The woman to my right certainly must have thought it was worth $35, because she continued her critique, "You wrote that you should always do everything possible to eliminate people, and then you have the chance and you don't do it."

"I see your point," I respond as politely as possible. "But you might have me confused with someone else. I don't remember ever writing that."

The truth is, you should seldom make this type of raise with anything but a major advantage, especially if it will cost you a significant portion of your stacks. Even if you have a great deal of chips and your opponent has only a few, it is not incumbent upon you to put that player all-in in hopes of eliminating him. Also, it is not required that you make a courtesy call when you have a large stack and your opponent puts himself all-in for a pittance. The later it is in the tournament, the more beneficial it is for you to eliminate opponents. Early in a tournament with, say, 201 players remaining, there is very little value in taking the worst of it in an attempt to knock out an opponent. We'd better examine this further…

WHAT IS THE REAL COST OF TRYING TO ELIMINATE OPPONENTS?

Let's use the same $35 in tournament chips, as in the previous example, to calculate the real cost of eliminating opponents in a tournament. Then ask yourself how much you will gain from eliminating an opponent. This is tricky. The answer is that you will actually gain in prize money, on average, about 1/200th of the value that eliminating this player will have to the entire field of competitors. In other words, whatever value eliminating this player adds to the expectations of all players, you, being only one of 200 then-remaining players, will profit only the same as everyone else will.

So, here's how it appears: If it's costing you $35 in chips, then the value of eliminating this player right now needs to be at least $7,000 (200 times $35). But, wait! Since I'm only going to succeed in eliminating Tim once in four similar raises, the value of eliminating him needs to be four times as large as my sacrifice. That means, the value to the entire field of players of eliminating Tim right now needs to be $28,000 in tournament chips. You read it right.

You might see this better if you think of it as costing $140 to eliminate Tim. That's because on average, it will take four similar tries, each costing $35 in sacrificial money, to get him out. Since $1/200^{th}$ of $28,000 is $140, and that should just about balance your books.

If you're beginning to suspect that the value of eliminating Tim cannot possibly approach $28,000 in a tournament that has roughly $100,000 in total chips, I'm glad. You are seeing how silly this sacrifice-to-eliminate opponents advice can be in the early stages of a tournament.

Now it becomes clear why the advice to always try to knock out opponents is bad. Most players sacrifice too greatly in their attempt to send opponents home early. The logic I've just presented is not quite pure, though. Small stacks often benefit more than large ones when an opponent is eliminated. This is easy to see at the final table, because small stacks move up in money position when they might otherwise have been eliminated. We'll return to this topic in a minute. But since I've touched on the subject of stack sizes, think about this...

WHEN BIG STACKS COLLIDE: GOOD OR BAD FOR THE SMALL STACK?

One of the best things that can happen to all remaining players is for two opponents with huge stacks to collide and for one of them to get eliminated. You then face the same number of opposing chips, but you have fewer opponents to contend with.

Contrary to the opinions of some, this does not make it harder for you to win a tournament. Your chances of winning first place are about the same with $10,000 against two players each with $45,000 as against one player with $90,000. In each case, ignoring other minor factors which I've discussed elsewhere, your chance of winning are about 10 percent. That's because you have 10 percent of the chips.

Of course, your chances of taking at least second place are greatly improved against the single opponent. In fact, your chances are absolute. That's why you want big stacks to go to war. It's also why, when you have a lot of chips, you do not want to go to war with another big stack.

THE TRUTH ABOUT ELIMINATING OPPONENTS

Back to the main issue under discussion. The big argument players give for wanting to eliminate an opponent is, "They might come back and beat you." So what? They also might come back to beat somebody else. Besides, they're more likely to beat you if you call and lose, because then they have more chips to build from and to attack you with. Why is it so much more tragic if a person you might have eliminated comes back to beat you than if someone else knocks you out of a tournament? When you're out, you're out.

There is no logic to the popular "eliminate players at all costs" advice. The only factor that matters is whether sacrificing your normally profitable strategy in an effort to eliminate an opponent will add or subtract from your expected payoff.

"The big argument players give for wanting to eliminate an opponent is, "They might come back and beat you." So what?"

In the late stages of a tournament, where fewer players share large benefits when a player is eliminated, it's often worth making some sacrifice. In the early stages, it isn't. That's the simple truth. You may not like the sound of it, and it may run contrary to everything you've heard before. But it is the truth, nonetheless.

HOW MUCH ARE YOUR CHIPS WORTH IN A TOURNAMENT?

Don't be discouraged if you only have as many chips as you started with late in a poker tournament. Most players think it's necessary to gather chips, but it isn't. If you have the same $500 you started with after three-quarters of the players are eliminated, the same amount of money is out there against you as when the tournament began. The situation regarding the total amount of opposing money relative to your stack hasn't gotten any better or any worse. But what has gotten better is that there are fewer players contending for the cash prizes. Mathematically, your prospects of profit have increased.

So, you're always better off with the same amount of chips later in a proportional payoff tournament than when the first hand was dealt. Remember, the trick is to survive. Don't panic if your stacks don't grow. You'd rather they would, but you're still better off, even if they stay the same.

THE BIG TRUTH ABOUT HOLD 'EM TOURNAMENTS

Remember, before you enter a hold 'em tournament, you need to decide whether you're playing for the trophy or whether you're playing for the most profit. In a proportional playoff tournament (those where first place wins, say, 25 percent of the prize pool, second place wins 15 percent, and so forth), the profit comes by ignoring many of the everyday aggressive tactics you'd use if you could quit anytime.

That doesn't mean you can't play aggressively in pursuit of profit. If opponents are intimidated, it's often proper to attack. And sometimes you'll attack in order to limit the field of opponents, thus limiting your risk of elimination. But you shouldn't take additional risk simply to target every extra penny's worth of profit the way you would in a non-tournament game. That's because there isn't any extra profit in those marginal plays. Yes, in the long run, they add to your bankroll in everyday action. But in a tournament, they do just the opposite. They increase your chance of elimination.

THE TOURNAMENT PENALTY THAT MUST BE FACTORED IN YOUR STRATEGIES

Always keep in mind that the first-place winner of a tournament is penalized. That player must gather all the chips, but doesn't get to spend them. Instead, the winner must give away most of his chips to those already-conquered opponents who finished second, third, fourth, and so on. That's a steep penalty. If it were winner-take-all, the correct strategy would be entirely different. Then you could use every advanced, risky trick in your arsenal, and you'd be playing *both* for the most profit *and* for the trophy.

The perfect hold 'em tournament strategy in a proportional payoff event is to play sensibly and conservatively throughout *all* stages of the action, except when it becomes heads up. (I'll talk about heads-up in a minute.) You're goal is to survive into the money, knowing that you can eventually lose all your chips and still get paid, specifically because whoever ends up with all those chips will give you a large consolation prize!

Many players don't like me to say this, because it diminished their delusion of tournament mastery, but I'll say it anyway. From a mathematical perspective, the object of a tournament is to play rationally while *avoiding* taking first place! Sure, you hope to win the tournament, but you want to back into the championship, while mostly playing to survive into the money.

HEADS-UP STRATEGY

I said that the concept of playing sensibly and conservatively doesn't apply when you're playing heads-up for the trophy. How come? Well, it's like this: Once you're heads up, it's no longer a proportional-payoff tournament. Sure second place gets less money than first place, but the prize-structure is now an illusion. Actually, *both* players have already secured second place money and are playing winner-take-all for the rest. If first place pays $1,000,000 and second place pays $700,000, then each contestant has already won $700,000 and the two are now playing winner-take all for $300,000. At that point, you can use every dynamic hold 'em trick you know.

But until that point, play to survive. The fact that you must sacrifice everyday poker skills in pursuit of the profit is one reason I seldom play tournaments. But if you decide to travel the hold 'em tournament trail, please take this advice about survival seriously.

15 QUICK INTRODUCTION TO HOLD 'EM RULES AND PROCEDURES

HOW TO PLAY

As I explained in a similar optional chapter in my book *Caro's Fundamental Secrets of Winning Poker*, I'm including this section because some novices may find it useful. If this doesn't apply to you, skip immediately to the bonus chapters that follow.

This material is borrowed from the *Fundamental Secrets* book, with permission of its author. First, you need to know that every traditional poker hand consists of five cards and that the 52 cards in a standard playing deck are individually identifiable by two features: rank and suit. There are 13 different possible ranks. The ace is the highest-ranking card, and then, proceeding down in rank, there is the king, queen, jack, 10, 9, 8, 7, 6, 5, 4, 3, and finally the 2 (also called "deuce"), the lowest.

Following is a listing of hand rankings from highest to lowest. Sure, you probably already know this, but here's the damn chart, anyway. Share it with someone you love.

CUSTOMARY POKER HAND VALUES
(APPLICABLE TO ALMOST ALL POKER GAMES WHERE
HIGH HAND WINS)

Rank	Example	Described	Ties
Royal Flush	A♣ K♣ Q♣ J♣ 10♣	Five cards of consecutive ranks from ace down to ten, all the same suit. (A royal flush is the best straight flush.)	Two or more royal flushes divide the pot.
Straight Flush	9♦ 8♦ 7♦ 6♦ 5♦	Five cards of consecutive ranks, all the same suit. (Ace can be used low to form a five-high straight flush.)	Higher ranking straight wins. (Judged by the rank of the card that begins the downward sequence.)
Four of a Kind	3♣ 3♦ 3♥ 3♠ K♣	Four cards of a matching rank, plus an extra card.	Higher rank of the four of a kind wins. If tied, higher extra card wins.
Full House	9♣ 9♥ 9♠ Q♦ Q♠	Three cards of matching rank, plus two cards of a different matching rank.	Higher rank of the three of a kind within the full house wins. Extra pair doesn't matter.
Flush	A♠ J♠ 7♠ 6♠ 2♠	Five cards of the same suit that do not qualify as a straight flush or royal flush.	Highest ranking card wins. If it is tied, next highest card wins, and so forth.
Straight	8♦ 7♠ 6♦ 5♣ 4♥	Five ranks in sequence. (Ace can be used low to form a five-high straight.)	Higher rank beginning the sequence wins.
Three of a Kind	A♦ A♣ A♥ Q♦ 4♠	Three cards of a matching rank and two extra cards whose ranks do not match.	Higher rank of the three of a kind wins. If tied, higher extra card wins.
Two Pair	K♥ K♦ 4♥ 4♦ A♠	Two cards of a matching rank, plus two cards of another matching rank, plus one extra card.	Highest pair wins. If tied, higher second pair wins. If still tied, higher extra card wins.
One Pair	7♠ 7♥ Q♥ 10♠ 3♣	Two cards of a matching rank, plus three extra cards of all different ranks	Higher pair wins. If pairs rank the same, highest ranking extra card not matched by opponent wins.
No Pair	Q♥ J♠ 8♥ 6♦ 2♠	Any hand that does not qualify for one of the categories listed above.	Highest card wins. If the hands tie for high card, the second highest cards are compared, and so forth.

Remember, the order in which your poker cards are arranged doesn't matter. Therefore, 9♥ 10♦ Q♦ 8♣ J♠ is exactly the same as Q♦ J♠ 10♦ 9♥8♣. It makes no difference whether you go to the trouble of sorting your cards or not; you still have a straight.

Oh, and one other thing—the ace is not always the highest rank. Sometimes it can be used as the smallest card in this straight or straight flush: 5-4-3-2-A. Five-high is the *worst* straight or straight flush you can get, and it doesn't beat 6-5-4-3-2, even though it contains an ace.

SIMPLIFIED HOLD 'EM PROCEDURES

Maximum number of participants: Usually 10, but sometimes limited to nine. Hold 'em can theoretically be played with up to 22 players, still leaving enough cards for the "board" and for "burning." But I've never seen a game with more than 12 players.

Hold 'em is a cerebral game, requiring both strategic and people skills. It is the form of poker traditionally used in championship competition.

In all, if the hand doesn't terminate prematurely because a bet is uncalled, seven cards will be dealt to the players, but five of them will be held in common! What does that mean? Well, in hold 'em you only get two cards for your individual hand. As in seven-card stud, you will eventually try to make your best five-card high hand from among seven cards. But in hold 'em, five of those cards are the same ones everyone else has. Those communal cards that belong in everybody's hand, are spread face up in the center of the table, and collectively are called the **board**.

1. There is usually no ante in hold 'em. Instead of an ante, blind bets are used to stimulate the action. A **blind** bet is a wager a player is required to put in the pot before receiving any cards. In our example game, the player immediately to the left of the dealer (or the assumed dealer position, if a non-participating dealer is used) puts in a blind bet of $2 and the player two seats to the left of the dealer puts in $5.

2. The dealer shuffles. This might be a non-participating house dealer paid by a casino. In most home games, players take turns dealing, and after every hand the task passes to the left. This means you must deal when it's your turn.

3. The dealer offers the cut to a player on right. Cards must be cut at least five cards deep, leaving no fewer than five cards on the bottom.

4. The dealer distributes one card at a time face down to each player (self included, if participating), beginning to the left and continuing clockwise, until each participant has two cards. These two cards are the only ones each player will individually receive during a hand of hold 'em.

5. The action begins three seats away from the dealer, with the player to the left of the **big blind** (the $5 forced bet), the larger of the forced blind bets. Each player, acting clockwise in turn, must call the previous bet, raise it ($5 in this example game), or throw the hand away.

6. All bets are added to the pot, along with the original blinds, in the center of the table.

7. If you bet or raise and all your opponents fold, you win what's in the pot, and there is no subsequent betting. (In this case, a new hand will be dealt.)

8. If there are callers and no raise, the $5 blind (big blind) may raise, even though he has only been called. This is

called a **live blind**, meaning the big blind, being last to act, will have a chance to act.

9. If two or more players remain after the first round of betting, the deal continues. The dealer turns over three cards all at once in the center of the table. These three face-up cards are called the **flop**.

10. Players coordinate the two secret cards held in their hand with the three cards face up on the board, estimating their chances of holding, or later forming, the best five-card poker hand. There is a second round of betting, beginning with the first active player to the left of the dealer. In a no-limit game, all bets must be at least as large as the original big blind ($5 in this case), and all raises must at least double the previous bet or raise. This is true for all rounds of betting. In limit games, all bets remain at the pre-established limits, $5 in this example.

11. If two or more players remain after the second round of betting, the deal continues. The dealer turns over a fourth communal board card in the center of the table. This is called the **turn** card.

12. There is a third round of betting, beginning to the left of the dealer. In limit games, all bets now double. In this example, they go to $10.

13. If two or more players remain after the third round of betting, the deal continues. The dealer delivers a fifth and final communal board card in the center of the table. It is called the **river** card.

14. There is a fourth and final round of betting, beginning to the left of the dealer. In limit games, all bets remain at the double level ($10 in our sample game).

15. If two or more players remain after the final betting round, there is a **showdown** to determine the winner. Players turn their two secret cards face up on the table,

and the best five-card hand chosen from those two cards and the five communal board cards wins all the money in the pot.

16. The dealer button moves one spot to the left, the blind bets are made for the next hand, and the process is repeated.

16 HOLD 'EM ODDS CHARTS

The following tables are adopted from the statistical tables I contributed to Doyle Brunson's original *Super/System-A Course in Power Poker*. While it isn't necessary to memorize these or to read them now, they're provided for later reference—or to satisfy your curiosity.

PROBABILITY OF BEING DEALT SPECIFIC
HOLD 'EM HANDS BEFORE THE FLOP

Probability of Being Dealt...	Expressed in Percent	The Odds Against
Pair of aces	0.45	220 to 1
Pair of kings through pair of jacks	1.36	72.7 to 1
Pair of tens through pair of sixes	2.26	43.2 to 1
Pair of fives through pair of deuces	1.81	54.3 to 1
A-K suited	0.30	331 to 1
A-K offsuit	0.90	110 to 1
A-Q or A-J suited	0.60	165 to 1
A-Q to A-J offsuit	1.81	54.3 to 1
K-Q suited	0.30	331 to 1
K-Q offsuit	0.90	110 to 1
Ace with less than jack, suited	2.71	35.8 to 1
Ace with less than jack, offsuit	8.14	11.3 to 1
Any pair	5.88	16 to 1
Any two cards suited	23.53	3.25 to 1
Any two cards adjacent and suited with *maximum stretch* *	2.11	46.4 to 1
Any two cards adjacent and offsuit with *maximum stretch* *	6.33	14.8 to 1
Any hand with a pair or an ace	20.36	3.91 to 1

Total Hands: 1,326

* Two cards in order, allowing the maximum chance at a straight. The lowest eligible combination is 5-4. The highest eligible combination is J-10.

FLOPS FOR SELECTED HOLD 'EM HANDS
YOU HOLD A♦ K♦

Probability that the Flop Will Be...	Expressed in Percent (%)	The Odds Against	Note
Q-J-10	0.01	19,599 to 1	*Makes royal flush
A-A-A or K-K-K	0.01	9,799 to 1	*Makes four aces or four kings
A-A-K or K-K-A	0.09	1,088 to 1	*Makes aces full or kings full
Three diamonds other than Q-J-10	0.84	119 to 1	*Makes flush
Two diamonds with an ace or king	1.68	58.4 to 1	*Makes aces or kings with four-flush or four parts of straight-flush
Two diamonds with a pair of 2's through Q's	1.68	58.4 to 1	*Four parts of flush or straight-flush, the pair is unfavorable
Two diamonds, not with a pair of 2's through Q's and not Q-J-10	7.53	12.3 to 1	*Four parts of flush or straight-flush
Q-J-10 (not all diamonds)	0.32	310 to 1	*Makes straight
Pair less than kings, with one or no diamonds	11.79	7.48 to 1	*Unfavorable
Three of another suit	4.38	21.8 to 1	*Danger, even if Q-J-10
A-K and smaller card	2.02	48.5 to 1	*Makes aces and kings
Three-of-a-kind 2's through Q's	0.22	444 to 1	*Unfavorable unless no one holds fourth one or pair
Any flop which includes an ace or king	32.43	2.08 to 1	*Makes key pair or better
Any two diamonds	10.94	8.14 to 1	*Four parts of a flush or straight-flush
A-A with 2 through Q or K-K with a 2 through Q	1.35	73.2 to 1	* Makes key three-of-a-kind

Number of possible flops: 19,600

YOU HOLD A PAIR OF KINGS: K♠ K♠

Probability that the Flop Will Be...	Expressed in Percent (%)	The Odds Against	Note
K-K and card other than king	0.24	407 to 1	*Makes four kings
King and 2 through aces	0.06	1,632 to 1	*Kings full
A-K and smaller card	1.80	54.7 to 1	*Three kings, possible trouble if 2nd ace fails
King and smaller pair	0.67	147 to 1	*Makes kings full
King and unpaired smaller cards	8.98	10.1 to 1	*Makes three kings
A-A-A	0.02	4,899 to 1	*Makes aces full, but you lose if someone has the last ace
Two aces and other, 2 through Q	1.35	73.2 to 1	*Dangerous
Three-of-a-kind, 2's through Q's	0.22	444 to 1	*Dangerous
Three suited cards, clubs or spades	2.24	43.5 to 1	*Four parts of a flush, much better if it includes ace
Three suited cards, diamonds or hearts	2.92	33.3 to 1	*Unfavorable
Q-J-10, other than all three spades or three clubs	0.32	315 to 1	*Open-end straight (probable trouble)
Pair of 2's through Q's, and another card (but not king)	14.82	5.75 to 1	*Kings-up and trouble
Q-J-10, clubs or spades	0.01	9,799 to 1	*Open-end straight flush
Any flop including at least one king	11.76	7.51 to 1	*Generally very favorable
One ace and two cards, 2 through Q, (including a pair of 2's through Q's)	19.31	4.18 to 1	*Bad news
1 Ace and two cards, 2 through Q, excluding a pair	17.96	4.57 to 1	*Unfavorable

Number of possible flops: 19,600

YOU HOLD Q♠ J♦
(FOR RELATED FLOPS, SEE CHART SHOWING A♦ K♦)

Probability that the Flop Will Be...	Expressed in Percent (%)	The Odds Against	Note
Q-Q-Q or J-J-J	0.01	9,799 to 1	*Makes four queens or four jacks
Q-Q-J or J-J-Q	0.09	1,088 to 1	*Full house: Q-Q-J is better (2,177 to 1)
A-K-10	0.33	305 to 1	*Makes ace-high straight — 3.13% of these will also be four parts of a straight-flush
K-10-9 or 10-9-8	0.65	152 to 1	*Makes straight — 3.13% of these will also be four parts of a straight-flush
Any straight when combined with your hand	0.98	101 to 1	*A-K-10, K-10-9 or 10-9-8
K-10 and any other card, or 10-9 and any other card (no straight)	6.04	15.6 to 1	*Open-end straight — 16.22% of these include a pair of jacks or queens, 8.11% include a cold pair
Three suited cards (your suits)	2.24	43.5 to 1	*Four parts of a flush or straight-flush—0.03% of these already make straights, 25% include a pair of queens or jacks
Q-Q-other, or J-J-other (not full house)	1.35	73.2 to 1	*Makes three-of-a-kind
Any flop without an ace or king	58.57	0.71 to 1	*Sometimes helpful, but often hopeless
Any Flop without an ace	77.45	0.29 to 1	*Generally helpful
Queens or jack with smaller pair	1.65	59.5 to 1	*Queens-up or jacks-up
Any Flop without a queen or jack	67.57	0.48 to 1	*Not good unless a straight, four-straight or four-flush
A-A or K-K with a queen or jack	0.37	271 to 1	*Makes a very unfavorable aces-up or kings-up

Number of possible flops: 19,600

FROM FLOP TO FINISH
YOU HOLD A♠ A♦ AND THE FLOP IS K♣ Q♣ J♦

Probability that the Strength of Your Final Hand Will Be...	Expressed in Percent (%)	The Odds Against	Note
Four aces	0.09	1,080 to 1	*Lock
Aces full	1.67	59.1 to 1	*Could lose to four kings, four queens, or four jacks (whichever pair is on the board)
Other full	0.83	119 to 1	*A player holding the 4th jack, queen or king wins, otherwise you have a lock (could tie)
Straight	16.47	5.07 to 1	*Okay, but a tie is threatened and opponent could have a flush if the three on the board are suited—or full house if a pair is on the board
Three aces	5.92	15.9 to 1	*Very favorable (unless all three board cards are suited, you can only lose to a straight)
Aces-up	33.58	1.98 to 1	*You're better off without the 'ups' on the board
Aces	41.44	1.41 to 1	*Might win

Number of possible outcomes: 1,081

FROM FLOP TO FINISH
YOU HOLD A♦ Q♦ AND THE FLOP IS 7♦ 4♦ 2♣

Probability that the Strength of Your Final Hand Will Be...	Expressed in Percent (%)	The Odds Against	Note
Flush	34.97	1.86 to 1	*The last two cards will both be diamonds 3.33% of the time
Three aces or three queens	0.56	179 to 1	*Strong
Aces over queens	0.83	119 to 1	*Strong
Aces over sevens, fours or deuces	2.22	44.0 to 1	*Dangerous
Queens over sevens, fours or deuces	2.22	44.0 to 1	*Dangerous
Aces or queens	13.32	6.51 to 1	*Might win
Three-of-a-kind on board (no flush)	0.65	153 to 1	*Slight chances

Number of possible outcomes: 1,081

ABSENCE OF ACES BEFORE FLOP
BY NUMBER OF PLAYERS

Number of Players	Probability that No Player Has an Ace, (including yourself) Expressed in Percent (%)	If You Have One Ace, Probability that No Other Player Has an Ace, Expressed in Percent (%)	If You Have No Ace, the Probability that No Other Player Has an Ace, Expressed in Percent (%)
2	71.87	88.24	84.49
3	60.28	77.45	70.86
4	50.14	67.57	58.95
5	41.34	58.57	48.60
6	33.76	50.41	39.68
7	27.27	43.04	32.05
8	21.76	36.43	25.58
9	17.13	30.53	20.14
10	13.28	25.31	15.61
11	10.12	20.71	11.90
12	7.56	16.71	8.89
15	2.70	7.86	3.18
20	0.18	1.12	0.21

NOTE: Your hand will have no ace 85.07% of the time

BASIC HOLD 'EM DATA

The Probability That...	Expressed in Percent (%)	The Odds Against
You will hold a **pair** before the flop	5.88	16 to 1
You will hold **suited cards** before the flop	23.53	3.25 to 1
You will hold **2 kings** or **2 aces** before the flop	0.90	110 to 1
You will hold **a-k** before the flop	1.21	81.9 to 1
You will hold *at least* **1 ace** before the flop	14.93	5.70 to 1
If you have four parts of a **flush** after the flop, you will make it	34.97	1.86 to 1
If you have four parts of an open-end straight-flush after the flop, you will make a **straight-flush**	8.42	10.9 to 1
If you have four parts of an open-end straight flush after the flop, you will make *at least* a **straight**	54.12	0.85 to 1
If you have two-pair after the flop, you will make a **full house or better**	16.74	4.97 to 1
If you have three-of-a-kind after the flop, you will make a **full house or better***	33.40	1.99 to 1
If you have a pair after the flop at least one more of that kind will turn up (on the last two cards)*	8.42	0.9 to 1
If you hold a pair, at least one more of that kind will flop	11.76	7.51 to 1
If you hold no pair, you will **pair** at least one of your cards on the flop	32.43	2.08 to 1
If you hold two suited cards, two or more of that suit will flop	11.79	7.48 to 1
If you begin suited and stay through seven cards, three more *(but not four or five more!)* of your suit will turn up	5.77	16.3 to 1
If you begin paired and stay through seven cards, *at least* one more of your kind will turn up	19.18	4.21 to 1

Includes unfavorable full houses

HOLD 'EM: LONG SHOTS

The Probability That...	Expressed in Percent (%)	The Odds Against
If you hold suited cards, a flush will flop	0.84	118 to 1
If you hold a pair, four-of-a-kind will flop	0.24	407 to 1
If you hold 6-5 offsuit, a straight will flop	1.31	75.6 to 1
If you hold 7-5 offsuit, a straight will flop	0.98	101 to 1
If you hold 8-5 offsuit, a straight will flop	0.65	152 to 1
If you hold 9-5 offsuit, a straight will flop	0.33	305 to 1
If you hold 9-8 suited, a straight-flush will flop	0.02	4,899 to 1
If you hold 9-7 suited, a straight-flush will flop	0.02	6,532 to 1
If you hold 9-6 suited, a straight-flush will flop	0.01	9,799 to 1
If you hold 9-5 suited, a straight-flush will flop	0.01	19,599 to 1
No one hold an ace or king in a 10-handed game	1.40	70.5 to 1
Heads-up hold 'em, both players hold paired aces	0.00*	270,724 to 1
You will not hold a pair or an ace before the flop for the next 20 hands	1.05	94.0 to 1
You will not hold a pair or an ace before the flop for the next 50 hands	0.00**	87, 897 to 1
You will hold a pair of aces before the flop each of the next four hands	0.00***	(2,385,443,280 to 1)

* Actually 0.00037%
** Actually 0.0011%
*** Actually 0.00000004%

17 TAKING IT ALL TO THE BANK

On these pages we've covered a lot of topics that are seldom discussed in other hold 'em texts. Oddly, these are precisely the most profitable, long ignored concepts that flow from hold 'em's fountain of success.

My goal wasn't merely to add to your collection of hold 'em tactics, but to provide you with a whole missing arsenal of tips and techniques that can add enormously to your bankroll. Please forgive me for the repetition in the preceding chapters; that's how I teach. I believe that by repeating a concept and exploring it from different angles, you can truly understand it. Using this method, you can move beyond a vague acknowledgement of an idea's importance and begin to actually own it. It's the same method of repetition and examination I use at my seminars. If I've succeeded, you now own these new weapons; they've become a permanent part of your winning game plan.

So, good luck on your future hold 'em adventures.

Straight Flushes,
Mike Caro

VIDEOS AND STRATEGIES BY MIKE CARO
THE MAD GENIUS OF POKER

CARO'S PRO POKER TELLS
$59.95 Two-Video VHS Set
$49.95 DVD
This video is a powerful scientific course on how to use your opponents' gestures, words and body language to read their hands and win all their money. These carefully guarded poker secrets, filmed with 63 poker notables, will bring your game to the next level. It reveals when opponents are bluffing, when they aren't, and why. Knowing what your opponent's gestures mean, and protecting them from knowing yours, gives you a huge winning edge. Says two-time World Champion Doyle Brunson: "Mike Caro's research will revolutionize poker!" Prepare to be astonished!

CARO'S POWER POKER SEMINAR
$39.95 VHS 62 Minutes
This powerful video shows you how to win big money using the little-known concepts of world champion players. This advice will be worth thousands of dollars to you every year, and even more if you're a big money player! After 15 years of refusing to allow his seminars to be filmed, Caro presents entertaining but serious coverage of his long-guarded secrets. The most profitable poker advice ever put on video.

CARO'S MAJOR POKER SEMINAR
$24.95 VHS 60 Minutes
Caro's poker advice in VHS format. Based on the inaugural class at Mike Caro University of Poker, Gaming and Life strategy. The material given on this tape is based on many fundamentals introduced in Caro's works and is prepared in such a way that reinforces concepts old and new. Caro's style is easy-going but intense with key concepts stressed and repeated. This tape will improve your play.

CARO'S PROFESSIONAL POKER REPORTS
Mike Caro, the foremost authority on poker strategy, psychology, and statistics, has put together three powerful insider poker reports. Each report is centered around a daily mission, with you, the reader, concentrating on adding one weapon per day to your arsenal. These highly focused reports are designed to take you to a new level at the tables. Theoretical concepts and practical situations are mixed together for fast in-depth learning in these concise courses. *Caro's Professional Reports* are very popular among good players.

11 Days to 7-Stud Success. Bluffing, playing and defending pairs, different strategies for the different streets, analyzing situations—lots of information within. One advantage is gained each day. A quick and powerful method to 7-stud winnings. Essential. Signed, numbered. $19.95.

12 Days to Hold'Em Success. Positional thinking, playing and defending against mistakes, small pairs, flop situations, playing the river, are just some sample lessons. Guaranteed to make you a better player. Very popular. Signed, numbered. $19.95.

Professional 7-Stud Report. When to call, pass, and raise, playing starting hands, aggressive play, 4th and 5th street concepts, lots more. Tells how to read an opponent's starting hand, plus sophisticated advanced strategies. Important revision for serious players. Signed, numbered. $19.95.

FROM CARDOZA'S EXCITING LIBRARY
ADD THESE TO YOUR COLLECTION - ORDER NOW!

SUPER SYSTEM *by Doyle Brunson.* Jam-packed with advanced strategies, theories, tactics and moneymaking techniques, this classic work, widely considered to be the most important poker book ever written! Chapters are written by six superstars: Mike Caro, Chip Reese, Dave Sklansky, Joey Hawthorne, Bobby Baldwin, and Doyle—two world champions and four master theorists and players. Essential strategies, advanced play, and no-nonsense winning advice on making money at 7-card stud (razz, high-low split, cards speak, declare), lowball, draw poker, and hold'em (limit and nolimit). A must-read—every serious poker player must own this book. 628 pages, $29.95.

SUPER SYSTEM 2 *by Doyle Brunson.* The most anticipated poker book ever, SS2 expands upon the original with more games and professional secrets from the best players in the world. Superstar contributors include Daniel Negreanu, winner of multiple WSOP gold bracelets and 2004 Player of the Year; Lyle Berman, 3-time WSOP gold bracelet winner and founder of the World Poker Tour; Bobby Baldwin, 1978 World Champion; Johnny Chan, 2-time World Champion and 10-time WSOP bracelet winner; Mike Caro, poker's greatest researcher, theorist, and instructor; Jennifer Harman, the world's top female player; Todd Brunson, winner of more than 20 tournaments; and Crandell Addington, no-limit legend. 672 pgs, $34.95.

CARO'S BOOK OF POKER TELLS *by Mike Caro.* One of the 10 greatest poker books, this must-have classic should be in every player's library. If you're serious about winning, you'll realize that most of the profit comes from being able to read your opponents. This book reveals the the secrets of interpreting *tells*—physical reactions that reveal information about a player's cards—such as shrugs, sighs, shaky hands, eye contact, and more. Learn when opponents are bluffing, when they aren't and why—based solely on their mannerisms. Over 170 photos of poker players in action and play-by-play examples show the actual tells. These powerful eye-opening ideas can give you the decisive edge at the table. 320 pages, $24.95.

CARO'S GUIDE TO DOYLE BRUNSON'S SUPER SYSTEM *by Mike Caro.* Working with World Champion Doyle Brunson, the legendary Mike Caro has created a fresh look to the "Bible" of all poker books, adding new and personal insights that help you understand the original work. Caro breaks 36 concepts into the following categories: analysis, commentary, concept, mission, play-by-play, psychology, statistics, story, or strategy. Lots of illustrations and winning concepts give even more value to this great work. 86 pages, 8 1/2 x 11, $19.95.

CARO'S FUNDAMENTAL SECRETS OF WINNING POKER *by Mike Caro.* Learn the essential strategies, concepts, and plays that comprise the very foundation of winning poker play. Learn to win more from weak players, equalize stronger players, bluff a bluffer, win big pots, where to sit against weak players, and the six factors of strategic table image. Includes selected tips on hold'em, 7-card stud, draw, lowball, tournaments, more. 160 pages, $12.95.

MILLION DOLLAR HOLD'EM: Limit Cash Games *by Johnny Chan & Mark Karowe.* Learn how to win money at limit hold'em, poker's most popular cash game. You'll get a rare opportunity to get into the mind of the man who has won 10 World Series titles—tied for the most with Doyle Brunson—as the authors pick out illustrative hands and show how they think their way through the bets and the bluffs. No book so thoroughly details the thought process of how a hand should be played, how it could have been played, and the best way to consistently win. 368 pages, paperback, $29.95.

MY 50 MOST MEMORABLE HANDS *by Doyle Brunson.* Great players, legends, and momentous events in the history of poker march in and out of fifty years of unforgettable hands. Sit side-by-side with Doyle as he replays the excitement and life-changing moments of the most thrilling and crucial hands in the history of poker: from his early games as a rounder in the rough-and-tumble "Wild West" years—where a man was more likely to get shot as he was to get a straight flush—to the nail-biting excitement of his two world championship titles. Doyle brings to life the high stakes tension of sidestepping police, hijackers and murderers, competes for hands worth more than a million dollars, and sweats out situations where his last dollar relies on the outcome of a card. Engrossing, captivating, riveting, and ultimately educational, this is a momentous and thrilling collection from the living legend himself. 168 pages, $14.95.

FREE BOOK!
TAKE ADVANTAGE OF THIS OFFER NOW!

The book is **free**; the shipping is **free**. Truly, no obligation. Oops, we forgot. You also get a **free** catalog. **And a $10 off coupon!!** Mail in coupon below to get your free book or go to **www.cardozabooks.com** and click on the red OFFER button.

WHY ARE WE GIVING YOU THIS BOOK?

Why not? No, seriously, after more than 27 years as the world's foremost publisher of gaming books, we really appreciate your business. Take this **free** book as our thank you for being our customer; we're sure we'll see more of you!

THIS OFFER GETS EVEN BETTER & BETTER!

You'll get a **FREE** catalog of all our products—over 200 to choose from—and get this: you'll also get a **$10 FREE** coupon good for purchase of <u>any</u> product in our catalog! Our offer is pretty simple. Let me sum it up for you:

1. Order your **FREE** book
2. Shipping of your book is **FREE!***
3. Get a **FREE** catalog (over 200 items—and more on the web)
4. You <u>also</u> get a **$10 OFF** coupon good for anything we sell
5. Enjoy your free book and **WIN**!

CHOOSE YOUR FREE BOOK

Choose one book from any in the Basics of Winning Series (15 choices): Baccarat, Bingo, Blackjack, Bridge, Caribbean Stud Poker and Let it Ride, Chess, Craps, Hold'em, Horseracing, Keno, Lotto/Lottery, Poker, Roulette, Slots, Sports Betting, Video Poker.

Or choose one book from here: Internet Hold'em Poker, Crash Course in Beating Texas Hold'em, Poker Talk, Poker Tournament Tips from the Pros, or Bobby Baldwin's Winning Poker Secrets.

When you order your free book by Internet, enter the coupon code **PROFIT**.

HURRY! GET YOUR FREE BOOK NOW!
USE THIS COUPON OR GO TO OUR WEBSITE!

YES! Send me my **FREE** book! I understand there is no obligation! Send coupon to: <u>Cardoza Publishing</u>, P.O. Box 98115, Las Vegas, NV 89193. <u>No</u> phone calls please.

Free book by website: www.cardozabooks.com (click on red OFFER button)

*Shipping is FREE to U.S. (Sorry, due to very high ship costs, we cannot offer this outside the U.S. However, we still have good news for foreign customers: Spend $25 or more with us and we'll include that free book for you anyway!)

WRITE IN FREE BOOK HERE _____

Name _____

Address_____

City _____ State _____ Zip _____

Email Address* _____ Coupon Code: <u>PROFIT</u>

*Get our FREE newsletter and special offers when you provide your email. Your information is <u>protected</u> by our privacy guarantee: We've been in business 27 years and do NOT and never have sold customer info. One coupon per address or per person only. Offer subject to cancellation at any time.
